DUDE, BRO

BREAD FOSTER

DUDE, BRO

THE HOW-TO GUIDE TO COLLEGE YOUR PARENTS DON'T WANT YOU TO HAVE

BREAD FOSTER

Skyhorse Publishing

Skyhorse Publishing books may be purchased in bulk at special discounts for sales promotion, corporate gifts, fund-raising, or educational purposes. Special editions can also be created to specifications. For details, contact the Special Sales Department, Skyhorse Publishing, 307 West 36th Street, 11th Floor, New York, NY 10018 or info@skyhorsepublishing.com.

Skyhorse® and Skyhorse Publishing® are registered trademarks of Skyhorse Publishing, Inc.®, a Delaware corporation.

Visit our website at www.skyhorsepublishing.com.

10 9 8 7 6 5 4 3 2 1

Library of Congress Cataloging-in-Publication Data is available on file.

Cover design by Brian Peterson

Print ISBN: 978-1-63450-311-2
Ebook ISBN: 978-1-5107-0093-2

Printed in the United States of America

There are too many to dedicate this to. The staff at BroBible.com and The Rooster for teaching me to write for college kids again, to Cat Kovach my editor who had faith in a rookie writer, to H who hired me after college.

Mainly, to my grandmother who once told my family, "Leave him alone, he's strange and he's always going to be strange. He's going to make mistakes but he'll figure out what he's gonna do and be great at it." Then she pulled me into her lap as she sat in her wheelchair and whispered, "Just make sure you make every day a story."

And to my family, who never thought I'd get published . . . Please, stop reading.

FOREWORD

Sam Haft

When Bread Foster asked me to write the foreword to his very first book, it struck me how few friends he must have. I've known him for just under two years, in which time we've laughed at each others' failures, scoffed at each other's successes, served as each others' alibis, and exchanged a *shocking* amount of hate speech (although the Anti-Defamation League won't return my letters). Honestly, it's difficult for me to describe Bread Foster. I've always felt that we were comics first and friends second. So, for a moment, let's ditch the fiction of the whiskey-swilling, lady-poaching, depression-mired comedian that is "Bread Foster," and focus on my friend Bread. And Bread is the kind of friend that comes with a verbal fucking warning:

"I'm sorry about him, he's really just a bad person."

Bread loves sex, liquor, fighting, drugs, kittens, hiking, and anything else that fills the gaping emotional chasm of a person sincerely afraid that they're utterly unloved (i.e., a comedian). He spends a lot of time justifying his very delicate sense of confidence by attempting to serve as a source of mistake-earned wisdom; helping his fellow man understand the explicit particulars of why one shouldn't do the stupid things Bread does. This, in turn, gives him a sense that his hideous lifestyle has a purpose and allows him to sleep at night. (Also, the muscle relaxers help.) Speaking as one of his close friends, he's a really fun time. But speaking as a person, this seriously needs to stop.

I am appealing to your sense of humanity—begging even—do not allow this madness to continue. Do not let Bread Daniel Foster, the ne'er-do-well scamp from farmland New Jersey, to add layer upon layer to the horrifying, twisted, Tinder-using, alcoholic mask that is "Bread Foster." Quit validating him. Stop it. Right fucking now.

Put this book down, and *stop reading*.

...

Fine, I guess that isn't happening. You know what, reader? You two deserve each other. You have absolutely no common sense, and you're definitely not gonna gain any from reading the ramblings of a horny drunk toddler contained within the pages of *Dude, Bro: The How-To Guide to College Your Parents Don't Want You to Have*. Sure, he might save you a herpes scare or two (sometimes that lip ring is hiding something), or help you avoid being the "Ultimate Frisbee Guy"* in your freshman class (spoiler alert: that guy gets date-raped), but he's not going to make you a happy, well-adjusted, successful person. You're going to party yourself into an empty husk—a happiness vampire that can only coexist with others when covered in cheap liquor and genital warts. You're going to turn into some kind of mini-Bread (a muffin?), ruining the world with your malt liquor vomit and your shitty Borat impression. You disgust me. Fuck you. I mean it, reader. Suck a dick.**

---

* Speaking of which—seriously do *NOT* be Ultimate Frisbee Guy.
** Also, when do I get a book?! Come on. Fuck you, Bread.

PREFACE

In all honesty, I wrote this after I was finished so it's not really a preface. This book has a lot of truth, because the truth is funnier than lying so a book sells more. Some of these are stupid, sometimes you're going to read this and think, "No way," and other times, "That ending was terrible." If I was writing a guide for how to do college, I wanted anyone reading to understand that it's not always amazing, it's not always crazy, it's mainly what you make of it. These stories aren't completely outrageous, they are strange and quirky and I hope slightly informative, funny, and endearing. College is about making mistakes and learning from them, so it was the perfect subject as I'm considered a "freshman author."

My insanity happened a long time before college. I grew up in a Catholic household with strict parents, no matter what they may say. Most other kids I knew were out drinking and being crazy in high school, and I didn't really start doing that heavily until I had already graduated. After that I ended up still living with my parents and going to community college. Community college is where the waitress next to you hopes to some day get a degree and become an executive assistant. No one really hangs out. They smoke weed in their cars and take classes then go home to their parents. There were no weekends in community college. There were Saturday classes and jobs. It was oppressive and nothing like what I wanted out of college.

So when I got to Montclair State University through a guaranteed admissions program into a business school, I knew life was going to be amazing. I wasn't there to be part of an institution of higher education. I was there to destroy it. I wasn't going to college. I was drinking and doing crazy shit on a deadline. I was pent up from community college and went to a college where no one from my town or high school ended up going. It was a fresh start to carve a niche and find a group of friends who wanted to have more fun than anyone else.

At college I found people who accepted and antagonized my craziness, and I have yet to feel as comfortable with people as I did then. Those who stuck with me were the people who stayed out till 4:00 a.m., who got great grades, and who knew this might just be the very best time of their lives. So I wanted you, the reader, to relive some of this insanity and laugh along with me. I wanted there to be some sort of collection of all the things I wish I had known, and realistic stories for me to set my expectations against. I could write a tome of the stories and amazing times that happened in college. I didn't have time to write about the sex (which doesn't matter because anyone younger than me is facing a whole new and different set of sexual problems), the strippers, all my groups of friends, the time I punched the King of Medieval Times in the chest and bent his armor, about people trying to drag me into pagan rituals, and Alex CarDouchey who sucker punched me at least fifty times only to get his ass kicked.

This is it, this is the insanity, the imperfection, the vulnerability. These are the ramblings of a crazy person who may have peaked during college. This is what someone who was delayed in getting to have fun did when sweet, sweet independence was given to them. This was our life in college.

So let's begin what my friend and writing mentor, who made me devour books before writing this, called, "A glorified and worthless personal essay."

Chapter 1

DICKS AND SHIT:

Let's get this over with.

I wish I didn't have to write this chapter but we're all pretty immature.

Why We Whip it Out

Why guys have an obsession with showing one another their balls and genitals is a question that has plagued the human race for years. The explanations are much simpler than anyone would expect. There isn't some deep-down sick, psychological need that showing our penis fulfills. The main reason is, if you had something dangling between your legs that society judged the size, girth, and shape of, you'd be playing with it and showing it to people too. Fuck it, the Babylonians had statues with huge dicks everywhere. Leviticus has a rule about women smashing a dude's junk getting their hand cut off. We've always been obsessed with genitals. Point positive, girls showing their boobs during spring break—or as I call it, Spring Breast, because it's essentially a holiday thats been around since the beginning of time as an excuse to get naked.

Dicks are a strange thing. Since we're kids, we have one. They're a silly and weird part of us we use to pee and don't really think much of past that. Then puberty hits and all of a sudden they become really important. We learn that our dicks are something weird that not a lot of people have seen, and we're told how conscious of them we should be. Classes are taught in school about sex and how each organ works. Women are constantly looking down and checking their boobs, readjusting and sometimes pulling crumbs out of them. No one gives them shit. They're held on high and esteemed, while men are judged for readjusting or having their legs spread too wide on the subway. We have our spelunkers before girls get their tits, then all of

11

a sudden some hormones hit and everyone finally recognizes, "These things are a little weird."

When you get to the age when women start touching penises, you get reviews about cocks. You never see one, but they're constantly talked about. It's inevitable that, with all this emphasis and attention given to dicks, eventually someone is going to whip theirs out. It's simple logic, the more you talk about something the more people assume you want to see it. No one ever thinks about the size of their dick until someone tells them they *should* think about the size of their dick. This is inevitably going to lead a man to show it, for laughs *and* for the off-chance someone will let us know we have fantastic phallus. We learn that dicks come in different sizes and shapes and wetness from females, and we'll be damned if around college age we're finally confident enough to whip it out and giggle.

As we get older, guys show each other their genitals for an easy reason: we don't want to see someone else's penis or balls. Two people showing their junk at once is weird so more often than not we decide to be the first. Nothing is more vile to most men than having their eyesight invaded by an unwanted dick. They're veiny and bumpy and colored so strangely that, in all honesty, I believe even women don't really want to see dick. Knowing how awful and strange they are makes it so amazingly funny to force your friends to see one. Bothering a friend with a surprise dick is so stupid and lowest common denominator that there are very few ways it's not funny. That is why we even develop different ways to show off how awful our genitalia can be. Some people call this "puppetry of the penis." I call it loneliness.

We also develop games for showing them to each other. In college, I developed the "Cockness Monster," which involved lifting my balls over my dick so it looked like I had two humps then making my dick into the shape of Nessie coming out of the water. I'd cover the bottom portion with my hand so it looked like it was rising from the water line of Loch Ness. The saddest thing is the amount of time we, as men, end up spending playing with our junk, because we're bored and it's there. In all honesty, a dick is like a toy you can never lose and it's really hard to break.

Friends share their toys with other friends. That's why we show them to one another.

Dicks are hilarious. They're weird and gross and hang down outside of us. When we whip it out, we're trying to share with the world. "This is my dick, I'm loud and not proud, and is it supposed to have this vein here?" As soon as people stop putting so much emphasis on what dicks look like, we'll stop showing them to strangers. No matter what happens though, we still reserve the right to show them to our friends.

Shock- Does that guy have his dick out?

Questioning: I don't hve that vein, should I have that vein?

Questioning: I've been staring for a while now, does that mean we're in a relationship?

Anger: Why won't he put his dick away? I'm gonna push him once his dick is away. Can't push someone whose dick is out.

Questioning: Can I push someone whose dick is out?

Bargaining: I'm not taking my pong shot till its away. I'm going to pay a drunk dude to touch it if he doesn't put it away.

Depression: He took my hEYEmen. I wanted it to be someone special.

Acceptance: At least its not my Dad's.

Seeing Your First Dick:

If you're reading a manual on how to go to college, it's safe to assume you might not have played sports or had any friends. I get you. So you may have never seen another dick before except your dad's Dick. If you've never seen a dick before, it's time to prepare you. Here's what you can expect.

Shat Chat: Pictures

Oh god. Why did I start my book this way? Everyone is already judging. I can feel your glares. I just want to get these topics out of the way.

Most people look at food and think, "That's delicious." As a college-aged male, I looked at food and thought, "You're poop and muscles in training." These were the days before you could Instagram your shit, and people still sent pictures of it. I hope that sending pictures of your shit is still universal. My friends and I would send each other pictures of the road kill we'd splash into the toilets, the awful things we'd do in the porcelain paradise. That always leads to the questions of, "What is the matter with all of us?"

No one really knows for sure why people send each other pictures of their shit. I say this because even if we think it's horrifying, guys, everyone has done it. I'm not sure anyone knows for sure why it's funny. (Personally, I have two ulcers and the diet of a manic-depressive, so my friends still find it funny.) So I propose the next few theories:

What Just Came Out Of Me. It's actually an incredibly surprising thing to see how much you're holding inside you. Dudes are upset about their load size for the same weird reason. There aren't too many things that make all men feel manly, but taking a huge shit is one of them. It actually doesn't matter if you're a Blerd, Finance Bro, a loner, or even a lady; an enormous dump makes you feel special and you want to show it off. It's not quite a child, but it's as close as you can get without swollen nipples. Sometimes, after it's been inside you for long enough, it's impossible not to take a selfie and ask everyone if it looks like you.

If you've never taken a shit and questioned your life decisions, you're more repressed than a Jehovah's Witness in a porn store or a Scientologist speaking about Scientology. You don't let loose something that terrible and just flush it away. Sometimes it's a keepsake from that time you lived off only peanut butter and whiskey. Sometimes it's a grueling reminder of how little water you drink in comparison to your dairy intake. You'd be insane not to send a picture like that when you're in college.

You're Never Alone. Not only are you never alone in sending a shat shot, you're never alone pooping. When you're sitting on the toilet, you're one of millions who are on the toilet at the exact same time. Everybody shits, except for maybe Kim Jong-un even though he's the world's biggest ass. It's not hard to use this logic to think, "Why should I be ashamed if everyone does it?" The answer being, because it's gross. Everyone is a little obsessed with shit jokes and poop pics because it's completely relatable. Yes, it's gross but most people look at a shat shot and remember a time when they did something awful like that to themselves.

Shat shots, poop pics, fecal photos are things you are going to look back on and wonder why you ever did that to each other, and possibly why you're still doing that today. Shitting is universal, and Poop Polaroids are about showing the surprise and whimsy of life. It's sharing with your friends this weird thing that your body turns beautiful and wonderful looking food into. Sometimes it's like art work, and other times it's like fart work.

Four in the Stink, Only One Got the Pink

Let me set the stage for the rest of this book, as this is where most of the book takes place. The Village apartment complex sat atop the highest point at Montclair State University. I don't know if that's true but it always felt like it. Personally I can't remember many occasions when I felt warm there, when the idea of hiding under a blanket wasn't a comforting thought. It was more than the harsh weather that made all of us stronger as people, it was the harsh things we all lived through. We all had heartbreaks, we had family issues, but a few misfits came together and had a college stint that no one else in the world will ever experience.

While other college kids danced and learned the lyrics to "Colt 45," I was in the depths of a psychosis no one really recognized as a problem.

Instead of offering help there was an unspoken pact to encourage me to continue do things that were off the wall. When I drunkenly decided to get a mohawk, Four Fingas shaved my head. When I was snorting painkillers, Amber stayed up all night and rapped every Wu Tang album from start to finish with me. Later, I realized that everyone knew I'd eventually get my shit together and be okay.

Outside of the Spanish-style stucco apartments we lived in, just under a red thatched roof in the building called Alice Paul, there were two benches where smokers gathered and stories were created. I love those benches still to this day. Two cold metallic benches where I met my girlfriend who stayed with me for three years, two cold metallic benches where I met my first friends and got invited to my first party. Those sleek, square benches that had to be bolted into the concrete so we wouldn't throw them grounded me more often than not. Those benches were a place of wonderment and love and if I could, I would go back and lube them up and fuck them softly, caringly, and lovingly. I spent my first weeks in college alone with a crippling concussion from a car accident. It made me do things that shocked some, but mainly made everyone cry with laughter.

The first day of my third semester was stifling hot for September. Instead of chilly hilltop winds whipping at our faces and making our noses red, we were met with a light summer breeze that kissed our foreheads and made them pitter-patter with sweat. It was weather that made your scrotum hang low but not quite stick to your leg. September is traditionally a cooler month, so Montclair State University turns off the air conditioning and flips on the heat. Trying to get that changed is like trying to get a hillbilly to go to a dentist.

Our apartment was switched to heat with no signs of relief. The backs of our necks sweated even while we were sitting still. It was unbearable for the upper floors, but living on the ground floor made it cool enough for a bunch of guys watching *South Park,* relaxing with their hands down their pants. Truthfully, it didn't matter to me because it was a relief to be back in apartment 1A after a summer off. It was my third and final semester, and my roommates and I had already gotten to know each other. We had all shared enough stories about our mayhem on campus so everyone felt comfortable acting like themselves. In truth, college is about hanging out with people that cause the same type of trouble as you. Look at the Duke Lacrosse team.

I will always love 1A, with its extra high ceilings and its door lock that had to be wiggled just right to get in. You had to get used to the weird noises it made and it never felt quite normal; for all intents and purposes, it was like me as a child. My roommates were getting used to it too. The floor made of poured concrete created an audible slap when you walked barefoot over it. There was a tiny layer of cheap, stained rug the school laid over the entire apartment that did nothing to soften the floor or muffle the sound. There was also the unexplainable drainage hole in the middle of our hallway, and a stove that had weird marks on it. Those were explained by the fact I used the stove to heat my iron the previous semesters. I had even almost gotten all the butter off the kitchen floor from previous pranks. After I watched people go sliding, I was the only one to fall. (First lesson to the readers: the butter on the tile prank is funny until you miss a patch and need to get to the fridge.)

Just a few hours into moving in and everyone was smitten. The room felt like home, with its large common area and attached kitchen with a counter to do shots on. Behind the common area was the long L-shaped hallway with two bathrooms, one double room, and two singles jutting off like tree limbs. Yes, it always smelled a little funny, but so do the feet of terrible Jersey girls when they take off their Uggs. It was still our home.

There is comfort in new friends, especially after paying six thousand a semester in housing and having them assigned to you. I looked at my second set of roommates on the couches. Chris may have been Portuguese, but he looked like he belonged on the No Fly List. He resembled the by-product of a Mexican and an Arab, who both wanted to piss off their parents. Even though he chugged craft beer, listened to bands I'd never heard of and always kicked my ass at Soul Caliber, I could still see him praying to Mecca or looking for work outside Home Depot. He was always joined by Jinny, who at the time was so hot I'd have mowed her like a soccer field, if it wasn't for a scowl that reminded me of my mother. Jinny always tried to take care of everyone, but once her eyelids closed, jaw clenched, and her cheek bones popped out, she stopped anyone in their tracks. Perched furtively in a chair, legs crossed right over left, was Greg. More affectionately known as Beer Clause. Greg had a job where beer often disappeared and magically reappeared as gifts to his roommates. He was quiet, handsome and witty. At six four and I'd guess twohundred pounds, Greg had learned a lesson I still haven't: being the biggest doesn't mean you have to be the loudest. And finally, Lee. Oh, Lee. Lee had the ability to slouch so low into any chair he essentially melted into it. He and I shared stories about drugs that only someone from the sixties could understand. Lee was the world's most handsome, alien and conspiracy theorist. The only downfall to Lee was his luck always ran out before his beer did. More terrible things happened to Lee than his fellow Jews in the desert. He was humble and handsome but prone to destruction being blamed on him. All of my roommates wore plaid, played music, and were completely different than me.

Sitting in 1A with my new friends caused a sense of Zen to wash over me. It had been four or five days since anything had washed over me and the smell was apparent. We thought nothing of the strange noises on that stagnant September day, but Lee glared accusingly at me and asked what fucking stank. I ran my fingernails under my armpits and lifted them to my nostrils. The tangy scent might have made other people gag, but to me it was gratifying. I leaned over and placed my armpit pap smear under Lee's nose. I watched it crumple up when my scent went into him. It looked like someone had fingered his nostrils. His eyes bunched up and cheeks loosened and I wanted to whisper, "Now I've been inside you." We came to the conclusion it wasn't my ungodly body odor causing the smell, but I still decided to shower.

When you pull back a shower curtain and see half a gallon of your classmates' shit bubbling up out of your shower drain, you wonder if there is a strange conspiracy going on in the dining hall. Shit is a weird thing when it's not yours. Looking at a pile of someone else's shit makes you wonder what type of a life they lead, how many meals that took to make, or whether they need vitamins. That's exactly what I was met with. It looked and smelled and bubbled like Third World drinking water. I did what any self-respecting man would do when faced with a disgusting situation. I started laughing and made everyone look. We all quizzically examined each other and knew we were standing, staring at fecal trimmings in a warm stink box with no idea what to do. We still weren't thinking twice about the noises coming from the pipes while we stared at our neighbors' insides. The pipes gurgled like a student trying to get rid of their first case of strep throat, and shortly after we left the bathroom we figured out why there was a drain in the hallway.

Faced with a problem that left all of us scratching our heads, we called a roommate meeting in the common area. If none of us knew what to do, we might as well do it together. That's when the pipes let out another gurgle and we learned that weird drain in the hallway was an overflow drain for a septic system that was unprepared for the gastrointestinal system of thousands of students moving in the first week. They say the truth always floats to the top, but so do undigested vegetables from the cafeteria's attempt at Asian stir-fry. A slow, steady, deliberate flow of viscous brown sludge was seeping into our hallway. I had never wondered how the Ninja Turtles must have smelled until that moment. It was like a rolling fog, making everything feel sticky as it crept and expanded, rolling out of our apartment and into the hallways of the entire first floor. I opened a window and purged what little was in my stomach.

We were daunted. The tiny little bit of carpeting over the concrete was even less prepared than we were. The mood turned violently, as giggles turned to gagging, and we all had the realization that being up shit creek without a paddle was much worse than the saying made it out to be. I sprinted outside my apartment and found the tiny apartment offices. I was met by a useless and uninterested student, who was only at the desk because he needed his rent paid. When he told me he was helpless and suggested I call building services, I didn't hesitate.

"Hi, I live in 1A. There's shit in the shower."

"Someone shitting in the shower isn't our problem."

"I mean there's a lot of shit in my shower."

"I don't care how much you guys ate, shitting in the shower is not my issue."

"It's in my hallway too."

"It sounds like you need new friends, not a building manager."

"It's coming up out of the drains, you really need to get here."

"So you didn't shit in your hallway?"

"Do people really just shit in the hallway?"

"This is a state university."

"I forgot."

"I'll be over soon."

Everyone cracked open beers while we waited for building services. I was jealous of men who went to spas and sat in saunas and talked business. We sat in a hot room sniffing strange prostate while playing "Who's going to vomit the least?" Every now and then, the drain would let loose a terrible "glub" and a bubble would work itself to the top. It sounded like a tuba player who had a sudden stroke playing the lowest note. It took over an hour for the tide of fecal matter to subside. I was met with the harsh reality that the likelihood of building services coming was the same as me passing Calculus the first time I took it, so I picked up the phone and started prank calling him.

"Hi, it's 1A, it's been an hour and the shit is starting to cake the rug. Should I try to stop it or do something proactive?"

"What are you going to do?"

"I was thinking of taking a dump in the hallway. Maybe a fresh dump will soak up the wet stuff?"

"I'll be there soon, I don't think you should do that."

"What if I put some rope around it and convince some girls to wrestle in it?"

"Then you'd still have sewage in your hallway and girls covered in sewage too."

"That's a really good point. If I was going to do that I'd film it."

"I'll be there soon. Just be patient."

Click.

"Hi, it's Bread in 1A again."

"I'm on my way."

"How long?"

"You're not the only one with shit in your hallway."

"Yeah, but we didn't put it there."

"I'm coming over now."

"Is it still considered toilet paper if you use it in a hallway?"

Click.

"Hi, it's Todd in 1B. I think there's a dead body in 1A."

"Nope, they just have pipe problems."

"I think you're wrong."

"Nope, they already called and complained."

"No, I killed Bread. I just needed to tell someone."

Click.

"Hey, it's Bread in 1A again. Are your arms tired?"

"Listen, I can only go so fast. Stop calling me."

"I'm just busting your chops. When you come over I'll give you a beer. Are your arms tired?"

"Cause I've been flying through your dreams?"

"No, because I wanted to let you know they're gonna be sore as fuck after you're done plunging."

Click.

Deliriousness was making its way into our brains. I drifted off, wondering how the first floor meeting would go. "Hi, students, help yourself to the free pizza and sign in. I'm your Community Advisor. I know we all heard Bread screaming about feces in the hall, but today's meeting is about letting you know something special. I may be your CA, but I'd also like to be your friend. Also will anyone admit they wrote, 'Give me mixers fuck face,' on the vending machine? Hmm. How about you Bread, did you forget you signed it?"

Chris ruined my delusions by farting out of jealousy; he couldn't stand the smell of other people's assholes. He wanted to see which would smell worse. I explained to him he was a gentleman for taking such great care of us, the smell of his farts were quite refreshing. His intestinal problems cleansed my palate of the taste our room was leaving in my mouth. I compared his farts to sorbet until I actually got a whiff of him and dry heaved. Chris will always have pipes inside him that produce smells that are so offensive, my body purges itself out of whatever hole can open wide enough. Lee was sarcastically telling us how gross we were. "Gross, guys, you're so gross. I can't handle this, you're, like, so gross." A quiet smile crept over Greg.

We rejoiced at a knock at the door and raced each other to open it. I dwarfed the man who stood in the doorway, but he outweighed me by fifty pounds. The portly black man, with salt and pepper hair and poorly shaven face, meandered into our room. Instead of assessing the situation and fixing anything, he regaled us with stories about living in the ghetto of Newark and the hell that is working around college kids. He sat after a bit and drank our beer. There was a methodical amble to his speech. His slow ramble and vocabulary made us feel like he was a single nostril short of ending up a mouth breather. This guy's entire life moved on the timeline of someone who knew he had job security and never actually had to work. I grew restless and paced around him. It had been another fifteen minutes, and he drank two more of our beers.

Chris finally asked this human sloth to look at the hallway. After begrudgingly getting up, he paused for a moment, looked at Chris and I, and stated so non-chalantly, "I know what they're gonna do this year. They're gonna shit in diapers and smear it on the walls on Halloween."

Chris looked at me like a kid who got what he wanted on Christmas and said, "That was too specific. Really specific. How do you think he knows that?"

I rebutted with, "That's one month away. Maybe you should consider a career change."

"Yep, it's something every year. It's shit this year. Look at your hallway."

"I'm sorry, is it a different fluid every year? Is this like a Chinese Zodiac calendar or astrology?" I was astounded.

With the biggest smile on his face, Chris said, "If it's like astrology, I want to see the drawings."

We watched him slowly pace over to the drain. I turned to Chris and said, "I bet his wife never asks him how his day was."

"What's there to ask? It's a shit year."

He grabbed a broom handle from a cart he left outside, then stood over the drain and stared into it, pupils constricting to a pinpoint, and poked the drain. If there is one thing I learned from the staff at MSU, it's that broom handles are actually magic wands. When used properly, MSU staff believe you can solve any problem. For some reason broom handles were in no short supply, but broom heads were. At my college everyone but the teachers had one. It was like walking around Hogwarts: Polytechnical Institute, where the wizards who never applied themselves to magic ended up learning how to do plumbing and repair Honda Civics. I was now faced with a window licker who was poking a crap hole with a broomstick. No amount of college education can prepare you for that.

"Doesn't look like there is anything coming out of it now."

"Oh really? Are you sure? Maybe you should poke it a few more times to make sure there is no shit coming out of it, since we clearly can't see that plain as day."

"I don't think we need to do that. I'll send someone over with a carpet cleaner in a few hours."

"No, you do something about this right now. This apartment smells like a thawed freezer after the power goes out at a deli. Maybe you're so far gone that this is nothing to you, just another day and another person's bowel movements, but not me. You fix this."

The roommates had removed themselves from the situation. They were handing beers to another building services worker who had decided two people doing nothing were better than one. I tried to resolve the problem while they sat back laughing with a white dude whose facial hair was shaved to such a razor sharp line around his jaw it screamed, "This is where my jawline used to be." I resented him for drinking our beer and I resented him even more for being completely content getting drunk in a room that had more dried shit in it than a homeless man's shoes after someone gave him Taco Bell. My building services manager was worthless. My blood still rises when I think of his awful pathetic face. A simple request of, "Figure out how to make my room livable," was met with him staring at me like I was asking him to shoot his dog. He was honestly puzzled by someone asking him for help. I was unsure as to whether this man had ever cleaned anything in his life.

In his laborious attempt to make one nerve ending fire off into the other, somewhere he got an idea. When he told me, I was prouder than a papa who watched his son hit a homer. For just a moment I considered that maybe, just maybe miracles do exist. I thought I heard a bell ring off in the distance. But lo and behold, like my own parents, I found myself disappointed when he brought nothing other than an industrial sized fan into the room. I walked over to it, plugged the industrial fan in, and screamed my frustration into it. Why this guy thought a piece of equipment used to keep child laborers from dying of heat exhaustion would cure my shituation, still causes a sharp pain in my temples.

"Please do not put that fan on a pile of drying shit. All that's going to do is send it into the air and give us all pink eye. It's going to be like the dust bowl in here, a cloud of hard and dried butt clippings and Woody Guthrie singing songs about it. There is going to be butt crusts in the air, on my table, and all over everything. I'll be wiping dried ass juice off my counters and tables for weeks. Putting a fan on this is going to be as effective as handing a Band-Aid to someone with hepatitis. It's not going to fix anything."

He moved the fan behind the pile and, without any regard for human life, that devil man flicked the switch that turned the fan on high while I stood directly in front of it. I begged and pleaded for mercy, but his idiot, half-formed brain destroyed me. Exactly like I had said, microscopic—and not so microscopic—particles of my peers' insides invaded every part of my home and some parts of my body. Nothing would ever feel clean again. It was like the air was made of spiders. I wanted to run screaming out of the room, but I was so shocked by the blatant stupidity my mouth opened and curled into a frown as particles floated in and around it.

Yes, eventually they brought a carpet and a shower cleaner into my apartment to clean the feces. A younger gentleman cleaned everything and even helped me to wipe down the counters and tables. My roommates and I laughed and made jokes about the shituation for days. We bonded over our sewage issue and came to deeply love the smell of Chris's farts because, for nearly five hours, he was able to pump them out to lighten our mood.

In the end, after our room was cleaned up and we were relaxing, there was a knock at our door. An RA walked in and said, "Hey, we're really sorry, so you should have this." It was a cold pizza. Everyone stared in awe. We had been sitting in human shit for hours and our consolation prize was a cold, and half-eaten, pizza. It was clear there wasn't an appetite among any of us, but in college free pizza is free pizza.

But one week later, I woke up with a contact lens crusted to my eye. Not only did my school ruin my day with unprepared pipes, three individuals I came to love tormented me because my right eye was beet red and crusty. Pink eye is adult lice. It lets everyone know who the filthy kid is. As soon as people realize you have it, they treat you like they just found out you were adopted. It doesn't matter how you get pink eye, the results are always socially devastating. Thanks to an eye infection the only pink I'd see for a week was stuck under my eyelids. My eye was so bruised, beaten, and crusty I could have been living in a trailer park, explaining to the police how much he loves me. Yes, I thought about suing the school. Instead, in October, I handed a drunk kid a diaper and forty bucks.

Life never gets easier. The moral of this story is sometimes people go through a shit situation together and bond for life. If it wasn't for a terrible case of pink eye and back wash from a thousand students, four roommates wouldn't have become best friends. We all valued our education a little bit more. We all valued each other a little bit more. We had the realization that even in the crappiest situations there was a silver lining, even though there was also other peoples stomach linings. Never take a shituation for granted, and hope that you have the right people in your life to help make it bearable. If it wasn't for the sarcasm and brutal berating from three other almost strangers, I may not have bonded so well with my new friends.

We all learned that laughing was really important. Laughter is especially important when someone you're friends with has pink eye. Laugh at them nonstop while they have it, then once it's gone, remind them of that time they got pink eye.

Getting a BFA, Butthole Fuggin Atrocity

Real Germans are pretty awesome. Sure they read the fine print on a Groupon out loud, but they do know how to have a great time. I imagine Germans look at German Americans the way Italians look at guidos. I don't trust German Americans anymore. It's not my fault really, after you hear what one did to me. He made me look for reasons to hate them. He gave me a reason to hate myself.

German Americans latch onto the worst parts of their culture. They focus on drinking too much, but they're still not as good at it as the Irish. They're about sufficient, but not completely gratifying or amazing, sex. I've only known two German Americans and they ate bratwurst, drank out of boots, and tried way too hard to get people to like them. I loved Steve, women liked him, and he could almost drink as much as me. He was my first real friend in college and, without our mutual love of havoc, my entire college experience wouldn't have been the same. Then all that changed. The thing I don't trust about any German American is their aptitude for being literal and their aptitude for factory labor. I learned all this because I needed something to hate about Steve. Steve's anus hurt me, it let loose stenches that only a German factory should produce. Steve blitzkrieged my soul with his ass.

The night before this incident I had made a quick dinner then Steve and I had killed a personal keg of Heineken to the face. Coming back from class (napping), I was still sluggish and the world was twenty decibels too loud. I had trudged the three miles from campus back to my apartment because if I stopped moving I knew I'd be spewing all over the sidewalk. When I swung the door to 1A open, I yelled, "Stevie Steve, how ya' doing brotha'?" mimicking the other roommate Four Fingas's Staten Island accent. What met me was hilarious.

I looked into Steve's room to see him half asleep, clutching the Beer Pong belt we had won and lost countless times. He got up and started kicking his laundry into a corner. As soon as it was folded over, the smell of ammonia was stronger than a subway in a summer heat wave or inside an Arby's. For the first time in his life Steve didn't smirk and explain himself. Instead he just stared at me like if I ever told anyone he'd kill me. The smell of urine was so potent, I knew I was about to piss myself too, and my bathroom was out of order again. Upon asking to use his, I was met with an embarrassed gaze and he uttered, "Um, I texted Four Fingas. He's gonna come fix it. I don't suggest using it." I didn't care at this point and

I told Stevie Steve I'd fix it myself. Until I saw it. I lifted the bowl with plunger in hand and I shivered as the life was sucked out of me.

The phrase shooting the shit became all to literal. Apparently after a courtesy flush, the water never made it back into the bowl, and Steve had shotgun-blasted a dry toilet bowl. He painted it. There were graffiti artists who couldn't get coverage like that. It looked like a Jackson Pollock painting if Jackson had irritable bowel syndrome and let one loose on a canvas.

The bottom of the bowl had a tiny bit of water, the rest had shit caked on like a spice-encrusted tuna filet. It was like someone went on a spinning carnival ride backward, after eating Indian food. This was the true darkness of humanity in front of me, I looked into the depths that day and it was black and green, a whirlwind of sadness. That bowl looked and smelled like depression and poor decision-making. It was a black hole, so black in fact I was worried my friend had ulcers. I asked him if he shit doing a 180, he explained he tried to clean it by peeing it off the sides but he was too dehydrated.

The smell was the worst part. It smelled like regret and pinky fingers after a kinky night. It was horrendous and made my skin crawl like bed bugs during mating season, or the knowledge that humans eat twelve spiders a year in their sleep. It smelled unnatural, like the toxic waste dumps that litter my childhood state of New Jersey. It smelled like he had eaten a polluted creek and looked like someone had pulled anal beads out of his ass by tying one end to a door and slamming it shut. The toilet bowl was like the sides of a food processor before it's quite ground everything up.

The toilet bowl was so horrendous I felt personally betrayed. He had thrown my trust out the window and offended the unoffendable. Because of him and only him I've wretched my stomach into human shit. I've seen too much human excrement for one sane person, but never in my life had I ever been so repulsed that I had to vomit on the spot. I purged everything I had eaten that day on top of that shit. The Pollock mixed with my own insides made me gag again until finally, I couldn't hold my piss anymore. Vomiting on top of your friend's poop doesn't bring you closer. It makes you completely distant from all people. He may have lost a small portion of his lower intestines, but I lost a large portion of my soul. I froze, crouched over that toilet, with the realization that I was going to be a different person now.

After I was done vomiting, he stood over me snickering for a minute. Then he walked back into his room. I plunged that toilet and afterward vomited into the sink too. Covered in piss and vomit, I cleaned up someone else's shit and realized this is what fatherhood must feel like; it was worse than I could ever imagine. I cleaned up a German American's barely-processed colon water and inhaled the sweet smell of death. I fixed everything in the plumbing but I've never been able to fix myself. Steve bought me a six-pack, but I had PTSD—Post Traumatic Sewage Drainage. Seeing what was in that bowl was like watching someone smear sand from Mars then throw corn in it. I will never forgive Steve for that day. I almost lost a friend and I'll never forget it. Although I fought against it, Steve and I remained friends. You don't forget the person who ruined you, and some day I plan on shitting in Steve's house so painfully his kids have nightmares like I do.

The moral of this story is simple: Learn to plunge a toilet. It's a simple task to learn. No human being deserves to see someone's shit in non-photo form, or while unprepared. A simple plunger and bucket of water could have stopped anti-German sentiment and someone from losing themselves in a torrid storm of poop. For $12.99 and some elbow grease, I could have saved my soul like a Southern Baptist church.

CHAPTER 2

CRYING IN COLLEGE

It's my toga party and I'll cry if I want to.

Real men have feelings . . . that they bottle up until they explode.

Crying: Not Just for White Girl Wasted Anymore

If we can just for a moment be completely honest with ourselves . . . college is fucking terrifying. It's this monster everyone talks about, both for being the foundation of your life and incurring huge debt. When you get there, you're left alone, realizing you have little life experience and there are a whole lot of other people who have had different experiences and the school is throwing them together in a loose framework called "higher education." I'm sorry, but higher education is when your room-mate hits the bong too hard and makes an attempt at a serious discussion about politics, race, gender, or religion and you realize those topics shouldn't be as taboo to speak about honestly. College is where you're supposed to find yourself, when in actuality you just find yourself in situations you're not equipped to handle with dignity. There are so many overwhelming life experiences to be had. So I propose a simple conept that I stood by throughout college: No matter who you are, you're going to cry in college. It's only okay if you do it around your friends, as long as they mercilessly make fun of you afterward.

Reasons to cry. There are a million reasons to cry in college, not limited to the first time you see how expensive a bar tab is. This is the first time in your life you're almost completely alone. Not having the support structure you did in high school can be incredibly intimidating and harsh. As one of the kids who didn't have many friends in high school, I was finally able to appreciate it. Having no friends in high school gives you the free time to get good at what you want instead of trying to fit into what everyone else expects you to be. However, for anyone who did have a close group of friends, I can honestly say welcome to maturity. Yes, most people are just a phone call away, but that will never hold the same clout as having parents or teachers who can give you healthy and reliable guidance. In college you get a spank of the ass and a "Go get 'em slugger," which isn't enough for all the things you'll be experiencing for the first time. A lot of things shape you as you become an adult, and having good friends in college is one of them. When you're overwhelmed by the first time you're cheated on, the first failing grade, getting put on housing probation, or just drinking too much, having a friend can be make or break. You may have never felt the range of emotions you'll experience when you're in the world trying to make it on your own.

College is a time for change as well. No one goes to college expecting to lose their best friends, but so many people do. The crippling regret of losing someone you were close to in high school is enough to make any person cry. Those are the people that helped you deal with the early stages of living. High school friends help form your first opinions of the world. Nothing is worse than one of them not picking up the phone when you're vulnerable, or rather, cutting you off completely because their new girlfriend Lindsay is a complete brat. We'd all like to think we're being oversensitive, but fuck if it doesn't hurt once you realize how different you all actually were.

Missing your dog is also a completely acceptable reason to cry. In fact, the manliest reason to cry. Some people are unlucky enough to lose their dog in college and when it happens, the making fun of them rule doesn't apply. A dog is your best friend, they lay in your lap when you're down and their soft fur always has a soothing effect no matter how heartbroken you might be. Having a wonderful companion, always willing to mindlessly carry a tennis ball back and forth, cannot be valued enough when you need time to think. Living with roommates and no pet is enough to make anyone buy something as stupid as a bunny or turtle in the hope of filling a void.

Having roommates is incredibly difficult. Everyone is a little bit different and having a roommate who idolizes Kanye West would make anyone with an IQ over one hundred tear their ears off. Trying to explain to someone how awful and arrogant that man-child is over and over again, while begging them not to play his music anymore, would bring a WWII vet to their knees. Yes they've been bombarded by Germans and seen friends die, but I'd rather that than constantly see Kanye West doing interviews, and be forced into talking about his new music videos. He's not an incredibly talented artist. He's a guy smart enough to have a good writing team (fuck you, publisher, for making me write this all on my own), and an eye for creating havoc and being unapologetic. Kanye West is just an avatar for what's wrong in society. We're all little children listening to what someone else told us to, and celebrating the personality flaws that make us unbearable assholes. I hear if you're roommate dies you get straight As, so it's killing two idiots with one stone if you don't get caught.

It doesn't matter if you're a guy who refers to women as "Slam Pigs," a shaved-headed feminist marching in an anti-slut protest, or a person who's questioning why they can't stop staring at feet, college is a time when you really develop your sexual identity. These are confusing and scary times for anyone. You might have your first pregnancy scare, you might be with someone who is willing to visit a sex shop and talk about your needs. The fear of rejection and that you're not normal is overwhelming. College was the first time I realized I had a thing for women with protruding hipbones, and the weird leather-wearing BDSM students sure made me feel like I was the weirdo. College is the time people who've never had sex are in the same enviornment as someone who has been tag teamed by football players. Don't feel guilty about what you like, feel guilty that you accidentally told your mom what you did last night when you were hung over.

Finally, and most importantly, college is an exceptionally weird time. You're old enough to be taking care of your own basic adult responsibilities, but you still have to bring your dad when you buy a car so the dealer doesn't fuck you over. It's an awkward stage when a lot of people call you an adult but no one treats you like one. It's so easy to get caught up in other people's expectations of you when all you want to do is smoke weed and write books. This is a time when the weak get sorted from the strong. Those who decide to chase their dreams with fervor and tenacity instead of letting others dictate their lives will go through overwhelming hell in college, but be really successful adults. This is a time when you're forced to develop a bullshit meter, which puts you in the incredibly awkward position of wondering who to trust.

Other good reasons to cry include: a girl missing the toilet and puking on your shoes, missing the toilet and puking on a boy's shoes, growing pains, your meth lab blew up in your parents' house, an elevator that's broken for the millionth time this week, your roommate catching you masturbating, suing YouTube to get the video of you masturbating down, your roommate being off their medication, getting stung by a bee, hangovers, hang overs (the kind where a person won't leave the next morning), and exploding your dishware in the microwave when you were just trying to make Ramen.

Why you cry with friends. This is your new, surrogate family. I repeat: this is your new, surrogate family. These are the people who live within a stone's throw, and will forgive you for hitting them with a rock. Friendships made in college are formed with the most powerful emotion of all—shame. Shame brings people together,the more dirt everyone has on each other, the longer the friendships are going to last. Nothing makes people keep in contact better than realizing they haven't talked to the person who knows about that one time they did that thing with the deli meat and a freshman.

If you're going to cry, do it around friends. If something happened that is so bad your eyes start to pee, it's selfish to cry alone. Since they are your new family, and your old one got to watch you pee your bed from the age five to fifteen, your new one deserves the same opportunity. Really though, not only is your new family there to support you, they might be feeling the same thing. As a society we're moving away from interpersonal communication and face-to-face contact. Enjoy having people around who care before you end up some angsty writer sitting alone in an apartment, realizing that just because you're funny doesn't mean people like you. In times of crisis, human contact is always better than texting. A hug from a friend is warm and soothing, your phone is colder than your girlfriend after she checks your phone without you.

The very best reason to cry around other people is that it inconveniences them. You're ruining an hour or so of someone's life, and if you feel bad enough to cry, you feel bad enough to take joy out of petty things. No one really knows how to handle another human being having a complete break down. Take a smidgen of joy that yes, this is shameful and you feel awful, but now everyone feels as awkward and embarrassed as you do. Additionally, it's a great excuse for roommates to share beers with you.

Why we make fun afterward. They say if you're not laughing, you're crying. That's an unfair statement because you could be cutting yourself, jumping off a bridge, eating your feelings, staring into a mirror talking to yourself, hiding in a closet, sleeping in a shopping cart in a common area, or a million other strange things sad people in college do. Laughing isn't the best option, but it's the easiest and most helpful. So after you get all your liquid emotions out of your eyes, it's best if people mercilessly and relentlessly make fun of you.

Humor is honesty. Most people can't tell you how they really feel about your situation unless it also makes you laugh. Trying to get honesty out of people is harder than trying to figure out where a bath salts user lost his teeth. Most people aren't comfortable enough to be honest with themselves, much less a friend who just spent time crying in front of them. Real opinions come out with a layer of sarcasm or satire, because it's easier than saying, "I think you're an idiot for crying over some guy name Trent, who gave you Molly and asked if he could finger you in his studio apartment. I know that was weird for you, Lou." It's hard to look at someone who is upset and explain to them that they're completely insane. But, relentlessly torturing you about how stupid you are, in joke-form, helps to put a Band-Aid on the wound and remind you not to be that stupid again.

Having people relentlessly make fun of you after a traumatic experience is polite. Let's not forget they just lost a precious hour or so of their life for you. When they're on their death bed and look back, remembering you eye sweating all over their shoulder, don't make them regret it. Let them smile, remembering how they told your brother the story about you crying. Humor makes everyone feel better, so being made fun of is actually a great way of thanking everyone for helping you through a tough time.

Humiliation is something everyone needs to get used to. While we're a society driven by narcissism, selfies, and follower counts (follow me on Twitter and Instagram @BreadFoster), our egos are starting to get obnoxious. We're turning into these weird adult-children hybrids that hold on to the reasons we're douches and cheers to it. Ratchet started off as something awful, but now people have embraced it as something to be proud of. We're ending up super-confident without the self-worth and hard work necessary to have something to be confident about. A great way to solve this is by making sure you get a healthy dose of humiliation as often as possible. It's an awful feeling, but it's a feeling everyone needs to remember exists. Sometimes you should feel bad about your actions because they were shitty and you were wrong. Humiliation teaches personal responsibility and helps you learn from your mistakes. Being made fun of and reminded of your mistakes in a way that makes everyone laugh helps cover the humiliation bit by bit while still reminding you that you were a douche bag.

Humor is the best way to face problems because it makes everything more bearable. It's almost unexplainable, but having your close friends busting each other's balls about the darkest moments of their lives seems to make everything a little bit easier to live with. Sure, it cuts a little bit, but I've always though you should cut at the dark stuff so it can scab over and start healing. Life, it can be really shitty. It can beat the ever-loving shit out of you, then kick you while you're down. Then as you get up and start walking, life will send a bunch of thirteen-year-olds to call you a faggot as you walk past them. Then life comes around a corner and pelts you with a ridiculous number of lemons and throws you into a volcano, and as you fall you stub your toe and get a million mosquito bites. Humor makes all of that seem a little bit easier to handle. Imagine how terrifying what I just said would be to actually live through. No one wants to die itchy. But when you get made fun of by friends, you develop a sense of humor about yourself and the world. It makes everything feel just a little more bearable.

My First Night in 1A: Crying in College

I went to Montclair State University for two reasons: a 3:1 girl-to-guy ratio and to run away from my hometown. In high school I was skinny, ugly, and frankly the most annoying person you could come across. I knew that every group had one person they kept around because they hated, and I always felt that was me. I was the kid who breathed at the wrong time and spoke down to people even though he was wrong. My mouth got me in fights and I had a wild streak no one understood. I acted without thought. One time, I broke into a construction site and painted an entire bulldozer purple. When the few friends I had asked why, I couldn't comprehend the question. No one in my hometown went to Montclair State University, so it was my chance to change who I was and finally get some real friends.

The problem with not knowing anyone is not knowing anyone. Time spent alone, without distractions, has a way of slowly eating at you. It pries into your brain and leaves you wondering about the darkest and worst things you've done. Before college, according to my own annoying masculine bravado, I was invincible and strong mentally and psychically. I had boxed, I had explored other countries without supervision, and I had gotten away with some incredibly illegal things. Sometimes life has the simplest ways of showing you your definition of strong is wrong. At nineteen, even if you're almost twenty, no matter how strong you think you are life will remind you're a scared, sniveling little child.

As soon as I arrived on campus, there was a slight ache in my chest. Being the youngest of three boys, my parents had already moved two kids in and out of dorms so they were sick of it. I watched as other families helped their kids arrange dorm rooms and carry furniture inside, while I pushed two shopping carts' worth of belongings into my room as my father looked on (he's been sick but I was happy for some company). My mother and brothers hadn't even come. He reviewed the dorm room, and told me about coming back from Vietnam, holding frat boys out windows for hazing, and drinking with black people for the first time (reserve judgment—he is old). Stevie Steve introduced himself momentarily and I took a shot with my father and them before they both left the Montclair campus. It was before noon and I didn't know a single person in fifty miles. I sat around playing Tekken Tag then jerked off and it was only 1:30 p.m.

I was forced to find ways to fill up time, so I poured a drink and decided to go buy a few groceries. Not knowing the area I was in, I decided to go over to good old Patterson, New Jersey, because my sense of direction decided if I was so bored on my own, I should be surrounded by people who could kill me. Patterson, New Jersey, is so bad that the eastern part of the city asked to be renamed. It's the type of place where, after you're done buying groceries, you can buy a reasonably priced gun in the parking lot but you'll have to shave the serial numbers yourself. Being a nubile kid, who still didn't have to shave every-day—puberty hit me like a prom queen's period, late—I wandered through the grocery store not understanding that literally everyone I walked past was eyeing me like meat as I meandered through with the subtle confidence only a complete retard could have.

It's amazing that I even got out of that place. As I'm writing this book I live in Newark, New Jersey, and I implore the reader to look up our crime rates. If I knew then what I know now, I'd probably do the same thing because I'm an idiot. Back in the parking lot, I got a running start then raised my legs feeling the asphalt slide by under my beat up sneakers. I giggled at my antics and started stuffing my food into the trunk of my beloved Grand Am. I had no issues until it came down to my last four bags. I turned to place two of them in my trunk when a short, clean-cut Spanish man grabbed two bags and made a mad dash.

I slammed my trunk closed and gave chase to the swarthy Latino man. I watched as he strained his calf muscles to try and go faster, they rippled with the strength of a man who had pushed a lawn mower for years. That's not racist—he was wearing a bright orange landscaping crew T-shirt, so smoke a joint and chill out, you white knights. He clearly wasn't fit to be a manager at the landscaping company because he wasn't smart enough to realize no one out runs a man with legs that look and move like crazy straws. I was on him faster than a liberal arts major on the jokes in this book after a bong hit. It took him five steps to match one of mine and, as I got near to him, I jumped and rode him at least three feet. He was out cold so I held him in my lap and moved his mouth for a minute.

"I'm very sorry I robbed you, Bread."

"Oh stop it, Latino man, I know you don't actually speak English."

"*Lo siento, Pan.*"

"How'd you do that? I don't speak Spanish!"

I put him down and slowly backed away. I've always used humor as a crutch. I remember backing away from him, and being horrified that all he had tried to steal was my milk and processed, individually packaged cheese singles. (Fuck you, pay me for a brand mention, Kraft.) I think deep down in that moment, I realized that my generation isn't racist, however, we are afraid of people without money or education. I didn't look at him and get angry with Spanish people, I got upset at dirt poor people. I was relatively poor growing up, but this was a completely different situation.

I drove back to my apartment blasting Spanish music and singing, "*Sol y Sambra aeh* Mama I said Yea Yea yea," because irony is never lost on people who might be clinically insane. Once inside, I stuffed the refrigerator with my food and reopened the bottle of whiskey my father was kind enough not to confiscate. He had no idea I had robbed bottles from two shit parties

Listen. Author here again. My publisher asked me to avoid the topic of race in that last paragraph, however, I can't. I am here to report how I thought. Whether it's right or wrong I am telling the reader what the mind of an immature twenty-something felt. Rake me over the coals all you want but I am being honest. Also, I will use Spanish and Mexican interchangeably. My current roommate who's Puerto Rican doesn't care that I jokingly call her Mexican and I laugh when she asks me to help her credit score.

that summer and was fully stocked. Drinking alone as an adult is a sign you might be sad, while drinking alone at nineteen screams to the world, "There is something horribly, horribly wrong."

I wasn't just sitting alone in my room drinking, in my defense. I wandered on campus to flirt with girls, but it's really hard to get numbers when dads are staring and imagining what you're gonna do to their precious once they're gone. It was a short-lived affair because I kept imagining a horde of dads angrily strangling me while another hoard talked to me about the dangers of unprotected sex. Nothing kills initiative to put it in a slippery mitten like half the girl's genetic material staring at you with brimstone in his eyes. So I skipped back to my apartment, blowing kisses at every girl who walked by and making a jerk off motion at anyone over the age of thirty.

I kept drinking and went to knock on doors. It was in this moment I met ReTodded (we called him ReTodded for reasons you'll discover later on), a massive meathead on the basketball team, who would eventually become one of my best friends for a semester. Being blitzed in front of someone's family is no way to make a friend, especially when his mother is wearing cheetah print. I also met a partner in crime, The Governor. I use these nicknames because I don't want to get sued, and at no point did I ever call him that awful name. ReTodded however, I called him that constantly. When I offered The Governor my services to help him move in, he politely declined and receded into his apartment.

I was getting desperate. I propped my door open and blasted my favorite music hoping to be the Pied Piper of friends. I hoped as Weezer's *Blue Album* filled the hall, a kid with plastic-rimmed glasses, wearing Keds, would stick his head in my door and say, "So much better than the *Green Album*!" Then I'd tell him how weird my day was and we'd laugh and find all the cute alternative girls and listen to The Cure together. I wasn't goth, but I was confused. Folks, my first day at college solidified I was a loser. A loser who had gained a ton of muscle, gotten a hair cut and contacts, but still a loser. What actually happened was night fell, and I watched people sitting on two beautiful cold black benches in front of my apartment complex and wondered why I was alone.

I imagined the stories they must be telling. My perception of college was completely formed by *Van Wilder* and *Animal House,* so while I watched a Siberian in a *Boondock Saints* T-shirt and an Arab kid—who a year later fell asleep at the bar and didn't get arrested because we explained he was Sri Lankan and they sleep at bars all the time—talk, I assumed it was about sex, drugs, and all the sick parties I was missing out on.

I switched from whiskey to a bottle of Absolut and things took a turn for the worse. The last time I drank Absolut, I ended up driving around New Brunswick, New Jersey, looking for a frat house (this was before GPS, people) and, after giving up, I found myself shooting my friend Mike Quill in the spine with blow darts for a half hour while he was wide awake and I was bored. I digress. I was sipping out of a NY Rangers mug, which I realized was stupid because I'm an Islanders fan. When left alone and drinking the average person will nap or call someone. I, however, stood in front of a mirror having drunken conversations with myself. At this point I was blacked out and don't remember the full conversation but I know from previous experience it probably went a little something like this:

"You're an alcoholic, you have a problem."

"I learned it from you, Dad, I learned it from you."

"Stop trying to make jokes about it. You vomited on Wyatt's cat two years ago, because you thought a white cat and Skittles vomit would be hilarious."

"I was just really impressed I caught that cat."

"Honestly, I don't know how we did that."

High fives self.

"Wait . . . stop tricking me, I'm trying to help you."

"Help me find a cat."

"Your roommates are gonna hate us."

"Probably, but this is college. This is our way of finding friends, we're gonna be fine."

"I don't think we're gonna be fine."

"Why?"

"It's day one, you're alone, and you turned a Spanish man into a human scab."

"I got confused and thought he was some sort of carnival ride."

"You know that actually scared us?"

"BLANKING IT OUT, I WILL DRINK MORE."

"I don't like you anymore, go away."

"I fucking hate you back."

I left the bathroom mirror upset with myself. I was drunk and alone and no amount of Weezer was going to help. I decided it might be best to turn in early and try to sleep. It couldn't have been later than 9:00 p.m., and I remember I still wasn't used to the smell of my new room. I've always vaguely smelled of musk and rotten meat, so cleaning solvent and fresh sheets were acrid. I was used to the silence of my suburban town and the pipes made strange, aggressive noises, and there was a constant buzz from the students who had friends outside. All this was adding up to tossing and turning in a half-asleep haze that no amount of booze would help. Normally the spins put me right to sleep, which made me wonder if someone shook me as a baby instead of rocking me.

I was in the middle of that thought when I heard what could only be described as a gunshot. The sound pierced me right to my insides and vibrated my organs. I looked outside and, although my windows were open, no one had hit the floor. The trivial drivel of drunken college students continued to fill the air while I was petrified and wondered if this was a panic attack. The noise was as if a crane had dropped its load onto a slab of concrete and I was scared, so I grabbed a knife and walked into the common area.

There are only five things in life I still can't understand, after recently figuring out how they put ships in bottles and what gender Criss Angel is. What I walked into in my common area is *numero uno*. I have never recreated it, and it's only happened one other time and Stevie Steve and I both witnessed it. I walked into the common area and saw that every single drawer had been opened at the same time, all the furniture had been stacked, and the windows slammed shut. I ran over and checked the lock, which was still bolted, and looked to see if the screens in the windows had holes in them. My spine shivered as I stood in the room holding a knife and wondering what the hell had just happened. Thinking it was my roommates arriving and playing gags, I put clear tape over the door and closed everything then put the furniture back.

That's when I lost it. I sat on my bed and let a few tears come out of my eyes. I had been abandoned by my family, with no roommates or neighbors interested in talking to me. I worried I might never actually make a friend in college, because it seemed so easy for my friends who went to Rutgers. I had ridden a Mexican man several feet in a parking lot, and I hadn't even paid him for a piggy back ride. Added to that a day full of rejection from women and now the possibility of a ghost, who played a prank that made me think he was clearly a frat boy stupid enough to be a TKE, and I was overwhelmed. My first night of college I cried for four whole minutes then buried my face in a pillow and went to sleep. Being young, alone, and drunk in the dark is clearly enough to turn the strongest of wills to a quivering crybaby.

I'm going to let the reader fill in the moral here. I just wanted to let all five people who read this feel a little comfort knowing that what they might be going through is scary. It's lonesome, but it's also a feeling millions of others have had.

> Hey, everyone. Look over here in the margin! So the second time something like this happened in 1A, Stevie and I both were there. I had mentioned earlier in the day the old myth on our campus about another set of apartments being haunted. My oldest brother went to Montclair, and talked about the other apartments having a pack of dogs in the back and ghosts inside. Stevie and I were leaving, and when he closed his door I heard the same noise from inside his room. We looked to see if anything fell or broke and found *nada*. I count these two events on the same finger. It's my thumb.

The Decimation of Delta Kyle

College is when the real bad shit actually starts to happen. You're faced with situations you're not worldly enough to handle, and sometimes it's abominable. Like I've stated, support your bros like they support you. He's in a weak moment and everyone can use a friend in situations like this. However, there are times when that's taken for granted. There are times when a man's crying becomes so selfish and dickish that immediate retribution and tough love needs to happen. Just because someone is in a bad moment, doesn't give them free rein to be an asshole.

Delta Kyle was a meek, short-statured, nerdy kid who everyone on campus had come to love. He was the epitome of a guy who joined a frat because he wouldn't have made friends otherwise. Normally that would be disgusting, but Kyle was also sweet and a little silly. He was a dwarf compared to me, with his crew cut only coming up to the top of my abs. His face was slightly riddled with acne that probably should have gone away years before. He had thin, silver wire-rimmed glasses that white washed his already pale skin. His body was untrained and unsavage. His oversized hoodies, with the Delta Kai frat logo, made his body look like it was swimming in fabric. Kyle was never my friend, but he was always pleasant and well mannered in a way that reminded me of a child who was properly raised and close with his family.

So as an orange sunset was cascading over the hills of Montclair State University and I sat alone smoking a cigarette, it was strange to watch Delta Kyle walking toward me incredibly slowly in the distance. I sat at the top of the staircase in front of those two infamous benches, in front of my favorite courtyard, enjoying a moment of quiet solitude, while a figure clad in all black gradually got larger as he progressed down the sidewalk. In life there was always a moment of solace before a storm happens, but being awash in orange colors and cool breezes could lull anyone into a state of bliss.

It took Kyle half an hour to walk four hundred feet. Once he got close, I saw his eyes were red rimmed and his shoulders were slunk. He looked like a human sigh, the definition of mopey. This bothered me because I had never known Delta Kyle to have anything but a smitten grin on his face, like he constantly just said in his head "Achievement Unlocked." I stood up and grabbed him, only saying, "It's time for a drink," like Lenny man-handling a rabbit, and pulled him down the hall and into my room.

I sat Delta Kyle down and poured him my current passion, Captain Morgan Tattoo. It's always foreshadowing of something terrible when I say, "Captain Morgan Tattoo." I loved the way getting rum drunk hit me, leaving me energized so generally I made terrible decisions. This night however, I was completely in the right. Kyle and I blasted a shot of Tattoo, and he let the water works go. In his defense, having a mouthful of pirate isn't for everyone. Kyle regaled me with the world's most boring breakup story. I was trying to be understanding and empathetic but it was just . . . so . . . boring.

> Side note in the universe of MSU: I do think it was this night that our good friend The Governor was at a party that was so terrible, he got obliterated and peed on the young lady's door mat.

She had seen him earlier that day and broken up with him. It was that simple. The reasons were valid too: they were in college they probably wouldn't build a life together after, so they should live it up. In my mind, this was all completely reasonable. I even wrote down what she said, right in front of him, in case I ever needed to remember how to have the easiest breakup ever. I kept doing shots and he occasionally tagged along. Listening to the meek little guy made me want to tussle his hair and tuck him in for the night.

Instead I suggested we smoke a spliff outside where I had found him. In all honesty, Montclair State had created one of the best courtyards ever. Directly to the right of the benches I preach about throughout this book, there was a perfectly maintained courtyard that my room looked directly into. There was clean and well maintained grass, which I would walk through barefoot throughout college, in a space perfectly sized to toss a Frisbee but not large enough to play football. It was surrounded on two sides by the apartment complex itself, and bordered by a gravel pit for drainage off the building's roof. The stone was not crushed, rather, the type of smooth pebbles you'd skip over a lake. They were dotted in blues and reds and greys, each rock either marbled with shiny quartz or completely flat toned. (I just spent three sentences describing gravel so to answer your question, yes, I did do mushrooms and stare into them for an entire night once.) Closest to my window, there sat heavily carved stone tables and seats, and most nights people could be found at those benches smoking cigarettes, drinking beer, and having their conversations cataloged with surprising detail by a strange drunkard who would later write a book about it.

Kyle and I stumbled through that fluffy, cold grass and sat on a stone table. I set the spliff aflame and watched as the smoke wafted and danced into the air. I passed it over to Kyle who took one drag and started coughing till his eyes were red rimmed again. I thought, *Poor kid can't catch a break today.* I handed him a rum and coke I brought out with me. After taking two sips and quelling his cough, Delta Kyle decided it would be a gentlemanly time if we both attempted to flip the stone table. Even as an adult, if someone asks me to throw something across the room or flip something I will do it. The flip and the crash are appeasing to the ears and therapeutic to the soul. When we realized we were outmatched, I decided we should throw a few rocks and yell into the air and call it a night. I had done my good deed and had other plans to get to.

Kyle was drunk, very drunk, drunker than Kyle should have ever gotten. As we stumbled across the grass, he stopped me and said, "I trained Brashilllian jew jutsu." Smiling, I asked, "Under who?" and was greeted by a kick directly to the side of my ankle. It was already throbbing and it gave a low moan then a crack when I attempted to move it. It doesn't matter how small someone is when it's a sucker hit. I can still pop my right ankle because one tiny bastard caught me off guard. I knew he was pretty drunk, so I did not plan to hurt Delta Kyle. I reached over and took the glasses off his face as he brought his hands up to guard it in a boxing stance that made him look like he had never seen lady bits before. I smiled and thrashed him across the top of the head with my open right hand. "I was being nice allll night to you, ya little prick." I smacked him with my left. "I gave you booze and let you cry." When Kyle tried to kick me, he fell on his back. I picked him up by his hoodie and threw him. The resounding noise of crumpling bones and egos echoed between the two surrounding walls. I then walked over to give him a hand and help him up.

I saw Four Fingas coming up the steps with Cookie Dough and I waved to them while I threw Kyle over my shoulders. I was fireman carrying the guy who had just snapped my ankle. My shoulders were hunching under his weight and I walked toward the courtyard entrance to greet

Four Fingas and avoid eye contact with Cookie Dough. Not only because he walked like the Pillsbury Dough boy and I couldn't stop myself from laughing at it, but I currently owed him money. I showed Four Fingas that my ankle was blacker and bluer than a frat boy's ass after Hell Week. When he asked who did it, I shrugged Delta Kyle up and down. Four Fingas looked at him. At that moment Delta Kyle got his second wind, squirming and writhing, and he brought his knee up directly into my nose so hard a little ribbon of blood started immediately coming out of my nose. Kneeing someone who's holding you over six feet in the air is stupid. Delta Kyle should have been smarter, because as soon as I realized what happened, I grabbed my nose and let go of him. Thankfully for him, I dropped him head first into a garbage can instead of onto the concrete.

Blood rushed down my face and I was pissed I had caught two cheap shots that night. I thought I'd leave him in the garbage can, his moaning and struggling was gratifying to watch after all I had been put through. Instead Four Fingas said, "Let's be nice and get him to his room." After taking the keys off his belt to open his door, and twenty dollars or so out of his pocket, I dropped him in the middle of the floor in his room and felt validated. Four Fingas, however, always had my best interest in mind. He laid Delta Kyle on his side, and opened the fridge.

Four Fingas is and always will be one of the most beautiful people on earth for this. I sat with a bloodied nose and an ankle swelling to the size of a grape fruit, while my roommate grabbed all of the lunch meat. I do not mean a little lunch meat. I mean there were four college students living in Kyle's apartment with him, and Four Fingas took all of their lunch meat out of its plastic bags and threw it as hard as he could into Kyle's face. Kyle remained passed out on the floor, as a resounding *splat* echoed through the room. Four Fingas looked at me and said, with the utmost seriousness, "Sandwiches need bread and mayo." Then he tossed me a squeeze bottle of mayo, and I squeezed it like a five-year-old holding a bunny. Eggs, vinegar, and whatever the hell else is in mayo splattered on Kyle's face and clothes, and then I painted the walls of his common area. By this time neither Frankie nor I were thinking; it was autopilot. We took the frozen food out of the freezer and threw it everywhere and covered passed out Kyle in raw hamburger meat.

Cookie Dough saw the fun and decided to jump in himself. He picked up an apple and as he was about to wing it at Kyles head we both grabbed him. Four Fingas, speaking like a teacher to a fourth grader said, "We only hit people with soft things." That started a rampage. We took all the condiments and food in that refrigerator and poured it on him. Mountain Dew, milk, cheeses, leftover spaghetti, a tub of margarine, maple syrup, sausage, pepper, and onions. We covered Kyle so gratuitously that if he had stood up the floor would have had a food angel imprint. His walls looked like someone yelled FOOD FIGHT at family reunion. They were dripping the type of poor college kid food that only someone living in a trailer would get jealous of. After eating half the mac and cheese in the fridge, we dumped the rest on his head and chucked some at the walls. We nodded and walked back to our rooms and I think had a party that night.

Three months later, I jokingly pushed Kyle as he passed by me. I said, "Thanks for the ankle, dick bag, how was your wall buffet?" Kyle's mouth dropped into an open mouth frown and he trembled, and no air came out when he tried to say, "That was you?"

I cracked my ankle and showed him pictures of my nose on my phone. I explained to him what he did and he said, "Dude, my roommates thought I got drunk and did that. I had to go to a therapist to stay on campus." I couldn't hide my glee at his statement and laughed in his face. I explained how I was trying to be nice and he ruined everything. He and I remained distant friends after this, but he said to me, "It's pretty weird because that girl wasn't even my girlfriend."

Chapter 3

DRINKING

I'm sorry I peed in your closet

Sorry I got drunk and peed in your closet at the party last night

I didn't have a party last night

Grand Theft Academics: Stealing is Only Awesome While Drinking

I'm a hypocrite. I know I am because I make fun of the very thing I go on to admit is fun in other parts of this book.

Drinking and stealing go together like the South and racism, the South and oversized portions, the South and . . . basically, the South sucks. Drinking leads to loose morals and huge ball sacks, so naturally you have the inclination to take shit for no reason. It's immature and stupid, but anyone who says it's not fun should be pushed in front of a crash landing jet. It's stupid and you're probably not going to use any of the shit, but it's still fun. You're going to do it eventually. Even one of my more moral roommates picked up a case of Red Bull from a school store and walked off with it, which made him a hero at the party. So here are the best, and kind-of safest, things you're going to inevitably steal.

Road Cones. It's stupid, it's unexplainable, but it's incredibly fun to steal these stupid florescent pylons. Nothing really feels as free as hopping into your friend's car after you've jammed one of these worthless pieces of junk into the trunk and giggling together. Think about it, that's maybe two dollars worth of plastic you've stolen, but the symbolism is enormous. You've stolen from the government, man. You did more than steal a road cone. You took something back from a government that oppresses people. Actually, you really just stole a road cone and that's kind of silly. There is absolutely nothing awesome to do with a road cone, it just sits there and looks obnoxious. You can try funneling beer through it, but that doesn't really work. The act of stealing it is way better than the aftermath. Throw it in your parents' attic until you get your first apartment, then be an asshole and use the cone to save your street parking spot at your first real place.

Construction Signs. These look like they'd make great decorations, until you realize they're too hard to hang on the wall. Also realize they are a bitch to steal if they're not already on the ground. The people who put these things up make it harder on you by bending the bolt and nut. If you're going to steal a road sign, it takes effort so make sure you get one of the good signs. Taking a "Blind Child in Area" sign means no one will see it's gone. Besides, letting people know there is a blind kid in the area won't stop someone stupid enough to hit a child with their car, it will just let them know a hit-and-run is plausible. "Deaf Child" is okay too. Just because they're deaf doesn't mean they're stupid. Sure they can't hear a honking horn, but they can still look both ways. If a deaf kid gets killed because of a missing sign, it just means evolution would have taken him out eventually anyway. The best ones are "Speed Hump" or "Do Not Enter," putting those on the door of someone you hate with epoxy leads to days worth of hilarity.

Pint Glasses. These aren't glasses, they're trophies. Steal as many of these as possible. This is the one thing you steal in college that makes its way to adulthood. For the rest of your life, you can look at the pint glasses you've stolen and remember the days before you had a shitty nine-to-five job and wanted to kill yourself. There is zero harm in stealing these, besides being an awful cost burden on the bar you steal from. But who cares, when one bar closes another one usually opens and you'll have a pint glass to remember them by.

Bottles of Booze at Parties. Yes, this sucks. It's awful when it happens to you, but so is the fact anyone wasted a night at your shitty party. Proper planning and care goes into a great party and, since you were oblivious, someone is going to steal bottles of booze. This goes both ways. Showing up at a crap party means you have the social responsibility to let them know how awful they are. Stealing booze shortens the party and lets people know they suck. Crush their soul so they think everyone hates them and they drop out of college. If you don't do it, a sophomore-level class will. Bottle Karma is a real thing, for every bottle you take you'll get one stolen from you, etc. That's why you go for big scores and try to steal five or six bottles at once. Karma will pay you back positively, if you throw a much better bash with them.

Behymens. I can't stress this enough, college is a time to experiment. Things are going to accidentally end up in holes and you're going to take someone's behyment. What you give is what you get, so try a finger up there if you're going to give a finger up there. Butt stuff is harder to get as people get older and gain self-worth. It can be impossible to do for weeks on end as a full-fledged adult. People actually get self-confidence around the age of twenty-six, so practice everything while people still feel bad enough about themselves to let you. It's a two-way street. If you've thought about trying it, there is someone in a class or on the Internet who'll do that for you. Stick a finger in every hole until you figure out who you really are.

Drinks. Sometimes chugging vodka in your car before you get to a bar isn't enough to make the night manageable, and that six bucks you have in your bank account won't help. This is when the art of stealing a drink comes in handy. Gobe (from a story or two in this book) once got drunk at a concert by bringing a long straw and drinking from people's glasses while they held it. No matter how you do it, it's dickish. Make sure you take the glass with you at a bar so the person you stole it from can blame a bus boy or bartender for stealing it. Bear Grylls can go fuck himself. College kids know how to survive on nothing.

BROBOT: The Art Of The Nickname

Whether you like it or not, everyone is kind of a bro now. There is a little bit in all of us. Sure, you may not pound Four Loko and wear a polo, but that doesn't mean you're not bro-ish. If you've ever drunk too much unapologetically, or done something amazingly stupid and pounded a beer to celebrate, you're kind of a bro. If you've ever skipped class and still pulled an A, you're kind of a bro. Most of all, if you have a nickname . . . you're a bro. I got my nickname when my dad got drunk and slurred my real name, solidifying me as a partial-bro from a very young age. In fact nicknames are a way of shedding the stigma of the name and expectations that your family has for you. Nicknames are more than just being a bro, they're about being a good college student. A nickname is more than just something someone yells at you from down the hall. It's part of your legacy.

A nickname is more than just a name given to you because of something you did. It's the start of the legend people share about you for years to come. You are going to end up seeing a lot of college friends after college, and while you're all drunk you're going to reminisce about the stupidity you accomplished. Any time a new girlfriend or new friend gets introduced, your entire backstory is going to be told to them. A nickname is a catalog of all the crimes against social etiquette you've managed to act out over the years.

A nickname softens the blow a little bit and makes you a bearable person. Saying, "This is Edward and this one time he got in a fight with three crackheads after shotgunning beers all night," makes that person sound like a terrible, terrible human being. Calling him Etown makes him a character instead of a sociopath. It's much easier for people to tolerate your terrible behavior if they think of you as a character instead of an actual human being, who's completely broken. Making yourself seem socially acceptable to others when you have done nothing but terrible and hilarious deeds is a glorious side effect of having a nickname. Simply put, it's better to explain that Wreckage slept with one of his teachers and only got a C than to say, "This is Evan and he's mediocre in bed."

A nickname is an alternate persona. We all have them, especially when we drink too much. There is a glorious few moments of drunkenness where we're bearable, fun-loving people who just want to enjoy a party. One or two beers after that moment, we all become monsters who have little to no control over our actions. Blaming everything on an alternate personality draws the line between who you want to be and who you actually are. Sure, you may have an alter ego called Svetlana or Spike, but they only exist to cover up the fact that deep down you're still a terrible, gutter-trash person. Save you real name for when you do nice or charitable things, or possibly graduate college instead of being a low life.

Getting a nickname isn't easy. The first rule of nicknames is, you're not allowed to make your own nickname. Giving yourself a nickname is the equivalent of masturbation: you're the only one enjoying it. Douche bags make their own nicknames and they're usually something way too flattering or seem forced. Those aren't real. The best way to get a nickname is to get incredibly, pants-shittingly drunk with your best friends and see what happens. No one in college ever gets completely smashed and just lays around; you'll end up doing something terrible or hilarious that inspires a name. Don't force anything, and eventually one of your friends will just blurt out something silly and it will catch on. It's the simplest and most gratifying way to get a nickname.

Sometimes, a nickname can just be a nickname though. Once I asked Four Fingas how he got his nickname and all he said was "I'm Italian and I like to gamble." It was that simple. Sometimes you don't need to assign anything more to a nickname than a a simple expression of who you are.

If that doesn't work, the only other solution is to come up with a simple word play on your name. It will be close and people will easily put the two together, but it's better than nothing when it comes down to it. It's much better to have something close to your real name and still have an alias than it is to have no alias at all. Nicknames are a glorious scapegoat, a brilliant little reminder that you aren't quite a person yet. When you have one and use it you can escape the crushing expectations of society and life with a little less responsibility.

Hangovers: Avoid Them More Than Someone Who Wants to Talk About Social Issues

Hangovers are the bane of everyone's existence, no matter what age you are. From fourteen to the age of forty, a hangover leaves you sluggish and makes everything you do feel like more work than a needy significant other. The headaches, the vomiting, the calling your mom and talking about how you want to turn your life around, almost makes the drinking not worth it. Actually nothing makes drinking not worth it. Alcohol is a wildly abused depressant that makes for incredible life experiences. It makes people more relaxed, but those same people become unbearable the next day. If you're going to abuse booze, do it responsibly.

SKYY Vodka. I wish I had a product sponsorship for this book. I would have lived a lot better while writing. SKYY Vodka was created by someone who had incredibly bad hangovers after drinking a single beer. The distillation process used in SKYY somehow makes the next day slightly more bearable. Drinking SKYY and soda water keeps you hydrated without ruining your buzz. My senior year in college, I was drinking a bottle or two of this a day to combat the damage I had done to my brain and liver. Personally I can attest that SKYY Vodka is the drink for any binge drinker who doesn't care about their credit card balance.

Vitamins. I have always taken shit from people who tell me this doesn't help, but those people are always the first to take my vitamin cocktail after they've had one too many. Drinking steals vitamins and water away from you. It takes everything you need and leaves you a broken husk, wondering what to do with your life, not that different from the higher-education system itself. This is why, before I even start drinking, I lay out vitamins and water. Sure, I often puked them up in the morning, but those few hours of absorption cut my hangovers down to almost nothing. My secret cocktail was a multivitamin, B-Complex stacked with extra Niacin, then a ZMA. I would take all of this with something greasy and fatty to help my body absorb the vitamins, and then chew two Pepto-Bismol tablets. It seems like a lot, but it took five minutes to do and I'd wake up and crank out all the papers and homework for the week the morning after. Everyone is different, so try a cocktail of your own.

Water and Aspirin. This is the old go-to to make any hangover tolerable. A trusted and wonderful way to make walking to the fridge bearable enough to gorge yourself on food until you feel better. Twenty or thirty minutes before you fall down drunk and asleep on the floor, chug as much water as possible and take two aspirin—it's foolproof. It won't get rid of the hangover, but it will make the next morning feel better until you get a look at what's in your bed from last night.

Weed. Weed helps cancer patients to feel better, so why wouldn't it be able to help with a hangover? It will disassociate you from the pain so you can function until you're able to be a human again. It encourages eating, speeds up your metabolism enough to process all the shit you've still got in you, and makes lying on a couch feeling crappy a little bit better. Weed is like water and aspirin but it costs more and you may find yourself doing a hair of the dog and partying again.

Cold Pizza. The be-all and end-all of the college experience, this stuff will make you show up to a hall meeting or even one of those international groups. Free pizza will make a college student show up for a cause they couldn't care less about. Free Tibet, Free Pizza. Cold pizza is still pizza and, when eaten during a hangover, it feels like it absorbs all the booze left in your system. It might be the grease, it might be the almost-vegetables, or it could be the incredible marketing campaigns from the nineties—cowabunga, dude. Whatever it is, cold pizza always seems to make a hangover a little better.

Hair of The Dog. Don't do this. This isn't a hangover cure. It's a bender starter. After about three days of hairing the dog, you'll have no idea what happened or why you're now living in a new apartment.

Closing Time

Congratulations, you've officially gotten to last call and you're still standing. That's a real accomplishment, not like arbitrary things like grades or honors. It's past 2:00 a.m. and everything's closed, but your friend keeps talking about keeping the party going while inhaling through his nose a little more often than normal. He's talked everyone into staying awake for a while longer, because the best stuff happens at crazy times. He's neglected to realize that if you're out at that time and inebriated, you're statistically going to be one of those incidents. But since everyone in college runs off hormones and Hot Pockets, there are still some unexpected places to go after every other party has died down.

Playgrounds. Look, this sounds perverted, but playgrounds after dark are amazing places. They're where you can buy weed from high schoolers, and see other groups of drunks try to fuck around on monkey bars. There are a million distractions for a drunkard at a playground, all of which they can get hurt on and end the night. I've witnessed a man running in only a tube sock as police chased him on more than one occasion. Playgrounds have enough half-physical distractions to keep you slightly awake enough to be drunk with friends. Puking on a slide makes it a water slide for the kids to play on tomorrow.

The Middle of the Woods. If you pass out in the middle of the city, some-one is going to steal one shoe at least. Passing out in a friend's place can be just as perilous, and you'll still wake up with a shoe gone. Personally, I often brought a sleeping bag and a tarp to wherever I thought I might be staying. Not drinking and driving does mean waking up and regretting. In all the places I've randomly woken up, the woods always seemed the safest. Grab some friends and let a stroll turn into a quest for Mordor, ending in you all waking up with mosquito bites. Honestly, if you have a sleeping bag and a tarp, it's warm, cozy, and quiet enough for when you wake up with that hung over headache.

Class. Holy shit, the bars closed hours ago and half the people you were with have dropped and gone to bed. It's just you and one or two other people awake and devoted to self-harm. The sun's coming up, and you're worried what the hell you're going to do now. It's probably time to go to class. Look down at your phone (if you still have it) and figure out when your first class is. There is literally nothing else to do at this time of morn-ing besides go get breakfast and get to class. At least in a classroom there's some nice white noise to lull you to sleep. Sometimes all you need is an hour or two of sleep, and class forces you to leave when it's over.

The Hospital. The later you stay out, the higher the inebriation level. The higher the inebriation level, the more likely there are to be injuries. Everywhere else may be closed but the ER is open 24/7. Dare your friend to do something stupid, or just do a heel tap and land wrong for a lifelong and chronic injury. Additionally, the ER takes forever to get anything done so you can stay entertained for hours watching the friend who got hurt sober up and be in worse and worse pain. Every now and again something gruesome to stare at for a while comes in too. All in all, the ER isn't a bad place to end the night as long as you're not the one hurt.

Convenience Stores. These are also 24/7, so they're always somewhere to end up. Sometimes this is a great place to go, because you get to watch a robbery or the severely wasted eat 2:00 a.m. hot dogs and buy lotto tickets. There is no loitering outside in the parking lot, but loitering inside is okay. Ask them about every type of E-Cig they have and hope someone drunker, and more pathetic than you, comes in. Keep an eye out for old guys buying porn and underage kids buying condoms. Anyone up that late is up to no good, so look out for the stories behind everyone that comes in. Is he a guy who gets off work at this hour, or perhaps a guy who's on his way home from cheating on his wife? This is better than any party you can go to.

Beirut is a fucking place, Pong is a game

Beer Pong is the most popular way to get drunk among college stu-dents. They like to put another step between themselves and the drinking to help them feel like there is a reason to keep going. Problem drinkers just drink, winners drink for sport. Beer Pong can be found at every single party, and nothing is worse than when a game drags on forever (i.e., lasts longer than ten minutes). If you're not good enough to finish, go back home and practice on your own. There are a few easy tricks to make yourself better at the easiest drinking game on earth.

Kill Yourself. Seriously—it's throwing a ball at a cup. This isn't rocket science. Although rocket science is throwing a huge piece of million-dollar equipment at a planet, so I'm not sure which is harder. A small ball going into a bigger circle is literally the simplest game on the planet. If you can't get mediocre at this game, just play it on your own until you can't play anything ever again. If you play ten games in a row on your own, you'll be good enough to play at any party. Don't be obnoxious and prolong everyone else's drinking while they're waiting to play a game that prolongs their own drinking.

Throw Stuff at Other Stuff. Literally throwing anything at anything will make you better at pong. Try throwing knives at a crosswalk or glass at your own wrist. Set up some bottles on a fence, aim at them, and then jump into a dangerous exhibit at a zoo. You shouldn't have to be told this stuff. Try throwing a baseball at a niece or nephew then work your way up from there. Next, throw a hot dog down a hallway, or a red cup at any sporting event. I'm not joking. If you threw snowballs at cars as a kid you should be able to play a game of Beer Pong.

Be Entertaining About It. If you're going to hold up the line, at least make sure you're entertaining about it. If you're too bad a shot then whip out a testicle, show an ovary, rip your gall bladder out and shoot with that instead. Being a sore winner or loser makes everyone's time a little bit easier. Taunt your opponents as much as possible, talk about how you'll sink a ball into someone's sister's cup. Go into your opponent's pockets, remove their cell phone, then choke on it. Climb under the Beer Pong table, have everyone climb on top of it, and then kick the legs out so you get splattered. The game doesn't even have its own equipment. It's so easy it took another sport's name AND ball. Stepping your Beer Pong game up is as simple as playing on your own for twenty minutes.

Master the Behind the Back Shot. The only thing you can actually do to up your Beer Pong game is to master the behind the back shot. You don't just master that shot either, first there's some weird yoga you have to do. Then, since the shots so hard, you have to make a deal with the devil in exchange for your soul. Then, to gain the sheer determination to successfully pull off the shot, you have to kill a basket of puppies to show the pong gods you're heartless and ready for the power they have to bestow on you. Seriously, the behind the back shot would probably take hours and hours to master. I've never seen it sunk. So don't bother wasting your time. I'm not even sure that mastering the behind the back shot would show how awesome you are at pong, or how lacking you are in every other facet of your life.

Beer Pong is an easy game. It's simple and straightforward. It's such an easy game that people who are shit-faced wasted can still play it. You're throwing a tiny ball into a pretty wide-mouthed cup while you drink the beer in your hand. Beer Pong isn't something to actually be proud of. It's basically an activity that slows down your drinking while doing it. If you want to get better at playing Beer Pong, throw a tiny ball at a cup in your room for a while. You should feel nothing but shame and self-hatred as you do that though.

All Hallows Summer's Eve: Why Halloween is Most Important Holiday

Halloween has always been the best holiday. Look at it clearly: at every age Halloween is the best holiday of the year. As a kid you don costumes, stay out past your bedtime with friends, and get free candy. Then you eat free candy until you feel sick and someone pukes. As a young adult, they add the aspect of "mischief night," A time to focus all those confusing pubescent feelings into rage, then go back to the houses you wrecked to get free candy. Then you eat as much as you can until you feel like crap and puke. Once young adulthood comes around, someone's brother buys some beer, girls start wearing costumes that make you feel funny, then someone drinks too much until they puke and pass out. High school is when Halloween gets even better. Girls slap the word "slutty" in front of anything and call it a costume. Really those costumes are gift-wrapping for all all the syphilis you're going to get. You get drunk around half-naked people, someone pukes, then you all go and pass out. You get the picture yet? Halloween is the best during your college years. There are a ton of different parties to go to and if you have social anxiety you can wander the campus and take in the sights or wear a mask.

Costumes are a source of constant entertainment on Halloween. When it comes to costumes there are three types: funny, "this again?", and sexy. College is where you start to really develop a sense of humor, and that comes out in the costumes. Every now and again, someone puts a lot of thought into their costume and comes up with something hilarious. Yes, they're showing a massive need for attention, but at least they're making an effort to make everyone else's night. Seeing a cool costume makes people smile and helps them to enjoy the night.

Then there are the costumes you're going to see at *every* party. These are uncreative pieces of shit and they should be shunned and banned. They don't take Halloween serious enough and should be forced to go trick or treating and supply whatever party they want to gain entrance to with bribes of candy while they eat apples with razor blades. If you see someone dressed as Hunter Thompson, then drug them, and anyone dressed as The Boondock Saints should have a toilet dropped on their head, The Blues Brothers and Tom Cruise in *Risky Business* should have their sunglasses broken and be forced to sit on them. These once-beloved characters have been watered down and destroyed by generations of college kids making last minute costumes.

The final type, the "sexy costume," is simple and easy. If you're a guy, be some sort of gladiator or Roman. If you're a girl, pretty much wear anything. It's confusing why we as a society have deemed that women should only look this way one night a year, but they can literally throw sexy in front of anything and it's acceptable.

The only costume that is never acceptable in any case ever is the "Sexy Bee." It's awful. There is nothing sexy about a bee costume. It's your way of telling everyone you don't give a shit about Halloween or about yourself. When the sexy bee walks in the room, everyone sighs and silently wishes you never showed up to the party. It's the least creative costume to ever exist and seeing it lets everyone know it was last minute and you probably don't leave your house often. No one ever looks at a sexy bee and thinks about anything other than spraying it with the chemicals under the sink. It's the worst costume and it needs to stop making the companies who put it out there money.

Condoms and morals have one thing in common on Halloween: they're not used. Dressing up then getting drunk leads to the best bad decisions you can make. It's like having an alternate persona for one night, an awful, drunk, slutty, and wonderful persona. It's always a treat to see what atrocious actions people will perform on a brisk Halloween night. Something about the cool air and lack of sobriety mixes in with a foggy October night to make people live out their weirdest dreams and fantasies. It's a night when Shrek might bang a contestant from *Legends of the Hidden Temple*. A night when Ms. Frizzle might have the first beer of her life and end up screaming at all of her friends for being idiots. Honestly, Halloween is a night when a volatile mix is in the air and absolutely anything could happen.

Warm cider is one of the very best things about Halloween parties. When you've been drinking for hours and you can feel the acidity in your stomach, nothing calms it and keeps you going like a warm cider. Sure, it's just store-bought cider with cinnamon and vodka, but it doesn't change the fact that it helps. Most people who are out on Halloween are half naked so a warm cider makes the night a little bit less nippy, for better or worse. Warm cider brings a little warmth to your bones, and that way you don't have to explain "it was cold out" when she sees your bone.

The walks of shame after Halloween keep the fun from the night before alive. There is nothing better than watching a Disney princess taking a walk of shame the night after Halloween. An amazing pasttime is to sit on a roof or porch or even bench and watch the walks of shame as they roll in. Staying drunk from the night before and watching as The Hulk's half-smeared body paint moves down the sidewalk looking sad is amazing, Captain America looks more like Colonel Canada. There are thousands of characters to watch as they all leave wherever they slept. Remember, she doesn't have to be Cinderella to have left a shoe behind.

The very best part about the holiday is that no one gives a fuck. Dad's taking kids out trick or treating get drunk and puke in sewer drains, Moms make hard cider and invite other adults over, giving kids places to throw parties. Everyone in college puts whatever dramatic bullshit they have going on aside and goes out to have a great time. It's several days' worth of costumes, parties, and bad decisions Everyone gets a free pass on Halloween, nothing is too scandalous or bad because Halloween is supposed to get as weird as possible. So don't say Let's Get Weird, then start crying when someone dresses as Hitler and ends up making out with Katy Perry.

Kidnapping is the Highest Form of Flattery

Average nights in 1A during my last semester of college involved craft beers, roommates playing music, and very close friends. Instead of drunk people scrambling out of the apartment like Mexicans when they hear, "*La Migra*," my friends loafed on couches and stared off into their own thoughts. Coming out of my room to find familiar faces asleep on the ground became an event I took solace in while I nursed a splitting headache leftover from the night before. Adulthood was reaching its slithery tentacles into my psyche, and I knew that once I had a degree, my world would end.

No matter how quiet and serene things were, having me as a roommate meant there was always a palpable toxicity in the air, an unquestionable knowledge things could get weird at any moment. On this particular night, I had come back from a class where the professor didn't know my name, but knew my grades and was happy to finally meet me. If having issues with authority and avoiding teachers was gradable, I wouldn't have lost 10 percent of every grade because of attendance. My feet were as tired as my mind, so I saw smoking weed as a treat I deserved. A flick of tinder and a flex of my lungs meant relaxation was seconds away as my brain reacted to THC. Dry mouth led to the desire for two fingers of whiskey and a night without The Girl I Was Dating.

I was smoking so much weed in college that I should have been wearing a poncho, with a liberal arts degree to match. My RA, a fellow smoker, thought I'd enjoy being invited over to listen to Bob Marley and drink yerba mate every week because the smell from my room was so pungent it would give a skunk an erection. I'm still not entirely sure he was just smoking weed, because not only should white people never drink mate, they definitely shouldn't tell people about it. My lungs were so polluted, the only reason I didn't end up with a bullshit degree like communications is because I knew marketing would look better to a corporate slave master. Other smokers would waste time playing video games and talking about legalization, while I sat on the couch pondering the joys of choking anyone who had ever talked about the benefits of hemp clothing. The world already knew the benefits of hemp, so when it was mentioned in casual conversation I drifted off wondering whether a stalk of hemp was strong enough to tie someone to while burning them alive like the witch they were. A grin would creep over my face at the thought of getting high from revenge instead of THC.

I was so accustomed to high-grade marijuana that an inferior batch made my mind a maze of paranoid delusion. The blunt I was smoking was so atrocious I looked over my shoulder more times than a racist about to tell an abominable joke. Police could be anywhere. Entering my room I noticed the normal, comforting, familiar faces, but in a haze of paranoia I forgot who these people were and was convinced my roommates had thrown a cult party and soon we would all drink the Kool Aid. At least I knew they'd have the common decency to fill it with tequila to dilute the taste of strychnine. I quietly drank beer and shifted around on my couch in an effort to get comfortable. Adding beer to this situation was like trying to put out a Californian forest fire by throwing Californian homeless on it, those sun beaten degenerates look like they'd light up faster than Paul Walker's Porsche. (Fun fact: the only thing more flammable than a sun burnt heroin addict from California was my liver in college.) When stoned off trash weed, my social skills were the equivalent of a blind man trying to put together a puzzle. Sure, all the pieces are in front of him, but he just can't put them together. When being reintroduced to a weasel faced guy named Mike, I called him, "The guy who ate poop on a dare," because his name escaped me. No one likes the guy who can't remember your name, but can remember your most embarrassing moment. Simply put, it's hard to talk to people when you're imagining how many objects in the room they can use to kill you.

Every single person in the room became a possible informant for the housing probation office, sent to finally get me kicked out of school. I made more rounds of small talk, while imagining getting the final notice that all my partying had officially turned me into a college drop out. I was walking the razor's edge between insanity and charm. Half the room was crying tears of laughter while I imagined the inevitable explanation I'd be giving my parents that my abuse of inebriates, dollar store toys, and anything I could steal had forced the dean to create a new level of expulsion. In my mind my parents opened a letter that said, "You are failures as parents and people. Whatever managed to climb out of your womb is inhuman and should have been shot on sight. Please castrate him. The only time he should have even seen a vagina was when he was being pulled out with a coat hanger. Your son managed to cause enough mayhem on campus that although he's only been caught three times, those crimes have forced us to send him to the Montclair State University Internment Camp for reeducation and reha-bilitation. You'll find his tuition has doubled." I wish I could say I was joking here, but those were my honest to god thoughts as close friends—and people who would soon know me as that guy who sort of kidnapped someone—surrounded me.

In college Scott Glazaar (name not changed, fuck you, Scott) was just as insane as I was. I once told him about how I drank too much and pushed an Australian down a hill and his understated response was, "I've been there." But he was also very likely to be the guy who would tell all the Australians on campus I was racist against them. Which isn't far from the truth, can we really trust people who survive on a continent where 75 percent of everything is poisonous? To my knowledge even the sunshine there has found a way to poison humans. Scott and I were close; I once let him squat in my apartment for a month. That night, I had been mutter-ing to myself, "You're only paranoid because of the pot," which wasn't true because I was getting more stares than yoga pants. Scott grabbed me and decided it was time for the type of enlightening, life-changing conversation that only men in college under the impression they're going to change the world can have. Scott was sure porn stars didn't actually enjoy sex, while I furiously argued the opposite. His argument was there was no immediate vaginal wetness while I argued sex is actually very mental. Looking back I'm surprised either one of us had ever given a girl an orgasm.

As my paranoia subsided at the perfectly wrong moment, the entrance door flew open with a slam that frightened the room. Everyone's heads snapped to the entrance. I also turned to identify what filthy barbarian I, the bigger filthier barbarian, was about to punch only to be met by a strange blonde. I didn't like the way she looked, her eyes were sunken into her skull and overshadowed by a blue and orange tinge she had painted around her eyes. It wasn't like a sunset, where orange slowly overtakes the blue in a beautiful array of colors, she looked like someone threw a Bears jersey in a grease trap, peed on it, and gave it scabies crusts. She clearly had an obsession with fake animal skin because the only thing more noticeable than the pleather jacket and cheetah print clothing was the fact she applied her makeup with a putty knife. I consider people who wear too much cheetah print worse than the liquid garbage at the bottom of a dumpster. Fake animal skin is an indicator of a fake person. Knowing there is some poor child in Bangladesh making false cheetah skin in a factory, while worrying about a real cheetah eating them on the way home, makes me hate it. I can imagine an older factory worker who survived this life, "In my day, cheetahs chased us uphill both ways." I can't understand why people wear a fake print from a hunter that runs eighty miles per hour without working for it. Wearing the real thing shows you're a badass, wearing the fake stuff shows you have self-esteem issues. Wearing a pleather jacket over it infuriated me. Fake skin on fake skin on fake skin, deception Inception. I hated her.

All the guests shared eye contact and shrugs, puzzled and disapproving looks as if to say "Not my friend." She helped herself to a beer, draining it so quickly Scott looked turned on, and then left it on the floor. I thought "I THC you, and I'm gonna do something about it." I watched her Clorox-bleached hair make its way through a crowd and back to the hallway where our bedrooms were. I was rather carefree because we were smart enough to lock the individual rooms, but saw an opening when she threw open a door again, this time to the bathroom. Instead of making an entrance she made two dents in our walls. A vein in my temple started throbbing and my pupils must have dilated. It was established no one knew who she was, so in my drunken paranoid mind I thought we needed to keep her contained in a cage. If she were a cheetah, I'd have been a poacher. I wedged myself against the bathroom door and placed my feet against the walls waiting for her.

There was a push at my back but the door stayed closed. I yelled, "Who the fuck are you?" My temples were pulsing and her lack of an answer had sent my heart into overdrive. Was it time to taunt her? I yelled insults through the door and tried to get a reaction. Every time there was a push on the door, I pushed back and yelled things like, "I'll waterboard you if I don't get some answers." After forty minutes my roommates had the faces of children whose puppy was just hit by a car. With their jaws agape, one asked who I was kidnapping and why. I explained calmly that I was holding a young woman of questionable reputation and intention hostage for information and yelled at the door my roommates were bringing a ball gag and a sock with soap in it if I didn't get an answer. All of this seems crazy until you realize she could have taken more beer and possibly our Xbox, the two things no college male can live without. Soul Caliber on Dreamcast sucks and don't let any nostalgic hipster tell you otherwise.

Four hands grabbed me and pulled me from the door, but I managed to keep one foot pinned so she remained caged. Finally, they dragged me away and saved her from my personal Guantanamo Bay. Out came the cheetah-clad woman. Her face looked like a Van Gogh if he had muscular dystrophy when trying to paint. She had been sitting in the bathroom whimpering and not answering me. Everyone else gave her looks of sympathy. I was not the type to feel bad for any actions at this point in my life. She got to her feet like a freshly born baby deer and definitely looked as sticky. She walked past us without a word. When she tried to escape I stopped her, and was promptly punched in the face. Luckily my body grew a thick skull once it realized the stupidity of the brain inside it, so when she hurt her hand she ran for the exit, with the door swinging so hard it bashed into her previously made dent.

My roommates went back to drinking and laughing about it. They remember a silly night, but I remember a sliver of shame. The truth is I chased her down and confronted her because I react to slamming doors the same as a man in an unhappy marriage. I should have imagined her fear as a lumbering six-foot-five, one hundred and ninety-pound man came sprinting down the hall screaming, "I wasn't going to waterboard you." I yelled it enough times to make anyone who heard it think I was actually going to waterboard someone one-fourth of my size. I easily caught up to her because as far as drunk runners go, I'm almost an Ethiopian. Drunk Bread Foster should get donations for every mile of drunk running—we'd have beat cancer and burned all the stupid "awareness" shirts. I realized how stupid this girl really was when she stopped . . . she was dumb enough to enter a stranger's apartment and even stupider for stopping to talk. I was moving so fast that if she had stuck a leg out I'd have been doomed. Instead, she turned and punched me in head then called me a string of curse words that would make a pastor burn his Bible and lose his faith. This string of curse words was so bad even someone who doesn't speak English would move back to the Third World to explain how terrible America was. Farming cocoa fields for a cartel was better than hearing what she said. Clearly I made everything better by responding, "I'm not going to waterboard you, but I do have a car battery we could play with." Anyone who doesn't find that hilarious can suck my dick, except for her, because although she did not find that hilarious I imagined her vagina was cheetah print too.

I prodded her until she confessed she only came into our room to use the bathroom. I told her she needed to tell me the fucking truth because no one is that stupid. I have met people who claim being a mouth breather is genetic, not a choice, and they're smart enough to know not to walk into a stranger's home. I don't think anyone has ever needed to pee so badly that they think, *Screw popping a squat in a stairwell, I'm going to make myself a suspect in a home invasion.* Even nearly blackout drunk and super paranoid, wrapping my head around that level of stupidity seemed impossible. I was right for locking her in the bathroom, it was her fault I acted the way I did, and I let her know it as loud as I could. A great way to get your point across is to throw a couch. Don't throw it at people, but let them know what you're about by hurting furniture with other furniture. Basically the conversation showed me I'd be great at being in an abusive relationship.

I went and read four chapters in a marketing book and *Things Fall Apart* to repair my brain after our conversation. She had no idea that walking into a stranger's apartment, drinking their booze, and pissing would be seen as unacceptable. Realistically I should have locked her parents in the bathroom and waterboarded them. Not only for procreating, but for not then giving that child up to an agency or to the streets where it wouldn't have a chance to become a spoiled narcissist.

So, future college students, current college students, and nostalgic readers, what have we learned? I do not always follow my own advice. Walking into a stranger's apartment is only hilarious if you don't get caught. If you get caught it is only hilarious for the people catching you. If you're going to commit home invasion make sure you know how to properly open a door. We've learned that kidnapping is completely acceptable given the correct circumstances. We've come to the conclusion that Stockholm syndrome is the best aphrodisiac, and if you scream you're not going to do something into a stranger's face enough, everyone around you is going to think you are capable of torture. Most of all, we've learned Scott Glazaar has probably still never given a girl an orgasm.

In all seriousness, that's a night that I was very lucky I wasn't arrested, and she was very lucky I was a human and not a serial killer or a rapist. Some poor girl was screaming and crying in a bathroom and no one even noticed or cared for almost an hour. Everyone got lucky because I could have gone to jail for abduction of an endangered animal and she could have been killed for her pelt. While drunk and surrounded by drunks, it's very easy to lose sight of what's actually going on. Campuses are dangerous and while you think what you're doing is harmless, others might be so offended they're willing to capture you in a humane no-kill trap. I'm sorry to say I still feel very little regret for my actions in this case. In my mind I was protecting friends; I will never know what went through her mind because she's probably stupid enough to laugh when her alphabet soup spells one of five words she can actually read. This all happened on a weekday as well. It's important to assess the situation you're in and react accordingly. Being in college, you're going to push the line to see what you can get away with, just stop and take a breath every now and again, because no one is invincible.

Love in an Elevator, Only Snitches are Going Down

Four Fingas will always be my favorite. He had the looks of a guido, but the heart of an Irishman. Four Fingas was a black-haired dago with deep blue eyes. It would be plausible that Sinatra knocked up his grandma, not only because of his looks, but because of the drinking. He was a vet, and still to this day he is one of the only people who has understood me. At my twenty-first birthday he, drunker than I was, stood up and lifted a glass and said, "You know, let's cheer for Breajamin Watson, you're not normal dude. You're not normal. He's like me. We'll never be normal. I mean it, no one else but him and I will get this toast. We're not normal. Fuck everyone else! Ha, ha, ha." Later that night he was kicked out of an Applebee's—don't judge him, we've all made the mistake of being in an Applebee's.

It was this very reason that I let Four Fingas take me out for what turned out to be one of the more insane nights of my life. It all started pretty normal I was designated driver so I was only drinking whiskey, but Four Fingas had his friends from down the shore, who knew how to fucking party, staying in the apartment. By 10:00 p.m. I had been punched by a Golden Gloves boxer and handed painkillers by a guy whose body type resembled a cylinder of cookie dough with perfectly done eyebrows. Golden Gloves had put my head into a wall and I in turn took Cookie Dough to the ground for some good old fashioned choking. I grew up with older brothers so this felt like home, which was fitting because we were bleeding and hadn't even left the apartment.

I am still not sure what type of shithole establishment lets an Irishman bleeding from half of his face and three bruised up guineas enter, but I will always thank The Rock Cellar for giving me one of the best/worst nights of my life. It's the type of shit hole where frat boys sponsor Beer Pong nights in half-hearted efforts to raise money for charity, and the only people who join them are the overweight girls from their sister sorority who over-compensate all night by doing the percolator. The smell of spilt beer and bloated frat boys dancing to Soulja Boy wafted into my nostrils all night as I, the designated driver, cranked back whiskey after whiskey thinking about murdering my fellow bar patrons who chanted their frat name, "Bulls, Bulls, Bulls."

Fingas and the goons had found some cute girls to talk to. I sat at a table spitting small talk with a girl in green-and-black-framed glasses who had approached me. At this point in my life, I would get too into any girl who approached me and shamelessly try to woo her with stories of my stupidity like they were trophies I got to bear. She quickly retreated and I laughed it off and drank more. Four Fingas and the goons were doing well for themselves and it was nice to see. That's a lie. It was terrible to see and I was alienated and jealous.

Frankly, I grew up jealous of Italians. Still to this day I am mildly jealous of Italians. They can turn any situation into a situation where they end up with a number. Even the worst looking ones pull tail like a retarded kid at a petting zoo. I once watched an Italian friend walk up to a girl in a library, tell her she had the type of hands that his mother would love, and asked her if she knew how to cook. When she said no, he smiled and said he'd teach her. He honestly told her she was homely and that her fingers would roll great cannelloni shells. They dated for two weeks. That kind of self-confidence took me years to build, so being the meek man festering with issues with women that I was, I stewed in my own self-pity for a few hours. Every now and again Four Fingas and the goons would circle me, tell me I was great for driving, buy me a drink, and then head off.

Shortly after the fifth or six such interaction, Golden Gloves hit me on the shoulder just hard enough that the bone screamed and my teeth grit, and the night spiraled into oblivion. A true celebration of Lotharios and highwaymen, criminals from the twenties would ask us how we did what we *allegedly* did. For all the fighting and drinking we did it was a tame night, until the very end of it. I watched as the goons and the bouncers got in each other's faces, and as always I jumped in the middle to find out what was going on. Apparently Four Fingas had run up a five hundred dollar tab, and like a real gentleman wanted to tip the bartender three hundred and fifty dollars. For any other place, this would be perfectly acceptable and encouraged, but in a place as shitty as The Rock Cellar it was a problem because

Four Fingas was "too drunk." This was personally offensive to us. All of us had jobs and lucrative side gigs in college, so we were able to afford to ball out occasionally. In a drunken stupor, I walked up to the largest bouncer and asked him if I looked poor. (I was poor, I grew up lower-middle class, but I'll be fucking damned if assholes working at a bar tell me that.)

The bouncer's nickname on campus was The Undertaker, and he was notorious for punching out college kids and leaving them in front of the bar to think about their poor decisions. He stood two inches taller than me and outweighed me by one hundred pounds. Simply put he was inhuman, the type of monster that if you saw it walking toward you in broad daylight you might call the police just to be safe. He was a super villain's sidekick. When he spoke to or breathed at you, shivers were sent down his goatee, mesmerizing like a cobra with an open hood. This was a man whom I had heard knock out every single drunken douche bag on campus, and I hoped it was my turn. I bellowed at the bouncers to let Fingas do whatever the fuck he wanted.

In my mind what happened was like an old western: two men met in a dusty road face-to-face and slinging guns mano a mano. What actually happened was all around me everyone was screaming and pushing in a bedlam of drunken Italians and guys with neck folds and security T-shirts. Over the din of bar stools falling and people pushing, there was a faint but noticeable, "Teach me how to dougie, teach me how to dougie," making it even harder to take any of this seriously. The Undertaker stared at me with a smile and I rushed forward toward him, like a fucking idiot. While a college education might give you knowledge (big might in my case), in no way does it actually mean you're not a fucking idiot. This heathen pushed me back with two fingers. He didn't move, he didn't reposition. He pushed me back onto the security guards behind me, who fell over, and my Italians jumped on top of them.

He was lumbering now, his arms swayed like Goliath, and the veins in his muscles bulged. He moved like a steam engine so when I got to my feet he was right there, ready to throw a knockout right hook. I could hear it coming. When it dropped from his jaw, his enormous hand changed the air pressure in the bar. His movements were a blur and when his fist fired forward again, I fell backward onto the pile again . . . but I brought the pad of my foot up onto his chin as I plummeted backward. You could hear the crack in the bar. A feeling of shock went through the air as a frat boy wearing two collars, who had been avoiding the chaos, screamed, "*Daaaaaaaammmmmmmmnnnnnnnn.*"

As I watched The Undertaker drop to the ground I smiled before I thought, *That was my driving foot, why the fuck did I accidentally hit him with my driving foot.* I managed to get to my feet and pull Four Fingas out of the bedlam, then I pointed to the bouncer and he smiled, grabbed everyone else, and we booked it for the door. Everyone was in great spirits after taking on the patrons and employees of a shit hole like that. More blood was coming out of Golden Gloves than I knew a person had. Four Fingas looked at a group of guys who were returning to their car and said, "We're fighting right?" I realized then he was too drunk to remember what had just happened inside.

After a huge win like that, having an addict's personality is terrible because you know you can go bigger and that's exactly what happened. I thought the night was over. I had put everyone to bed in my car for a twenty-minute drive home where I thought we'd sober up and be hungover and bruised tomorrow. Instead we got out of my car and started walking toward the apartment, when two drunk girls grabbed Four Fingas and told us to follow them. Cookie Dough laughed and asked if there was booze, Golden Gloves walked up beside them, and Bread Foster wondered for the first time in his adult life if he had gotten himself in over his head.

Her name was Sarah or Savanah or Susan or Shelly, it didn't matter really and the other one never gave us her name. Two mediocre girls had taken a look at our rag tag bunch and decided they wanted us to come to their party. Four guys and two girls slowly dragged themselves two apartment complexes over and into an elevator that smelled like someone had peed in it. Because at MSU, most elevators actually had pee in them. She brought us into a cookie cutter of 1A, but with a dropped ceiling and a stereotypical girl's charm. It was empty though. I thought I was going to a party but she pulled Four Fingas and Golden Gloves into her room and left her door open. Her friend said she was going to change and locked her door. Shelly or Shelby or Sarah called for Cookie Dough and I to come into her room too and hang until people got there, but I was busy in the fridge stealing booze. I didn't have to drive anymore, so when in Rome, black out with a bunch of Italians at what's about to be a shitty party.

It felt like forever, waiting there after I finished her liquor. That's when I noticed straws in the shapes of penises scattered about. I wondered if we were about to get raped in some weird sex dungeon party. I knew I didn't have the body to end up a male stripper and my curiosity started getting the best of me. I heard Four Fingas and Golden Gloves being loud and talking in the other room, so I told Cookie Dough to look out while I broke into the other rooms. I could only get into one room and I opened a drawer and was met with the mother lode. I picked up a vibrator and sniffed it. I picked up two more sex toys and ran out into the common area and tossed one to Cookie Dough. He immediately dropped it and silently threatened me with a closed fist and a twitch of his shoulder. I knew it was time for us to go, so I yelled over to Four Fingas and Golden Gloves who left the room. As we ran out I threw the sex toys at them. Four Fingas was personally hurt that I stole without him.

This brings me to the *alleged* part of the story. While I hadn't blacked out, I did gray out. Legally speaking, this book is now fiction and will resume being non-fiction after this story ends. Four Fingas pulled the doorknob to the first apartment after Sarah-Beth and went inside. There we found enough booze to put down a horse. Four Fingas became Tarzan in the moment, a wild ape-man. He banged on all the doors inside the apartment to ensure no one was home.

Cookie Dough and I chugged half a liter of rum. With deliberation, Four Fingas walked out of the room, pressed the elevator button and told Cookie Dough to keep it open. The slob immediately sat down and fell asleep, letting the doors pin his legs in the doorway, then reopen, push, then reopen. It goes to show you that there is use for a fat useless person, mainly when you need a doorstopper. Fingas and Golden Gloves looked at each other, knowing it wasn't their first time doing this. I looked at them with quiet questioning and a level of fearlessness that only someone who didn't care about his own life could have.

It was like someone fired a starter pistol and everyone was off. We ran down the halls trying to find open doors while Fingas picked one door open with his credit card. For our level of inebriation, he showed who the real criminal was. He was clearly too drunk to get a key in a door, but never too drunk to pick a lock. As soon as one of us found an open door, we rushed inside. We weren't quiet, we weren't subtle, but we were fast. Fingas went and knocked on room doors to distract and verify no one was home, while I threw open kitchen cabinets stealing food and liquor and Golden Gloves grabbed PlayStations and any games he could get his hands on. Spending no more than five minutes in each room, we threw everything in the elevator on top of Cookie Dough and kept going.

After the top floor, I was surprised to find out they wanted to rob every single floor. I can't remember what day it was, but as I look back at the soulless monsters, drunk with pride and thrill, I wonder how we didn't get caught. All the odds had been stacked in our favor because if one person had seen that fat drunk Italian holding the elevator door open while it was filled with PlayStations, games, and more food than we could eat in days, every one of us would have been fucked. God knows that awful piece of shit with his perfectly manicured eyebrows and overly ChapSticked lips would have snitched and tried to suck his way out of trouble. I was thinking about that as we went down to another floor. So when the door opened and the slob still didn't react, I waited for Fingas and Golden Gloves to go running through the hallways screaming like teenagers who just got their license. I shrugged, grabbed him by his gelled guido head, and gingerly placed it in the way of the door. I watched as the door closed on it and reopened and I laughed at how stupid that fat shit was. I took solace in that moment, while two crazy ass Italians ran from door to door yelling and trying to break into people's places, I watched a fat ass get his head smashed time and time again by robot doors.

There weren't any open apartments on the next floor, so Four Fingas ruined three credit cards getting one open. Imagine trying to get those cards replaced at the bank. "Hi, I need you to send me replacement cards."

"What happened, sir, were they stolen?" the bank worker would say.

"No, but four PlayStations, an Xbox, a gallon of frozen sorbet, tons of beer and bottles, ninety video games, and a year's supply of chicken breasts were."

"I'm sorry?"

"Neva mind, killllllaaaaaaaaa, send me some credit cards." Four Fingas would say.

When Fingas got that door open, he made the face of a fourth grader proud to show his mom he didn't fail math. They both ran into the room excitedly, screaming drunken nonsense as I once again threw open all the kitchen cabinets, freezer, and refrigerator making runs to and from the elevator. Golden Gloves started stealing games while Four Fingas unplugged the gaming systems. This time was different though. On my second run back into the apartment a door opened from one of the rooms inside and a short, stocky dude appeared half asleep. We all froze. I could feel my heart pumping warm hot blood faster than it had ever pumped. In my mind this was it, I was about to get caught. I'd have to go running and that bloated guinea asleep in the elevator was gonna rat us all out when he was caught. He walked slowly toward us, nonchalantly grabbing the bulge in his boxers. I was frozen, but I watched as the most inebriated human being on earth slowly lowered himself to lying down with the grace and precision of an underage Russian gymnast. The stocky shadow moved farther down the hallway and I cringed. I was holding a bottle of Captain Morgan Tattoo and wanted nothing more than to drink myself to death in that moment, until the idiot lummox showed just how stupid people who go to state schools are. He walked into the bathroom and didn't notice he was being robbed.

That was it for me. I jetted with a bottle of Captain Morgan and a nut check that proved to myself I wasn't a pussy. I jutted down the stairwell, only stopping to take a cigarette out of a stranger's mouth and kiss them on the cheek. I sprinted back to the safety of my room and sat quietly in front of the refrigerator eating Four Fingas's food. I knew that everything was about to get nuts again when they arrived, but as my other roommates came in and asked how my night was, I played the idiot. I convinced them I had stayed in while Four Fingas and friends went back out, and the blood all over the walls wasn't half mine. When they asked where everyone went, I offered up Four Fingas's stuffed mushrooms as my own and we sat as I anxiously waited for the rest of the shit show wrecking crew to make it back to home base.

It was another hour before Four Fingas punched a hole in the window screen and threw an arm full of electronics into the room, with a laugh so devilish I took it upon myself to adopt it as my own. Stevie Steve and Max freaked out and I acted like I had no idea what was going on. Cookie Dough meandered in through the door holding the sex toy I had stolen and a bag of chicken wings. That fat son of a bitch had his priorities in check. Golden Gloves dumped games and booze in through the window as I watched Stevie Steve and Max start to flip out even more. Everyone was too drunk to remember I was even there, so in my mind I ended up the best criminal out of the group. The major problem running through my head was a charge of "receiving stolen goods," which was brought about by the long trail of dropped video games, electronics, and food all the way from one apartment building leading directly to my window. Steve and I ran outside and collected armfuls of stolen goods to carry back into the apartment, while Frankie and the crew decided to go to bed.

I looked at a pile of stolen gaming systems, games, frozen food, booze, and sex toys. My last memory from that night is Four Fingas saying, "Who the fuck stole my stuffed mushrooms?!"

I think about this story a lot as I've gotten older and it's never had a moral. I think it was just a few angry young men being angry young men. It was bad, what we did, but there are worse things that could have happened. I think most of college is a moral gray ground between a great story and a terrible thing you did. I think finding a distinction between the two is where adulthood is. When you get older you come to realize what's funny and entertaining and something you should always keep to yourself.

Which One Has the Water in it?

"You're an asshole. I can't believe you said that. What would possess you to say that?" the Girl I was Dating yelled at me while she was wearing *my* sweatpants. You don't fucking yell at someone when you're wearing their shit. I couldn't stop focusing on the fact she was yelling at me about what I had said while she was wearing something that was mine. My future flashed before my eyes—it was her eating ice cream on the couch while telling me I was lazy. My spine shivered.

"Well?" she was accusatory.

"Well what?" I was lost.

"You said something racist at that party."

"I said it to Will, Amber, and ReTodded . . . I'm the only white one!" Honestly, I always got away with murder when it came to racist jokes.

"ReTodded is racially ambiguous," she said with conviction.

"That's more racist than the joke everyone laughed at . . . but you."

"You're embarrassing, it's unattractive. Why do you have to do that?"

My TV was on low. These were the dark days, when Netflix was losing to Blockbuster because everyone watched cable or DVDs. I kicked over my PlayStation 2 and sat at my desk. It was a tiny single room that could only hold a dresser, a bed, and a desk. There was a half-hearted attempt at a rug that flopped on top of a cold white vinyl that had no give when you were in bare feet. I kept my walls bare except for a Wu-Tang poster signed by the Ghost Face Killah, GZA, Method, and Redman and a sparse number of redheads my blonde girlfriend eventually made me take down. Jennifer Garner, Deborah Messing, I even think one of Anna Kendrick—who would be America's Sweetheart if it wasn't for Paul Rudd—graced my walls in no order or even leveling.

She sat on my extra-long bed, complaining while I stared at her mouth and fought back the urge to get my sweatpants back. The compressed saw-dust bed, with a heavily stained mattress, was wrapped in a disgusting dark green sheet, childhood pillows, and so many comforters it resembled a nest. There was no escaping her in the tiny little room. There was a knock at the door and when I opened it a firing squad of Super Soakers and buckets launched a wave to knock me back. My jaw slackened and cracked as my shoulders dropped like a dog on its haunches. My hand wiped water off my face as I bellowed into the open door. The wall of humans clogging the hallway parted bit by bit until I met Tossi. She was a brutal wall to hit. Years of being on women's sports teams had honed her ability to play with the crazies. I attempted to push her back only to be met with the butt of a Super Soaker on my back. Upon falling, someone smashed me in the head with a water balloon. I crawled between Tossi's legs, that blonde wall kept her hair in a ponytail and her shoulders forward.

Drenched, I escaped the hallway and darted out of 1A. Leaning against the wall gasping for air, I clenched and unclenched my hands time and time again. The Girl I was Dating and the surprise shower had sobered me up enough to realize this was the second day in a row everyone had been drunk. No one had slept, but no one showed signs of stopping. The night before blurred, but I vaguely remembered filling a barrel-sized garbage can with water and kicking it into someone's room. After attempting to scratch my butt and failing, I pulled out my flask I discovered I had in my back pocket and chugged. I wandered in and out of strange doors and hallway closets while sloppy wet footsteps followed me. Like a bear trying to get into a locked cooler, I smashed, flipped, and turned anything in my path looking for anything to arm myself with against an army of squirt guns and buckets. After tearing apart a stranger's room, I fell onto the couch and stretched myself out. My breathing became steady again and I relaxed in a spinning world. Invading someone else's space always lowered my heart rate and helped me think clearer. If anyone ever found me I had planned for years to say, "Nah, Imma stay," like a yogi cat burglar. I kept imagining how they'd laugh so hard at my stupid comment, giving me time to kick them in the knee and make a daring escape.

"Why the fuck am I looking for a water gun in here?"

A reply from down the hallway of the room I was in made its way through a closed door and into my ear.

"Oy, who's there?"

"Nah, Imma stay," I blurted out. I didn't stay.

Soon I found myself in a janitor's closet. I wove my way through broom handles so prolific they made me feel like I was walking through a bamboo forest. Eventually I found a bucket that hadn't been cleaned out. The water gurgled from the base of the bucket. It looked thick enough to be considered plasma. It was a putrid brackish brown with indistinguishable bits floating along the top, swirling as a bubbles from the bottom pushed it around. The cold metal of my flask hit my lips again and I kicked the yellow janitor's bucket back toward 1A.

Every time I kicked it, a slosh of the brown bucket fluid hit my Adidas Sambas, staining the few unstained strips left on them. I cursed every single time, but kicked it anyway. Positioning myself directly in front of the door with the bucket on the ground beside me, I attacked even though it wasn't locked. I pounded, I thrashed, and I bombarded the door with fists and feet and knees and elbows and heads . . . well . . . head, until it caused a commotion loud enough for everyone inside to hear. I heaved the bucket up, the sinew in my arms tightened and the muscles clenched around my bones, which felt like they were bending with the weight of the bucket. Filled mop buckets are tremendous. My shoulders cracked, the door flew open and everything froze in time. Inside they had lined up, squirt guns aimed directly at me, all their mouths opened in a collective scream meant to scare me.

Life was in drunken slow motion. I heaved the entire mop bucket, throwing the filthy water into the doorway. Their faces morphed from playful anger into shock and awe, their mouths still open. The filthy brown substance moved closer and closer, some people jerked backward and Four Fingas started to mouth, "fuck." Two squirt guns went off in an attempt to counteract the filthy water, and time went back to normal. The water splashed off people's faces and shoulders, everyone fell back screaming in disgust. I picked up the bucket and splashed everyone again, tossing the bucket aside.

Everyone was silent or rubbing their tongues as they parted ways to let me through. "I use nukes motherfuckers." I stripped my clothing off in front of everyone, mumbling "Bitches." I bent down in front of everyone to pull my flask out of my wet jeans and heard a collective groan from a crowd of filthy friends. I laughed all the way back into my room.

"What the fuck is wrong with you?"the girl that I was dating asked, pointing her finger at me.

"What? I got attacked and I had to fight back."

"We were in the middle of a fight and you just left."

"Are you fucking kidding me? There is still water all over the floor. Was I supposed to get shot in the face and get pelted with water balloons then close the door?" Spit flew from my mouth, I was so mad. I thought about how funny and confusing that would have actually been. "You know what, we can argue tomorrow because I am going to go out and keep drinking with my friends." I grabbed a bottle of whiskey off my desk and went back outside. It was only moments later and everyone had scattered. I was completely alone. "Why does everything smell like NaTrasha?"

Four Fingas yelled from inside his room, "The fuck is wrong with you? The *fuck* is wrong with you?"

Snickering, I stood alone on the battlefield. The entire room was dripping. We had just cut up a Sports Illustrated swimsuit edition and taped the girls to the walls, the pages now curled and crinkled from splashes of water. There was a puddle in front of the door, and all of the couches now smelled like wet bunnies. No one came back out into the room. I stood there drinking until The Girl I was Dating drifted off to sleep.

"I fucking got it in their mouths. I'm fucking ridiculous," I drank right from the bottle.

"I'm going to violently fuck you in your mouth." Four Fingas yelled.

I dashed back into my room and locked the door.

That was the beginning of the end for my friend Tossi. She was stocky, the type of girl who'd shoot Jack Daniels and ruin people on a softball field. I have no idea when I met or how we started hanging out with her but I ruined at least a month of her life. Because for two weeks after that night, everyone carried squirt guns and water balloons on campus while she only had a water bottle. We memorized each other's classes and skipped out on parties to ruin someone's morning. Strangers were gunned down in the crossfire. All of us had to flee from the scenes of the crimes. In a marketing research class Four Fingas and I shared, Stevie Steve walked in and unloaded an entire Super Soaker on us. We stared directly at Mr. Hill like it wasn't happening. Stevie Steve walked away like a boss after drenching us and disrupting class for six long minutes. When he was done and gone, Frankie stared at the teacher and said, "Go ahead. Teach." When class began again, I turned to Frankie. "You ever realize how wasteful we are."

"You're not normal."

One brilliant day, something wonderful happened. It was an unseasonably warm day that I remember fondly because there was wind blowing through my latest bad decision, a drunken Mohawk. A drunken Mohawk from the night before, and a lingering buzz too. Oh god, someone needed to spear me for having that. I should have been forced to walk the Trail of Tears until my hair grew back to a respectable length. One fine day, I stepped off the bus and spied an unarmed Tossi holding a brand new iPhone. She was scrolling along on the bright new touchscreen as I crept up as quickly as I could. She must have been completely entranced, because my weapon of choice was carrying two completely filled buckets around . . . not the most secretive, but it always got all over innocent bystanders.

Tossi walked unsuspectingly and I followed her until she was alone. She was so into her phone, she didn't put it away as I doused her with both buckets before class. Oh the real joy in all of this came from how vindictive everyone got. Max's tennis arm threw water balloons that left welts, and I was the only person he ever got. It went from immature fun to blood sport faster than we knew what was happening. We'd purposely drench Four Fingas before class presentations so he had to stand there and act like nothing was happening. What I did was a nuclear bomb to the game.

"I've had this phone for four fucking hours and it's dead." I open-palm slapped it out of her hands and stepped on it.

"Now insurance will cover it and they can't tell there's water damage." It wasn't true and I was aware.

"You're a fucking asshole." Groups of students were magnetically pulled toward us. "Four fucking hours. Fuck you." A small crowd assembled. "Four fucking hours I had that phone."

"Can anyone tell me why this wet lady is yelling at me?"

"Do you know how expensive this is?" she fumed.

"Twenty questions, go!" I antagonized.

No one in the crowd was laughing, but as always I was looking to amuse myself more than anyone else.

"What is wrong with you?"

"Is there a Scantron I can fill out?"

Every sentence fired from her mouth was followed by a hunching, lunging set of shoulders. I treated her like an animal, making no sudden movements and slowly backing away. When she moved to pursue, I ran away laughing. Leaving her wet and phoneless.

After that moment, everyone stopped drinking for a while. It was hard to make eye contact with each other too. After a few days of detoxing, we figured out the amount of damage we had been doing to each other. A pile of wet text books and broken Razor phones sat in the middle of 1A, while all our heating vents were covered by atrocious smelling shoes. It took us all a week to speak to each other again, and plenty of bottles shared with one another to laugh about it.

College friends are friends for life, so break as much of their stuff as you can while they'll still forgive you. That's what you can take away from this story. If you care about someone, slap something out of their hand. This is your only time to be a complete idiot when everyone has the tolerance for you being a complete idiot. If you're in your thirties and your friend is pissing you off, nothing is more cathartic than remembering that time you took their shoes and hurled them into traffic. Slap that freshly made bowl of mac and cheese out of their hands and into their face; it will be a priceless picture for years. Do every funny and destructive thing you can because it feels fucking amazing and you have exactly four years to get away with it. Invest in a saw and a screwdriver. Nothing is better than completely dismantling someone's furniture while they're at class. If I had acid at any point in college it would have made my time there one hundred times greater, I know this because I was constantly trying to purchase acid because it would have been hilarious to literally make someone's stuff disappear.

Everyone is so drunk no one really remembers what happened. You're supposed to save your money for alcohol, not Apple products. Everyone would much prefer you to get them drunk than to have super crisp sound coming out of your phone. You can use excuses like, "No, Max, I don't know why your beer tastes funny," and people will believe it. Delete someone's entire music collection then say you couldn't figure out how to play Smash Mouth. It's really the only time in your life destruction in most forms is awesome. I once broke my friend's frat house door by throwing Wendy's baked potatoes at it then head butting it. It's still a story that lives on in a ZBT house.

Right now, if you're saying, "That sounds disrespectful," I acknowledge you hate reading this book. I sincerely thank you for your money, but you can stop reading now. It doesn't get any better. In college, break other people's stuff—it makes friendships last longer. Slap controllers out of people's hands, any controller: remote, Xbox, PlayStation, surround sound, toy helicopter, or Life Alerts. Be dickish and you'll find the types of people who become incredibly successful and stay with you for life. Dicks are the people who don't give a fuck and start businesses where you can be a professional and still reminisce about the insanity over beers at lunch.

There's No Such Thing as a Winning Streak

In every single college movie there is a scene where everyone gets naked and streaks, or one person gets naked and streaks and doesn't realize no one's behind him. Hollywood is lying to the students of the United States. Nobody gets so drunk they take their clothing off to run around campus anymore. We live in an age of cell phone dick pics and Internet cam whoring. If someone went running around campus naked, no one would look up from the nudity on their phones anyway. Nudity isn't sacred anymore. Now, if you saw someone running past you in the buff you'd just yell, "Save that shit for Snapchat!" It's a sad realization. Not that we live in a post-streaking society, but that we have never lived in a society where streaking was cool. The only people who ever considered streaking cool were strange kids in the seventies who wanted to take off their denim to show off their muffs. Even then streaking wasn't all that great for the onlookers because of the old rule: the people who want to get naked the most are never the ones you want to share a stool with.

I wish I had known this because I went in with the impression that streaking was a socially acceptable practice in college. It's real shame I have when I look back at my college years, because my streaking must have annoyed the shit out of everyone. Getting assaulted with the vision of my nudity must have been awful. I was shaped like a Pringles can with legs and arms. My body was a

If you don't know who Groot is, please watch *Guardians of the Galaxy*. This isn't a plug, it's best movie of all time and I liked Chris Pratt before anyone else did. Chris Pratt, please read my book and compliment how nice my skin looks. That's not creepy.

cylindrical mass of muscle and skinny fat, and I always thought it was the funniest thing on earth.

GayRa was never my direct nemesis. In the world of college housing, he was more of a paper pusher than anyone else. It's my understanding that he was like the head of the jail, and under him every floor was under the jurisdiction of a CA, community adviser. We were the luckiest bunch of students in the world because our CA was the single best authority figure I had dealt with ever. A black lesbian whose girlfriend was in the military, she understood our desire to do crazy shit and let Four Fingas get away with anything because he was a vet. It's what it must have felt like to be part of a mob, because she never reported us for shit we would have been expelled for. She was always on our side when it came to disciplinary actions, and on the books Four Fingas and I were exceptional students.

If D was ever on the fence about being a lesbian, my naked body probably solidified it for her. Not just because it was horrifying, or because she saw it so frequently, but because she always looked disgusted that I showed even a little bit of pride in it. Boxing and martial arts don't give you a Bruce Lee body. They make you a tree trunk meant to take and return damage. It's fitting to compare it to a tree trunk because my body would look exactly like Groot, if he was a beech tree. Gangly, big shouldered, and fingers skinny and creepy enough to be roots.

D was subjected to this attack on the senses monthly. Someone in the group would inevitably convince me that I should go streaking. I just realized my friends are assholes. D would always be in the wrong place at the wrong time. I never actually got more than ten feet before D would look at me in disgust and yell at me to stop being the creepy white guy on the floor. To avoid being so white, I decided to wear nicer sneakers and shave a line into my eyebrow. I was no longer the creepy white kid on campus. I was the creepy confused kid.

The first time this happened to poor D was at noon on a weekday. Four Fingas and I had gotten lunch drunk and were bored of telling each other stories. Frankie and I would one up each other for hours and it was a wondrous distraction from life. The only time I ever beat him at one-upping was when I talked about growing up near a mini horse farm that only had one male horse on it, which was also the only non-mini horse. (Wait for it . . . you all there yet? Yep! That was probably like Four Fingas's reaction too.) This specific time it led to a dart competition where the loser had to streak. The problem was that neither Four Fingas nor I knew how to play darts and thought it was an awful idea for Stevie Steve to have brought in a dartboard.

Frankie and I invented a game where there were no points and I'm not even sure how I ended up losing. The premise of the game was , but you tried to do the shot and get the highest number. If you threw the dart normally and got a bull's-eye instead, the other person got two letters. This started off with great intentions until we came to the conclusion we should see who could throw darts the hardest. We started off throwing them into the wooden part of the couches then the side of my TV, and Frankie won by denting a piece of metal. I missed completely and almost cracked the fish tank we had filled with turtles. So Frankie kicked me out of the room and closed the door. He yelled, "I don't want to see you naked," as I took my clothing off to run down the hallway. Five seconds later, D was walking out of her door while I came crashing down the hall wearing a only pair of socks.

"Bread. Get your ass back in your room. Put your nuts in something." As soon as I had run away from my room I was running back toward it. Four Fingas thought I chickened out until D came to the room to see if someone else had dared me to do it. Her motherly instincts were impeccable.

D never wrote me up or scolded any of us. She gave a disapproving look that set a precedent in my mind. I became the guy who wore his underwear everywhere. If there was a fire drill and I was in the shower I would come outside in a towel or a pair of boxer briefs. Remember readers, I was at a point in my life when I hadn't learned what shame was. As often as possible during the day, I could be seen in a pair of tight fitting boxer briefs smoking cigarettes even when it was cold.

The next time D saw my pasty white frame at the worst possible moment. I had decided to walk the two-mile trek back to my apartment instead of waiting for one of the busses after getting day drunk in class. There's no such thing as orange juice, it's just an incomplete screwdriver. It was a bright and clear day, until I was far enough away from the bus stop not to turn back when a sudden torrential downpour rumbled over-head. Thinking I could out jog a thunderhead, I ran out of breath after one hundred feet and lit up a cigarette. When the flood started, it was like a wave. A mid-summer storm flying in out of nowhere after days of sticky weather cracked the sky and darkened the once comforting sun. I was a mile and a half away from my apartment when a wave decided to fall from the sky. To call it a downpour does it no justice. In moments sewers flooded, being stuffed with the dangerous combination of foliage and inches upon inches of water that fell without warning. I trudged through back streets on uninhabited parts of campus. Stepping in puddles left me no wetter than I already was.

I ran into a couple also taking the back path, they snickered and stared from under their umbrella. I was standing in a puddle staring back at them as they laughed at me in wet hell, and then stopped laughing when I caught them in a group hug. He lunged at me after the hug and I sidestepped it. When he lunged again I pointed behind him to his exposed girlfriend, stand-ing cross armed while he still held the umbrella. I dashed and sloshed away, droplets coming up from the puddles my feet landed in and down from the sky.

Not showering has some pretty awful side effects. Not just social paranoia and alienation, but being filthy makes the slightest thing ruin your skin. First, I was not the non-showering *World Of Warcraft* player. I have plaque psoriasis and crappy skin to begin with. After I shower 40 percent of my body looks like someone injected pink food coloring into a shucked oyster. My face swells in patches that get irritated and the skin splits. The medications make everything worse, so I take the awful dan-druff and inability to shower over swollen joints and other side effects. No one realizes this but when you aren't freshly showered every day, a thin film of oil stays on the top of your skin. It's there to protect and keep moisture in but if it gets wet, everything itches like someone mated bed bugs and chiggers then shot the offspring with radiation to make them faster.

New Jersey also has rain that's made of 30 percent chemicals and not even the fun ones. They actually make medical cocaine in some of the chemical plants in New Jersey. What is medical cocaine you ask? Its cocaine that comes with a government approved warning label. The smoke stacks in the meadowlands pump more chemicals into our sky than Robert Downey Jr. can put into his nose.

The chemicals in the New Jersey sky mixed with the awfulness of my own filth led to an itch across most of my body more irritating then when my older brother played, "I'm not touching you." My shoulder burned and flaked with so much dead skin, I could have left a mixture of snow and rain behind me. The itch crept across to other parts of me. Trying to pull a shirt that was pasted onto me off to scratch got bothersome, so I took it off. Having no shame means not caring when people stare because your pale body looks like uncooked crabmeat removed from its shell. I came out of my shortcut and back onto the main road in front of the six apartment complexes. Plenty of students with half-efficient umbrellas were out in the downpour staring at the drenched shirtless guy who appeared to be oozing from fresh scratches all over his body. I took in the stares and decided to one-up myself. As I got in front of the complex I dropped my pants and decided to walk the rest of the way to my apartment naked. I took five steps before D came around a corner.

"You're shitting me." D was shocked but her girlfriend laughed hysterically. Her body keeled in front of her and her knees couldn't support the weight of her body and laughter.

"Actually, I'm flashing you." Her girlfriend laughed harder.

"He says he's flashing you. This motherfucker." I walked around D with my clothing balled up and folded over my arms.

"I wasn't streaking, I was trudging. I got caught in a downpour. I was in a situation where you just keep going."

"You were streaking."

"The only streaking this dude was doing is all over his body. Why are you red and white?" D's girlfriend couldn't contain herself. Her umbrella shook and little droplets beaded down in front of her face as it mocked me.

"D can I go now?? I can't put this clothing back on, it's too wet."

She forced me to wrap my shirt around my waist and let me go. "You should feel humiliated enough as punishment."

I didn't.

D saw my strange body in its natural (or unnatural depending on how you look at it) plenty more times. The final time being the best.

Every floor in The Village Apartment Complex had a common area that could be rented out for free. Whether you were a student activity leader or just some student who needed the silence, an hour and a half block was a signature away. It was always open too, whether it was 4:00 a.m. or, let's say . . . 10:00 p.m. . . . . . peak drinking hours. D was a part of one of those dance troupes where they stomped the yard, even if they were inside and on carpet. While at first it was kind of awesome to see, eventually I realized it was just obnoxious. It took human beings hundreds of thousands of years to perfect creating a drum. It almost went against evolution to rely on smacking your own arm to make silly noises instead. I constantly wondered if the people who danced this way just had some sick fetish for getting smacked because afterward they were covered in hand prints and I'm sure their knees were screaming in pain. (If you really want to hear the human body make some weird noises, have sex. That sounds like someone slapping the top of a bucket of cottage cheese instead of a stupid thigh.)

It was during one of these strange ritualistic self-beatings that we were all drinking in excess. Four Fingas had run into the room twice and showed he was surprisingly adept at mimicking their movements. D would laugh and shoo him out of the room, playfully slapping his arm and telling him, "I'll hit you hard enough to make a bass drum next time." Being the gentleman he was, Four Fingas would slap her back and leave, then secretly make jokes to me about how if a lesbian hit him hard, he might be inclined to hit back since they shared a sexual preference. That, everyone, is true equality.

They had been stomping the pre-booked communal room for several hours, hours that I had been drinking with the hipsters from my first real college party. While they stood on tables, Four Fingas and I kept making jokes about making a pillow fort because the floor was lava. From our room we could see through the windows as they choreographed their hits on themselves and tried the routines over and over and over. It was mesmerizing. Four Fingas forced a shot down everyone's throat, and that's when he and I started plotting. He grabbed my camcorder and started recording the routine happening in the other room while I ran into my room and got a pair of pants that easily came off. None of the hipsters (who were actually hipsters before it was cool) noticed as Four Fingas and I ignored them completely. Soon they were out of our room and I was in the bathroom alone, watching the tape over and over and over again. It wasn't terribly difficult to mimic their movements. With a half hour of practicing I had gotten the dance down enough to get by, but switched a few of their moves for comedic effect.

Four Fingas laughed once he realized what was about to happen. "I ain't watchin' that, killa, but you go do it, crazy ass." In minutes I was in the room with D and her dance troupe. She saw me enter and was going to kick me out until she saw I had the moves down pretty well. A smile came over her face at the notion of me stomping the crappy school carpet. After a round with them everyone smiled at me and congratulated my performance. I was sweaty but not tired, which was very important. During the next round when everyone started stomping and slapping I stripped my clothing off, I was in the back and D was dancing with them instead of leading them, so no one faced me. I was doing their choreographed dance, but I replaced two very important moves. When hands came down on thighs to create a slight slap, now my junk was doing the thigh slapping. After a round and no one noticing I started giggling at getting away with it. I had always been considered hung, but I knew that wouldn't be the case with who I was dancing with. D stopped everyone, still facing away. "Someone's not hitting their thighs."

Instead of stopping when she asked everyone to, I just kept dancing. Soon, all the dancers turned in my direction and noticed I wasn't just stomping the yard, I was slapping the bush. My creamy white thighs, covered in faint, ghostly red hairs, were turning red with phallic-shaped slaps. No one laughed. It was silent and D gave me the familiar look of shock.

"Cock the yard, motherfuckers. Wait. Beat the bush, motherfuckers. Wait, that sucked too."

One dancer chimed in, "Hey, I never thought of that, can we do that?" Everyone started laughing at him. "I bet ours will sound better too." They kept laughing more.

"Let me have my moment, dude." I was frustrated by my lack of a one-liner. Finally D shooed me out, after laughing at me, and locked the dance room. She didn't even tell me to put my clothing on. I was so defeated. "I may not have gotten them to laugh but I think I invented a new type of gay porn." When I got back to my room, Four Fingas asked me how it went and I explained I was showed up by someone funnier. "Get used to it," I heard as I waltzed off to bed.

People need to get naked more often. Nudity is fucking funny. We have these organs tucked or dangling and a hole in the middle of our bodies for life. Most people aren't in amazing shape but who cares? That's what makes it better. No one is shocked by a person getting naked and running around anymore, and it's barely even funny. We need to stop the societal infatuation with thinking the only way for nudity to be funny is if it's running past strangers for five minutes. Instead, as a society I say we can do better.

If you want to do something way more effective, hold prolonged eye contact with a stranger then slowly and robotically get naked in silence. What's even better is that for the rest of your life you'll have to apologize for the time that you got naked robotically at their family reunion in front of the buffet. It's hilarious because not only is it uncomfortable, but also your friend will have to hear about how hot/gross his friend who got naked was. Maybe you'll even give someone's weird cousin their first erection.

Get naked at the gym. Trust me, there is nothing less sexual and more hilarious than watching anyone do a naked squat. It's the most unnatural looking exercise ever. Being naked at the gym is hilarious, because you're even more of an asshole for not wiping down the machines when you're done. Nudity is even better in front of the mirror. Find a guy who keeps watching himself flex then put a leg up and let him see those spots you missed shaving. Mimic him, and I bet he won't say anything about it because . . . you're naked.

Do naked trust falls. What could make a stranger even more weirded out than you being in front of them naked? Yell, "Trust fall!" and hope they don't use you tumbling toward them as an excuse to cop a feel. Falling on someone naked is a hilarious way to leave an amazing first impression. Also, try this later on in life at business meetings—people will love it. Being that you're naked, they're twice as much of an asshole if they let you hit the filthy ground.

Men, get completely naked in the public restroom and don't go in a stall. It's hilarious when you go into the bathroom and some drunken idiot pulls their pants all the way down. Imagine the hilarity if you have your clothing neatly folded under your arm while you use the urinal. Get all the way naked then leave the door to the stall open because squatting on the toilet with the door open is brilliant once you imagine it. It also solves the dilemma of waiting in lines, if you're already naked and the urinals are taken up. No one fucks with the naked dude peeing in the drain in the middle of the floor. Just make sure you leave on your socks and shoes because those places are fucking disgusting.

Women, get naked in a strip club. There are dark lights and weird music and no one is really keeping track of what's going on. There's no way to make easier money than not actually being employed by a club and giving unlicensed lap dances. If you're not looking to make money, it's probably hilarious to be able to tell a stranger who asks for a lap dance, "Oh, I don't work here, I just didn't think anyone would mind." Go with a group of friends and everyone get naked! Then you can laugh and laugh as the bouncers brutally remove the guys in your group and leave you alone. Instant girls' night out!

Chapter 4

FREEDOM

Remember you can die.

You could die tomorrow. Someone you love could die tomorrow.

The Pros and Cons of Freedom

Welcome to the land of being on your own, kind of sort of. You don't have anyone to be responsible to except yourself. You can leave the house without ever being asked where you're going. No one is going to know where you are unless you tell them. *No one is going to know where you are unless . . . you tell them.* You could disappear for a week or more and no one would really notice. That's the scariest, yet most freeing thought ever. You're more on your own than you ever have been in life. What to do first? Get alcohol poisoning, eat enough candy to pee sugar and lose a foot, blow crystal meth smoke into a stranger's eyeballs? Probably just find someone who's twenty-one to buy you booze.

All of a sudden there are way fewer restrictions in your life. You can come and go as you please with little to no repercussions or anyone to answer to. You are finally unrestricted and that feeling is going to be amazing and wonderful while still being incredibly intimidating and error prone. Most schools have a dropout rate because there are people who realize they don't handle a lack of structure very well. Answering to no one but yourself can be a pain in the ass when you realize you have no idea what your own expectations are.

The first con of independence is the crippling identity crisis. With no one to explain what and who you should be everyday, all of a sudden left alone to wonder who you actually are. No longer are you out to please your parents, teachers, or friends. This is the difficult time when new college students are still figuring out their value systems. This can be a painful time when meeting new people

Also, this is the point at which everyone recognizes that most college kids have awful senses of humor. They're so desperately trying to hold onto something that anything that insults something they have feelings for could set them off. As part of your value system, I'd like every single one of you to put, "Not taking myself seriously" as number one. Trust me, it will make life easier.

and having new experiences can leave you feeling guilty for your old ways. The best thing to do in this period is to have as many experiences, with as many people you'd never speak to during any other time, as you can. Expand the fuck out of your horizons, and have friends your parents would disapprove of.

The pro is, you're completely free to do weird stuff. Living with your parents is a constant struggle, hiding things in your room while they're constantly looming and you're just trying to figure out what makes you tick. Now that their shadow is gone, you can get your kink on and explore what you honestly think and feel. Do mushrooms, get hand-cuffed to the bed, and take a global consciousness class. Whatever dumb thing you think you want to do, now is the time to do it. Some of my fellow friends in writing and comedy spent their first year of college figuring out they weren't cut out for college. This is a time when the only person whose expectations you really have to live up to is yourself. This is a time when you should find what you love and hold doing it in the highest regard.

Find what you love to do and do it as much as possible. Even with school and friends and drinking, you'll have enough free time to get really good at something you like. Do not waste this opportunity.

Trying everything leads to another con. You're going to make mistakes . . . learn to be humiliated but then forgive yourself, feel shame, and be a better person because of it. The only thing making a mistake and being bad at something means is that you're trying to get good at something. Freedom means you're going to fuck up, with friends, creative passions, social situations, and a slurry of other things. This is the beginning stage of real life, so there are billions of mistakes you have to make before you're good enough for the real world. Yeah, they're gonna hurt and occasionally they're going to make others feel shitty too, but this is how you're going to start becoming an adult.

The ready availability of alcohol and drugs is one of the best pros of a college campus. You're also in a secure enough environment to do them. College campuses have security, on-site medical care, and a reputation to uphold, which means they'll sweep anything under the rug if you threaten to go public. This is one of the only times in your life you won't have to worry about transporting drugs, because you can walk to the guy who's selling them and back to your place. Take advantage of this and do some risky things. Do your best not to get caught up and addicted, but if you don't dabble then the only thing you get out of college is an education, which really doesn't do that much anymore.

This next con is the reason it's every parent's job to buy this book for their kids, and every kid to hand this book off to someone else—or tell them to buy one (please). One of the biggest downfalls of freedom is that you don't know what your limits are yet and you're going to test them. This is an absolutely terrible and scary fact for everyone to realize. You're going to test what you can do creatively, academically, socially, drinking, drugs, and sexually. At this point in life, there are so many strange and new experiences to be had without the observation and guidance of others, that you're going to push the limits of what's acceptable and what you can do. Yeah, you might get your stomach pumped, have a bad trip, an awful one-night stand, lose someone's trust, or a million other things, but it's really important you push the bounds of what you think you're capable of doing. Now's the time to do things in a little excess, push what you can do creatively, and become the person your parents warned you about for a little bit. Personally, I think this is how people grow the most during their college years. Self-worth comes from proving to yourself, and others, you can do more than you thought you could.

The most important pro about the freedom you have in college is that you can have so fucking much fun. You have no idea how amazing these crazy nights and long days are until you look back. With your first taste of freedom, everything is still fresh and exhilarating. You'll never understand how awesome having sex in a pillow fort is until you leave college and it becomes considered immature, even if you take down the

"No Girls" sign. Every day, you'll have a few hours of classes, but tons of time off between them to get into shit and see your friends. After classes you're free to drink and go nuts because at that age you can still wake up the next day and function. Every moment belongs to you in college. You take internships and some of us had jobs, but you never have to think about how your actions affect a mortgage or other people. Your time doesn't belong to the corporation that's paying you or another person who completely relies on you. The freedom that happens in college . . . please don't take it for granted. Later on in life is still amazing, there's happiness to be had. But there will always be something special about college. It's your job to make sure you live it up.

The Do's and Don'ts of Your Parents' First Visit (Originally published on Brobible.com)

Your first year of college is a scary time . . . for your parents. You're out having the time of your life, if you live on campus. You're out narrowly avoiding your RA catching you for drinking, while they're sitting at home drinking. Being someone's parent takes up a lot of time, and now that you're gone they have nothing to fill it with. This is why the parents' first visit is so important. If they see you're doing well enough on your own, you won't have to call them as often. There are some simple rules to making sure they don't start to think you're some inept kid who'll never make it alive.

Do: Leave a pair of handcuffs out. Your dad will high five you and your mom will be too horrified to notice you left your bong out.

Don't: Leave your bong out.

Do: Put something else in your fridge besides alcohol, energy drinks, and Sriracha sauce. Parents always check fridges to make sure that you're eating.

Don't: Tell them you're going out to parties to try and get laid.

Do: Tell them you've met a cute girl, but she's a vegetarian. It'll give them something easy to worry about. Parents like to worry.

Don't: Clean your bed sheets.

Do: Clean everything else. It makes parents feel like they're still needed so they'll look at the bed and not at the bathroom.

Don't: Leave your bong out.

Do: Offer to take them out to dinner.

Don't: Actually take them out to dinner, unless it's Chipotle. You need that money for thirty packs.

Do: Ask them to bring your pet for the day. Not only do you get to see your pet, they now have to spend more time walking around campus and not in your room.

Don't: Forget to buy toilet paper.

Do: Light a scented candle to cover up the kitchen sink smell.

Don't: Let your girlfriend or the girl you're hanging out with meet your parents. Save that shit for adulthood.

If you follow these rules, your parents will be driving home thinking about how you're dating a vegetarian, sleeping in a gross bed, and needing more money for food. They won't be worried about the fact you're drunk five nights a week and experimented with a goth chick.

What Do You Want to do? I Dunno, What Do You Want to do?

College is the most expensive boredom you'll ever have to face. Not just the droning of every professor and counselor, but also trying to fill all the extra time you have. If you collected the money you paid for college, you could easily start your own business instead of wasting it on a half-assed college education. All that money could have been used to start a store that sells trick mirrors to self-conscious dogs. If you opened a small business, you'd end up learning all the same things you would in college, but have something to show for it. You'd miss out on all the craziness because you'd be busy building something instead of following what other people told you to do. Instead, you realize after school is over that you had hours of time to sit around with friends trying not to be bored. Some people play video games, some people put together sports leagues, some get really into cocaine, others purchase this book, which is probably better if you also do cocaine.

Booze mixed with boredom lies on the danger scale somewhere between booze and a cell phone and booze and a barrel of otters. It leads to time spent lying on a couch watching a friend play Super Smash Brothers while plotting your own destruction. Take a moment and appreciate that the decisions you make now have pretty much zero affect on your future, as long as you don't become an addict or get arrested. Now is the time to grab boredom by the jaw, pour as much Four Loko down its throat as possible, and hope something cool happens. This much free time should be devoted to doing things to change your life for the better, doing something creatively fulfilling, or just trying to get fucked up and laid as often as possible. It's really easy to get in with a bad crowd during this time too. Here is a list of things not to do in college.

Sign up for free credit cards. It's really easy to sign up for crappy $2000 limit credit cards in school, and all those free T-shirts will eventually block the space between your door and outside. It's alluring, but don't forget eventually you're going to have to pay back triple what you actually spend. Thanks to interest rates, and the fact you're a lazy piece-of-shit college student, the chances of making a payment on time are minimal. This means that $50 bar tab, with compounded interest at a rate of 7 percent, equals a bar tab so complicated I can't even figure out how much it really is. (You'll find out later how I passed finance.) If you are going to sign up for them, try spending $20 then bouncing it from credit card to credit card. Not only are you causing everyone more paper work and an inevitable shut down of the credit card system, but you're wasting time while you do it. It's just the kind of pseudo-political non-action action any college student would do to feel like they're a part of something.

Hacky Sack. Read the foreword of this book. Sam Haft is right. Nothing good ever happens to the guy who is really good at hacky sack or that stupid lighter game. These people wake up in townies' apartments after a three-day molly binge and find out they now have a kid growing inside some flower child named Willow. Fun fact: that girl also has hepatitis and now you do too. Hacky Sacking is the actually the number one leading cause of hepatitis across college campuses. It's also the number two leading causes of pulmonary embolisms and impotence. Getting into Hacky

Sacking is a great way to let everyone know you're probably not going to graduate.

EDM. As the former host of a documentary about EDM across the world that never made it to air or even post production, I beg all college students: Please do not get into EDM. It's dead. Your candy-heart-wearing, molly-popping music scene that started in the late nineties is like JFK: terrible and probably shouldn't even be in a car. You all ruined it for yourselves. A wonderful subgenera of music went from great songs like "Around the World" and real DJs to shirtless assholes fighting over the last ketamine while someone plays an iPod. If you're waving your arms in the air you aren't a DJ, you're a self-important, wannabe cult leader. Let's get back to the roots of EDM folks, listen to DJ Spinbad, and masturbate to a really talented DJ.

Get really into a band no one's heard of. We get it, in a desperate attempt to feel like you're part of a larger group, you've decided to follow around a band you really like. I'm sorry, you've become kind of a douche bag. It's really easy to do. I still religiously follow a band from Australia called The Cat Empire, who is the greatest band to walk the earth. See how douchey that sounded? It's great to discover and fill your time with new music in college. Explore all the different sounds and sights and shows, but don't get religiously devoted to one band in a genre. Instead get really into one comedian. Please. Please. Comedy is dying and we need more young people deciding they have a sense of humor. Show up to any one of my shows holding this book with this page bookmarked and I'll touch your genitals. Bands get groupies and fans and everything because they play instruments. *I put ideas and lessons into your system and I get nothing. Nothing.*

Smoking too much weed. Weed is wonderful, a fun little plant that makes you feel silly and slowly rots away your short-term memory. It opens your mind to experiences you wouldn't have had otherwise and it's also a really annoying habit to get way too into. No one at the party wants to hear you talk about legalization; it's already happening and the average person isn't anti-weed anymore. Your annoying pro-weed T-shirts and hoodies infuriate the normal people who partake. While we just want to smoke a joint after dinner and be productive, you're out there in the media giving people the wrong impression of stoners. Additionally, when you disappear at a party and come back with glazed over eyes, no one wants to have another conversation where you deny you're high until you giggle and can't hide it anymore. Smoke weed like a normal person, with a group of friends and no political agenda.

Stealing Road Signs. As addressed previously, I am a hypocrite. Stop it. Do you know how obnoxious these stupid signs are? Ugh, you're stealing road cones too? Jesus, what's with college students' obsession with stealing these things? Here is the life cycle of your stolen road sign. You go out at night, or daytime if you have the balls, and throw it in your car while you giggle. Now you have to hang it up somewhere in your dorm. This is twice as obnoxious as you thought it would be, the stupid sign is heavy, and nothing will really hold it up besides screws and those aren't allowed in the dorms. Now you're stuck with a sign that you throw in a corner of your already too-small living space. If you do get it up on the wall, then you have to deal with everyone coming into your room and asking the same questions.

"Dude, bro, is that a road closed sign? Where'd you get it?"

"A road that was closed."

"Dude, bro, is that a deaf child area sign? Do you think the kid noticed it's gone?"

"He's deaf not blind and after talking to you, I'm envious."

"Dude, bro, is that a blind child area sign, think he noticed it was gone?"

"The real crime is any parent who lets their blind kid run around unattended."

"Dude, bro, is that a U-turn sign?"

"It's actually a suggestion for what you should be doing."

"Dude, bro, did you steal a stop sign?"

"Yeah. See how I wrote, 'Saying "Dude, Bro"' underneath it?"

Inevitably that road sign isn't going to last more than a semester or two until you dump it on the side of the road somewhere.

Talking about your study abroad time. You spent one month studying art in Rome or Italy or France and now you won't shut the fuck up about it. Guess what, a month or a term isn't living abroad. It's barely enough time for one person to wonder where you went. You're not living abroad when you study for a few months, and no one wants to hear about the two-dollar glasses of wine in France or how in Spain catcalling is considered a compliment. You're eighteen to twenty-two years old. The only cultural knowledge you absorbed are the shallowest and easiest observations you could make. Guess what? People don't think you're more interesting and the fake accent you have is obnoxious. Just stop being so pretentious about it, talk about where you lived when you're in your late twenties and move to another city completely alone. That's how you earn bragging rights.

CrossFit. It's the Jehovah's Witness of exercise. Cross Fitters are the same level of annoying as vegans. We understand the health benefits, but there is something so unlikeable about it when it comes pouring out of your mouth. Guess what? Being college-aged means everyone should be doing something athletic. Thousands of students around you are rock climbing in gyms, playing sports, tackling their friends, lifting weights, and running. As a Cross Fitter, you're the only one unbearable enough to not shut the fuck up about it. Doing Crossfit alienates you from friends and society as a whole.

Reading. Actually, do as much of this as possible. Reading makes you awesome. Just don't be one of those English majors who thinks they're better than anyone else for reading. No one gets your literary jokes.

There are thousands upon thousands of things you can do while in college. You have enough free time to go hiking, work in a wood shop, become an apprentice leather maker, or make NSFW stained glass. Don't waste this time, figure out what you love to do and fucking do it because later on, that's what's going to really end up making you money. This isn't time to waste. To quote my grandmother, "Make every day a story."

The Abominable Snow Man-Child

Anyone who goes to college where it doesn't snow is missing out on the most fun a man-child can have. Something about snow returns you to childhood memories of making snowmen, but in college you put dicks on them. In fact, in college you can make enormous obelisk-sized snow dicks then watch school security try to take them down as you sit inside a hot-boxed igloo. In college, you can hit a stranger with a snowball and watch it turn into the invasion of Normandy as it spreads. Snow brings out that fun-loving child in all of us we should be in touch with, or that's how I spin it to make my own irresponsible actions seem less glaringly stupid. Snow is like a mother's love, cold and burning to the touch until you go numb and accept it.

MSU had a few snowfalls a year and we always capitalized on them. Living without supervision meant we leapt at every chance to exercise our freedom. After we had established a group of friends, even if there was only a slight dusting, 1A would put up a sign in our windows that said SNOW DAY PARTY and we'd all skip class to be idiots while taking everyone down with us. Before that sign it was a struggle to cause idiocy in my fellow student. Well, it was that sign and I realized college people will do anything if a hot girl joins.

Dezzie was exactly as her name suggested—desirable. She was short, slender with curves, and a button face that made you imagine bringing her home to your mother. She was a cheerleader for a major New Jersey sports team at one time before college. Her hair was brown and wispy with a crinkle in it, making her the type of Caucasian that was still a little ethnically ambiguous. Everything about Dezzie was perky, from her butt to her personality. She inspired as many smiles as she did erections. So I was surprised when I was running down the hall, holding a cookie sheet and laughing like a maniac, and she stopped me.

"What are you doing?"

I stammered and told her I was going sledding. Instead of judging, she asked me to wait there so she could get a cookie sheet too. In the time it took her to run back to her room, I had filled a flask and acted like I was waiting patiently in the same spot the entire time.

We ran outside, giggling like little kids and looking for the best hills to sled down. Like two children we carefully calculated where the fastest routes would be. Unfortunately for us, every hill ended with a parking lot, so we'd have to aim in between parked cars in a precarious and precise style of sledding that cookie sheets didn't benefit. Directly outside of the apartment building, on the opposing side of the benches, then straight ahead over a road was the best spot. The top layer of the fresh morning dusting had melted a little then refrozen as the temperature started to drop later in the day. It was a tight run: directly to the left were thorn bushes all the way down the hill and to the right was a stone staircase surrounded by metal railings. But those obstacles weren't worse than trying to fit between the parked cars at the bottom of every other hill.

We knew this would take precision and perfect control over our metal pans not to get hurt. Dezzie carefully showed me the route, wildly motioning with her hands and pointing out the nuances of the trip down. I followed her index finger as it showed me the way, and she took care to guide me in a way no one else had before. So after listening and agreeing with her, I took a running start and jumped down the hill headfirst. As soon as I was no longer airborne, my cookie sheet hit the snow and flew out from under me, but a slick nylon jacket propelled me forward over the top layer of ice that was much thicker than expected. Just like Dezzie's keen eye had stated, this was going to take careful steering, which I attempted by flailing spider-like appendages around and screaming, "My last thoughts are of vagina!" I spun backward uncontrolled and wobbly. This sent me feet first so far under a car I couldn't feel my spine. Then my cookie sheet slid down and hit me across the bridge of the nose.

It was like a midget having sex with a normal sized person. I fit somewhere I completely shouldn't have. I yelled for Dez, who sledded down with the grace and expertise that only someone who gave a shit about their life could muster. I moaned in a state of half-blackout, half-consciousness, 75 percent of me now wedged under a compact car, and I couldn't feel from my neck down. In a pitiful moment, held my arms out and moaned, "Deeeezzzz," like a child trying to get his mommy to lift him up.

Dez was tiny, she couldn't have been much over five feet, and most of her body was T&A. She grabbed my arms and pulled with everything she had. I just moaned louder and passed out. Underneath that car, my legs had wrapped together like headphones in a pocket and my rib cage had managed to shrink itself enough to fit under a car without collapsing. I laid there for a little while, processing how stupid my actions were. I was with a hot chick completely incapacitated under someone's crappy Honda. The only thing worse would have been being on a date with a hot chick and owning a Honda. I should have been ashamed but instead I felt warm and happy, which was probably because I had managed to cover my body in snow and water while sliding so my skin was burning from how cold it was. I came to and started clawing at the snow until I could grip something and pull myself out. Between Dezzie grabbing my shoulders and me clawing, we managed to dislodge me and a piece of a bumper off the car. I laid across the snow breathing deeply, since my ribs were no longer in the world's largest Chinese finger trap. Dez looked and me and said, "Guess we're done?" I smiled at her like she was the stupidest person I had ever met. "I can take a hint."

Before I knew it, she and I were running into the common area of our building, grabbing as many pillows from the couches as possible and yelling for everyone to join us. We screamed down the hallways, knocking on doors, trying to get people to come sledding. Ever reliable, directly after being informed, Stevie Steve joined up. The roommate with a butthole that was a direct portal to hell was dragging a mattress with one hand, while the other held a beer. Max, who I explain more in depth later, even followed—child-like splendor cannot even be denied by the cuntiest of cunts (I'm making jerk off motions to Max's name as I write this). Soon there were twenty of us out there flying down an icy hill on sleds made of school property. Twenty soon-to-be adults had given up on all responsibilities to jointly destroy as much Montclair property as possible. It was beautiful sight, standing at the top of a hill looking down at students trying to hit each other with broom handles from two dueling mattresses racing down a dangerous ice path.

After a few hours, everyone had moved their cars and we had free reign to battle on mattresses. As two went down simultaneously, I'd jump on a pillow and fly directly behind them trying to crash everyone. Needless to say it did not take long for me to become a target. Everyone had beers and booze lodged in holes made by snow cozies. As soon as booze infects everyone's bloodstreams, things go from innocent to vindictive quickly. We were all bruising each other with broom handles and it was starting to get dark. Falling off mattresses onto ice had snapped a few fingers and left skin across the asphalt at the bottom of the hills. Slowly people trickled back inside the apartment to warm up with rum and shitty pre-packaged hot cocoa from parental care packages. While most other people retreated to warmth and wound licking, one obliterated Irishman (of course I am referring to myself) wanted a last run.

I decided to ride the mattress solo one last time before we grabbed all the pillows and called it a night. Max and Steve stood at the bottom of the hill waiting for the final run of the day to be completed. Their knees were bent and their faces were red enough to let me know they were as exhausted as I was. I lay on the mattress and scooted it to the hill using my feet and flopping around. I dug my wet shoes into the slick snow and began the battle with gravity. Instantly, I knew something was wrong. Instead of going down straight, I had hit a rock and barreled directly toward the metal railings headfirst. Steve and Max's eyes widened and the bend in their knees snapped into movement. Somehow, in a second, they managed to throw the other mattress they had brought out between the metal and my head, saving me a concussion but not a crippling bruise on the top of my skull. I felt the coils crumple under the speed of my skull and spring back at me as my trajectory changed. I already had one concussion from a car crash and thought this was the end. I didn't see a flash of my life before my eyes. I just saw another metal railing getting close. I fell off the mattress and spun around in the snow, eventually stopping after a pole eloquently caught my foot then spun my entire body and slammed my ribs directly into another pole. The crunch of my ribs made Stevie Steve and Max flinch. We sat in silence while I got my breath back.

"I think this is the start to a really great friendship, guys."

"You should be dead." They grabbed their mattresses and walked in, leaving me alone at the bottom of a hill.

"You think you're honestly ready for all this, dude? Do you think you're going to survive this?" I stared down into my beer.

"I sure hope not, the world seems scary." I replied to myself.

Freedom is being able to do what you want when you want. Sometimes you're going to have to make decisions about whether what you want to do is right or not. Having fun is incredibly important, the most important thing in the world. The problem is at college age, most of us don't think about death or the consequences of our actions. The simplest and most innocent sounding fun can make for a perilous and deadly situation.

Aussie, Ozzy, Ozzy, Oi, Oi, Ouch

Being away from your parents gives you the freedom to make decisions on your own in a relatively safe environment. This means you can make a multitude of mistakes and deal with minimal repercussions. Some of these decisions will be minor in the scale of life. Others will be life altering and will change you forever.

The apartment complex I was assigned to was as unique as the people who dwelled inside it. I learned more there than I ever did in class. They say you can learn while you're asleep so don't say I didn't even try. Not only was it an amalgamation of characters not fit for higher education, like myself, it also had an entire floor of international students. I was one of a very few who were invited to their parties. I was overjoyed to be surrounded by different races and cultures and to learn all about the world while still in New Jersey . . . until they started to talk about soccer. I took it as my personal duty to show them how strange and terrifying the American college experience was, while they showed me edible delicacies that I ate politely before vomiting from something besides cirrhosis of the liver. I was begrudgingly taught about the customs in each country and did my best to be accommodating whenever possible. They quickly bonded to me one evening, when they were all sitting outside drunk, and I pretended to be an Irish exchange student and spit this lovely line at a German girl: "I'd like to take a vacation between those legs."

One night we charlatans in 1A decided to be extra hospitable and throw an "American" themed party (a normal party but we are Americans), with the ulterior motive of plowing some foreign soil. I had planned it out for a few days. Like a real American, I had Russian vodka infused with American Skittles, Irish whiskey paired with more Irish whiskey, Everclear gummy worms, JELL-O shots, and I even invited an obese person. It was so American we took the things we loved about other cultures, ruined them, and then added sugar. The only thing missing was a pregnant teen on welfare wearing designer sunglasses. Stevie Steve, Frankie, and I were prepared to have a rager where everyone got so drunk it didn't matter what languages were spoken, they'd be slurring too much for anyone to understand them anyway.

To my astonishment, the party was empty way past when we had planned for it to start. Ever the optimist, I assumed that they were on CP Time (cultured person time). In the US, fifteen minutes late is fashionable, so maybe in Europe two hours was common. I prepared in the most American fashion, drinking by noon when the party didn't start until ten-ish. After a few hours of waiting, I wasn't having it so I decided to head up to the international floor to impose my "freedom" on them. I was horrified to find the entire international floor at a party being held by dear friends, Australian Mat and Austrian Andreas, who had both tried to make out with me telling me, "It's not gay, it's European."

I'd like to say I was hurt by my international friends back stabbing me, but if my veteran grandfather taught me anything, it was never to trust foreigners. Knowing these countries were vulnerable to a blitzkrieg, I ran in unannounced and grabbed everything party related in their apartment and screamed, "Party in 1A!" I ran down the staircase holding booze and every flag that could be found at the UN, only stopping to steal a cigarette out of a stranger's mouth and kiss them on the cheek (I did this as often as possible). My penchant for yelling in the hallways was apartment-renowned, so I screamed, "Free booze and cheap labor in 1A!" It always amazes me how yelling something racist will fill an apartment in minutes.

Slowly they trickled in as the booze attacked my bloodstream. A frequently occurring problem throughout my life has been my tendency to be the guy who everyone tries to catch up with because I drank much more than them. It's a serious issue because it forces people to drink in excess way too quickly and makes my toilet look like the vomitorium during a Roman feast. As the host of an American party, it was my duty to explain why we're the worst. The best part about being as drunk as I was, I didn't have to speak a word to explain why we're the worst. I was grabbing strangers to dance with me, feeding everyone Everclear gummy bears, and calling people out for awful "post-shot face." As a terrible person, it's always a joy to be in the social context where this was an expectation.

At no moment during what I thought was a successful party did it occur to me that I managed to offend every single person in my apartment. I had asked a girl whether her blow job had an accent. It came from a wholesome curiosity but left my mouth misogynistic and forward. The fact that it might bother someone that I hijacked someone else's party didn't occur to me either. The action that infuriated people the most is that when I drink, I tend to grab people, lift strangers, spin them, and generally not listen to things like, "Hey, don't fucking do that." Most of my shittiness comes from a complete lack of understanding of social cues, being a social space cadet. In all honesty, I try my best to have innocent and silly fun, but me becoming a human carnival ride is something that most people cannot stand. After three hours of lifting Europeans and Asians I was getting peckish. Four Fingas had made mac and cheese, but he didn't grow up poor enough to make it right.

Mac and cheese is only good when made by poor people. It's an honest fact that everyone should admit. If it's going to be your only meal for the next two days, you overboil the noodles and add extra individually packaged cheese slices. (Fuck you again, Kraft!) It's a food source that needs to make you so tired you can actually sleep instead of thinking about surviving until your next paycheck. If your bowl of mac and cheese doesn't block up your stomach and intestinal track for two days, go eat dried kale then jump in a fire.

I was hankering for food and black-out drunk when Australian Mat convinced several United Nations rejects that we should all go to a diner that was within walking distance. At this point I have zero clue what happened. So excuse me for a moment while I let my impression of Four Fingas and what Australian Mat later recounted write this part for me. I can't quote them exactly but this is what I was told days later:

Four Fingas said:

> Brenjamin Watson, you got sooooo drunk last night, playa. You were swinging bitches around on your shoulders and shit. I was like, 'This fucking guy, look at him swinging bitches around like its nothin' Haaaaaaaaaaaa.' I made mac and cheese but you said fuck that. Dunno what that even meeeans. Like, you're a weird dude, but you took the fucking bowl and threatened to throw it. Naaaaa, playa. I'm not letting you throw my noodles. So this British dude said he'd take you to the diner and we didn't think nothing of it. You were drunk as fuck and no one should have brought you out but we said fuck it, you were goooooonnne. Two and a half hours later Mat is fucking drinking in our room. I'm like, 'What happened to Brenjamin *Waaaatsoooooooon*?' He just smiles and says in that accent, 'Dunno, mate,' so like three hours later you come back. You're mad covered in mud and holding a stick or something.

Mat replied:

> Well, mate, we left your room and you started running. Just took off. We were gonna have a good chat but off ya go. We looked at each otha' and said, 'Well, hope that jackass turns out okay.' You were pissed and acting like a maggot. We all just thought, 'American party, American rules, off the wacka goes, right?' We had a nice roundabout, going to the diner and all. Walked down some nice hills, right? It was real pretty, lotsa pretty sheilas

walking down too. All of a sudden you pop out of nowhere and scare everyone. I was a tad bit screwin'. Wasn't funny, mate. I decided to push you—we don't muck around in Australia, someone gets us mad, we do something. Yep, pushed you down a hill. Watched you roll really far too. You were all wobbly and went limp. Dags get treated like Dags. I think a tree stopped you. You got right up and came to the diner. You were talking with stranga's and it was kinda funny. Lots of drunk people acting drunk. You had a few plates of corned beef hash, weird. After we ate I was still screwin', added I was a bit pissed myself. We walked up that same hill, I pushed ya again. Same tree stopped ya. We just kept walkin.

In all honesty, my only memory from that night was watching blood pour out of my eyebrow and some poor freshman yelling when I asked him for a Band-Aid. There is an hour and a half after Mat last saw me that is unaccounted for, so the rest of this story will be my imagination filling in.

As I hit the tree, I felt my spine wrap around the old oak and my spinal column burst into splinters. Fool me once, shame on me. Fool me twice, I shouldn't care because my country isn't in a water crisis like Australia. I looked as the forest around me started spinning and decided this was my life now. I pulled some leaves on me for warmth, and I knew that sometimes hippos covered themselves in mud to protect their skin from bugs. I've never been one for naps while single, but I thought this might be a time where one was called for. I napped in the forest for a little while, and when I woke up I had no idea where I was. But for some reason the magical forest around me was spinning. Not being able to remember my own name, I decided to take on a new life in the woods.

I gathered some sticks for a shelter and wished I had a copy of *Walden* to guide me on my new way. As I was lacking any tools whatsoever, I picked up a stick and began sharpening it with a rock. I used my previous knowledge of nature to build a lean-to that would temporarily guard me from the elements and held my stick close. The idea of bears terrified me, but I knew in my drunken stupor I could kill one if it weighed under five hundred pounds. When a squirrel or rat ran by I did my best to spear it, while

I wished I had listened to my Eagle Scout friend when he tried to teach me trapping. I lit a cigarette with my lighter then tried to rub my spear against some bark to start a fire. When that didn't work I smashed two rocks together into a pile of dried grass to make me warm for the night. Booze saved my life that night, because at no point did I put two and two together to realize lighters could make a fire. I took solace in the fact that I had shelter and protection for what I assumed would be a long night.

All of a sudden a surly young man with the letters TKE printed on his hoody yelled down from what appeared to be a mountain. "Hey, faggot, why are you in a ditch?" This infuriated me, as I hated the idea of civilization encroaching upon my new woodland home. "Get off my land if you're not here to trade furs or teach me how to ferment!" I bellowed up the mountain. When he laughed I understood he had no conception of the rules of the wild. I sprinted up the mountain at him holding my spear. I saw he was unarmed and undersized, so when he ran I knew I would track him and overtake him. I would be eating well tonight; no one but me would wander into the woods without provisions. I dreamed of tearing into what delights from civilization he might have brought with him. I missed the comforts of home. As I reached the top of the mountain, a cement trail led back toward civilization! I smelled the sweet smells of home but knew I'd miss the freedoms of the wild. I looked back at my time adventuring in the woods and thought, *Why the hell was I playing in a ditch?*

I journeyed back to my apartment a stronger man from my time spent fending for myself. I knew that I could survive in civilization if I could survive in a land with no rules or safety. I entered my apartment and slept in the first bed I had seen in what felt like a fortnight. Waking up clutching a stick and covered in mud felt right.

Three weeks later I had decided to get revenge on Mat after he told me he pushed me down a hill into a drainage ditch. While he was using the bathroom, I switched his vodka for Everclear and had a drunken gummy worm eating challenge. Once he was drunk enough to slur his words even worse than his accent normally butchered English, I suggested we go eat food. While walking down to the diner, I pushed him into the same ditch and left him. Two days later he looked at me disapprovingly and said, "Got me now, didn't ya?" It was his first taste of real American freedom.

There are many different types of freedom in this world. Not all good, not all bad. It's important to understand that it's a responsibility how you handle being allowed to do what you want. So before you push that Australian in a ditch make sure it's the right ditch. A ditch he deserves to be in.

CHAPTER 5

ROOMMATES

Perfect strangers my ass. Legally assigned Friends.

Hi, I'm your new room mate, don't worry I wont masturbate while you sleep

That wasn't even a concern until you said it

I'll jerk off in the shower

I'll jerk off on the toilet, but never in bed while you're asleep next to me

Dude...I don't even know your name.

Types of Roommates to Look Forward to

Welcome, this is the world where people who are completely different play the lottery to find out who they'll have to fall asleep with. It's petrifying to think that your most vulnerable and easily murderable moments are going to be shared with a complete stranger. This person, whom you've never met before, is going to spend nights listening to you breathe. (In my roommate's case, Max had to deal with my night terrors, sleep walking, and a REM cycle that shot gas out of my anus that was as thick as a storm on Jupiter.) The only thing a college looks at as a judge of character is grades and financial documents. Plenty of murderers are rich. This person could be a pagan, or worse a Christian. The only difference between college and being in the Army is that one of the two institutions has the common courtesy to teach you to defend yourself. So, let's give you a little glimpse into the types of roommates you might be faced with.

Alcoholic but Young Enough That It's Still Fun. This person is a fucking wild card. (The author slyly smiles into a mirror.) This is the type of person who will saw the furniture for no fucking reason. They didn't get drunk at noon. They got drunk two days ago and have kept it going. They're the most fun roommates, if you don't care about any of your shit and don't mind throwing someone across the room every now and again. In college you're too young to know if you have a problem yet, so everything with these people is just a story to tell. Right now, you're bragging you fell asleep on a roof, but when you're thirty and in AA you'll be crying about how much time you wasted.

Bathroom Nazi. You can't even call these assholes Nazis because the Germans never gave anyone grief when it came to etiquette in the shower. (Oh my god. You can't say that. That's incredibly insensitive. Someone call the student activities board and report this book as vulgar. Please. Then I could do a college tour.) The bathroom Nazi is so strict they treat every hair like it has hepatitis. They keep Purell in jugs. The bathroom Nazi would rather dive into a tub of Purell than risk a mold mark on the shower curtain. They use shower cleaner directly after they shower and expect you to do the same. I hate to break it to these people, but everyone pees in the shower. Your shower. While you're asleep, we all sneak into your bathroom and pee in the sink and the shower. Bathroom Nazis will bother you about a hair in the shower drain no matter how late it is. Congratulations, this semester is going to involve enough Clorox it'll be a legitimate excuse for why you have nosebleeds.

Off the Meds. Enjoy explaining to anyone who comes over your roommate is off her meds and has decided to stop flushing the toilet again. Oh, the joys of a depressed and chronic masturbater sleeping within arm's reach of you every night. This can be scary as hell, so make sure you have a Taser or a Prozac. For some of us, living with someone who's off their medications can feel like home. For most though, this is a scary and crippling type of roommate. Schools aren't very good at getting these people help, unless their grades drop or you can prove it's an emergency. Until then, it's your responsibility by proxy.

Misses Home. These people are completely unbearable but still hilarious. You never see them on the weekends because they go home. If they're from another state, prepare for a lot of Skype calls. It's mommy-daughter drinking time for the third night in a row, or two bros from high school lying to each other about all the vagina they're getting. Either way someone else knows more about you than you know about them because "Misses Home" lives vicariously through other, more outgoing people.

The Phantom. The Phantom roommate is the only time it's good to have a ghost in your apartment. This one doesn't stare at you when you look in the mirror or hang out just outside your peripheral vision. They're The Phantom because they may or may not exist. The books on their desk have moved, but you've never seen them. They treat the room like it's storage, so it's super fun to go through their stuff. What mysteries do they have and what skeletons are hidden in their tiny, school-provided closet? What's wonderful about these people is whether they spend most their time in their girlfriend's room or they're taking twenty-one credits, you get to enjoy essentially having the place to yourself.

The Leave Behind. We all know the leave behind trick for trying to see someone you banged again (if you don't, learn it). However, with roommates The Leave Behind is a person who, even in a apocalyptic setting where you were the last two people on earth, you'd still leave them behind. They're about as helpful as booze that costs over seventy dollars a bottle is to an alcoholic. These window lickers are helpless because their mom and dad did everything for them until now. They stare at the laundry machine like it's a monster that eats quarters and killed their entire family. The Leave Behind is the type of person who only knows how to boil water, and asks you to do everything for them. They're not completely bad, but you should probably sniff them to make sure. Get ready to be responsible for another human being's life. Unattended, these people will manage to set raw chicken on fire or explode their sheets trying to make their own bed.

There are plenty of roommates you're going to have throughout the next few years of college. Some of them will clean dishes, and others will leave handcuffs around the radiator in the bathroom. Make your life easier and accept people for their weird little kinks. Embrace who you live with, around the neck. Tightly. Don't let them go. Love them. Love them until they can't love anymore.

Blues School Clues: That Art of Passive Aggression

Congrats, you've decided to become passive aggressive. This is your first step into adult interactions with other people. Instead of an all out brawl fest, you've decided that you're going to keep tabs on a person and be deniably vindictive to them. Passive aggression is the fun way to be a complete wuss, slowly getting back at someone while completely avoiding any real confrontation. Being passive aggressive isn't just for ladies anymore. Now, passive aggressive comes in male too. It's pretty much the same things as female passive aggression only it's blue instead of pink. Whatever this person did to you must have been irritating enough to cause you discomfort but not bad enough to warrant a complete brawl. Now that you've decided to take out your emotions in the most immature and adultish way, there are some rules to being a ninny.

Find a Reason to Hate. This is very important. This is the most important thing. Once you've decided to be the type of human everyone feels no remorse hating, it's important to find something you hate as your target. It's really important to be shallow here. If you're going to be passive aggressive, you're a shallow husk so it's time to start acting like one. Find something that bothers you about your target that is meaningless and incredibly difficult to change. Try things like where they were born or that mark they have on their face. If you're confused about this, just talk to any father who lived through the sixties, they'll find any reason to get angry.

Let Everything Bother You. Now that you've found a reason to hate them, everything that person does is going to be annoying. Make sure you never directly tell them what's bothering you. Try sighing a lot and hold prolonged gazes that say, "Why are you even here?" Do they bite the silverware when they eat? That's a great reason to get annoyed, if your life has no meaning and you're an incredible piece of shit. Do they skip when they're happy? Nothing would bring an asshole more joy than making someone feel self-conscious about that. Now that everything they do forces you to be intolerable, try saying things like, "really?" in response to every statement they make. If their breathing itself annoys you, a great passive aggressive topic is sleep apnea. Almost everyone in the room will hate you, but it's so easy to act like it's in everyone's head.

Keep Score. Nothing in life is free, so make sure you keep constant score with your target. Never mind that you should probably become a cutter if you're humanly capable of acting this way, but every little favor you do for that target needs to get blown out of proportion tenfold. Did you take out the trash today? Instead of jumping in that bin too, you're going to be passive aggressive and remind them later that you take out the trash *all the time,* so next time it's their turn. Did you change the toilet paper roll? Try asking if they were born in a barn then laugh and say whatever their hometown is is close enough. These are the traits of a really great passive aggressive person, or a really shitty human being.

Inconvenience Everyone. Never forget, being passive aggressive is all about you. The fact that your target needs to get to class doesn't change the fact that you randomly decided to take an hour-long shower. This is about you doing what you need to do to feel okay. If you normally cook Taco Tuesday, it's time to stop when your target is still around. Make people choose sides without actually choosing sides, break up friend groups. It doesn't matter because you're completely fine with being an asshole.

Be Argumentative for No Reason. Remember, you've decided be a five-pound bag of wet dicks. So make sure every little thing becomes an argument. If the person you want to be passive aggressive with is in the room, try Googling everything they say to fact check them. Did they say something that was only 97 percent correct? Make it into a bigger argument about them being untrustworthy. Once that's ignited, try leaving notes everywhere. Make no attempt to be courteous, just leave notes that say, "Fix This." This is about making every single thing that's not the reason why you're angry into a huge deal. Avoid the problem so it never gets fixed. Being passive aggressive is about nitpicking until every one else tries to avoid you.

Make Shit Disappear. This is a very important part of giving yourself a passive aggressive and punchable face. Making everyday essentials disappear is a great way to be passive aggressive. Since everyone uses them it's impossible to blame one single person. Start off with something simple: use all the toilet paper and wait for someone else to replace it. Toilet paper is as valuable as a freshman's term papers.

After that, be an even bigger shithead and take the easily stolen and plausibly deniable foods. These are foods no one misses until they're gone and the evidence of theft has already left the intestines directly onto someone's front lawn. These include: dried pasta, trail mixes, salsa, hummus, any liquids, and most of all condiments. Being passive aggressive is all about making someone's life slightly harder and acting like they deserve it. Stealing a pack of Ramen might not seem like much, but it's actually a fucking asshole move.

Righteous Indignation. Remember, to be the type of roommate that no one likes isn't easy. Don't forget that people who are passive aggressive treat everyone like white people treated anyone with AIDS in the eighties. Being passive aggressive means knowing you're right, no matter who, or how many tell you otherwise. People who are passive aggressive are little jerk offs, so make sure you never admit defeat and always act like you're better. If forced to apologize, act like an eight-year-old and do it while throwing a fit. Remember no one will ever understand the quest you're on . . . because other people have souls and friends.

> One time in college my roommate brought home a thirty pack of toilet paper. We wiped our dicks with a TP bib after pissing. Ladies, you don't get how luxurious that feels. Stop complaining.

Leave Wildly Different Clues. It's not your fault that they didn't put together the snide look you gave them when they ordered curly fries and the fact that you left construction paper in their slippers. They're even stupider than you thought if they can't put all these things together. If Steve could understand a dog, they can understand you. However, he did dye his dog blue all the time and spoke to salt and pepper shakers. He was also really excited to get the mail. What were in those packages, Steve? Being passive aggressive is like playing *Blue's Clues* with someone who doesn't know that they're supposed to be paying attention to you.

As you can tell, passive aggressive people are the best and sarcasm and satire have no place in society. Being a passive aggressive roommate will get you nowhere, even if you've convinced yourself otherwise. Life is filled with passive aggressive backstabbers, and college is a time when you don't have to be a cunt. The only way to survive living and dealing with others is finding compromise and speaking candidly. College is when you can nurture those skills and maybe change the post-college world for the better. Don't be a passive aggressive and vindictive prick. Just be a blunt and honest prick.

STEAL YA CHOWDAH

When in college, canned soup tasted like the sweet nectar that came out of the tip of a throbbing angel cock. Canned soup, Ramen, and potato flakes are the staple foods of broke college students. They're also the staple foods of broke adults and people who need to lose weight. Soup is a magical food that's ready in fifteen minutes and still feels like home. You can steal pretty much any other food from your roommates. As I write this I'm eating my current roommate, Rob's, pierogi. He's only twenty-one and I'm twenty-seven. Stealing a roommate's soup means karmically you're going to fall in a freak sinkhole filled with skunk spray and sea urchins that know magic spells that hurt even more than spines. Look, just don't fucking steal soup.

Soup is like home. It doesn't matter whether your parents burnt you with cigarettes and always left the ironing board in the living room, or you were so well-off you had a nanny who was a different race than you, everyone eats canned soup. It's one of those amazing and lovely items that fills you up, arteries and all. You can't help but love it. It's scientifically designed to make you think that's what love feels like. Even if you came from a bad home, few things make you feel better than a good cry over a bowl of Campbell's Chunky Clam Chowder. It soothes the pain of the news that your brother "lost" your third pet turtle this year.

Soup is cheap. It's like three dollars for a can. The price point may scream, "I'm okay to steal," but let me offer a differing opinion. If it's only three bucks, there is no excuse for ever running out. If you clip a coupon, the supermarket actually gives you free stuff for taking it off their hands. If you buy five Manhattan clam chowders the company will give you anything for taking it off their hands. It's so cheap you can buy a million different flavors so there is bound to be at least one can of a weird flavor you hate in the back of your pantry at all times. Italian Wedding soup—if that's what they serve, I'd get a divorce. It's so cheap there is no excuse why your pantry shouldn't look like an episode of *Doomsday Preppers*.

Giving someone soup seems way more thoughtful than it actually is. This girl I was dating asked to make our relationship exclusive after I got her soup when she felt sick. It cost me fifteen cents for a girlfriend and I took like eighty-five saltine crackers with me for when I got high later. When someone is hungover to the point that there is no food left, cold soup feels amazingly filling for the few moments it stays down. Cold canned noodles feel like a massage on the larynx when they come back up. Chicken Noodle soup and a splash of Pedialyte seems way more thoughtful than admitting, "I put two things I had on the same shelf together." You don't steal someone else's chance to make people feel better.

There's no need to steal it if people will let you have it. Soup is just tea made from veggies and meat, and if someone won't share a can of tea, you don't want it from them anyway. No one asks for soup when everything is going well. When things are going well, you always have soup, when things are bad you don't even want to leave your bed, much less go buy soup. Just give each other soup. It tastes better if you throw it at someone anyway.

Killing Someone is Always an Option

We've covered that I hated my roommate Max. I will always hate that guy. I could get called to his bedside after some horrible accident and I would gladly pour just enough water into his throat to drown him. I will always imagine Max's dying breath to be more refreshing than a cold autumn breeze as it rustles leaves down the sidewalk. Sometimes, I used to sit next to him and show him pictures of other people's naked girlfriends on the Internet. I don't know why but it always seemed to piss him off. "Hey dude, look at this girl's chest, who would break up with that?" I'd wonder out loud. He'd take one look then go back to doing nothing and sigh, "She's probably terrible to talk to." A valid point, since she does date the type of men who'd post her naked pictures on the Internet, but I hated the pessimism. If you can't think highly of a naked stranger on the Internet, who can you think highly of in college?

Max was intolerable for a slurry of reasons. It was more than his good looks, how he thought he was better than everyone else, and scowled at fun until he was a senior. Max was the most inconsiderate and passive aggressive dick head I've ever met and it only got worse when his fat, bitch, and bitch again girlfriend was around. She had the personality of low tide. Although she was an Irish girl, she had the body type of a pastry bag that someone just kept loading more icing into without any coming out. Her head was too big for her body and she had a mess of unkempt curls that couldn't hide the neck of an athlete. She may have been a soccer player, but she kept her body in a state that was much more like a softball pitcher. The only thing I liked about her was that I could never eat around her no matter how high I got. She always hunched her shoulders and scowled because she hated me as well. I tried to adjust to her constantly, pervasively entering my space but just the sound of her breathing made me contemplate the pros of beating myself with a heated clothes hanger.

One lovely weekend I had the joy of running a 103-degree fever with fluids dripping down my throat. It was a brisk winter and I turned my heat off because fuck it. ReTodded dumbly meandered into my room where I was attempting to make myself feel better by doing push-ups. "What're you doing?"

I responded "Push-ups."

"Oh," without thinking or even reacting, my favorite lummox got on the floor and started doing push-ups with me. Friendships like ours are once in a lifetime. As we continued to push down on the earth, telling gravity to go fuck itself, ReTodded explained to me he'd be blasting the best music in the world tonight with tons of girls and it was my obligation to come over. Although playing the best music in the world was a lofty goal, I loved that can-do attitude that only someone who could bend a frying pan could have. I was sold. I knew I'd watch that behemoth dance to Gorillaz and death itself was worth it to see that.

I consulted my then-girlfriend, because there's a wondrous change in what it means to be a man after you have decided on monogamy. I admit fully I was at her very whim—she was intelligent, attractive, and everything I'd never considered myself to be. (Guys, she's now a yoga instructor. I was dating out of my league.) I did what any man does when faced with a beautiful woman and horrible constitution. I lied. Stared directly into those oversized brown eyes I admired, and told her I had a hangover and I wasn't sick at all. Some may think that is a little lie, but she always prided herself on the fact she was the only person on campus that tried to help me make it out alive. Saying you're not sick when pus from tonsil fissures drips down your throat, you choke on more than just your words. Lying was my strong suit in high school, but once you don't have to practice on your parents every day you get shitty at it. Her brow furrowed and her wisps of brunette hair fell over her cheek. Her skepticism made me grin. She didn't smile back and I scampered down the hall to read the colorful boxes in the margins of my textbooks and sleep off my "hangover." Max and Pastry Bag were in the room lying in the dark not talking, as people who are bored in their relationship do. Being polite, I reached for the light switch but decided against it. I would crawl into my poorly sized bed and get a much-needed hour of sleep. Until a horrible hacking sound started forcing itself out of my gullet.

It was worse than nails across the chalkboard, it was a heaving from my lungs that permeated my stomach and made rest impossible. Every attempt at being horizontal resulted in a wet heave than left me swallowing a rancid broth of stomach stew. The sky dimmed and the lights outside the windows turned on as I crumpled the blankets, tossing and turning, trying to sleep. The sheets stuck to my back and arms as moisture from my pores leaked out at a surprising rate. An audible groan came from the opposite corner of the room, where Low Tide and Max still hadn't exchanged a word while I struggled for sleep. The hacking from my gullet continued, the back of my throat set ablaze, and the moisture in it menacingly disappeared. I coughed again and Low Tide whispered, "Can't he go somewhere else?" When that wafted across the room and into my eardrums I was hot, but not just because of the 103-degree fever. I sat up in my bed, without a word I alternated eye contact between the two of them for as long as it took to make their skin crawl. In that moment I couldn't cough. I couldn't feel the feverish brow that was pouring burning sweat into my eyes or the entire-body ache that follows when someone is incredibly ill. I hoped they felt like animals trapped in a corner while a predator slowly stalked them.

An alarm blared through the awkward and menacing silence, breaking the tension in the room. It was time for my biweekly shower and to prepare for ReTodded's shit show. I held eye contact as I removed myself from my own dwelling. I stepped over to the shower, threw the dial to hot, and waited until steam humidified the bathroom and my throat stopped pulsating. That water felt like the first morning in winter, the type of chill you only get when you step out of bed and the cold hits completely unexpectedly. Ice water shot down onto porcelain and swirled about the drain, until it disappeared with a gurgle. I stepped in anyway, knowing the water was scalding hot, but my body was most likely hotter. An old Irish mother's trick is to fill a tub with warm water and force your child to jump in to bring down the body temperature. When your temperature is as high as mine was, thinking is difficult, but I had done this enough times that muscle memory acted instead of my brain. Time doesn't pass when you're really enjoying a shower. While I gargled and sang, "Soulja Boy Up in it HOO," I could feel the heat dwindling out of my body against its will. I stepped out, put back on the same dirty clothing, and brushed my teeth.

By the time I was finished preparing, I could hear the music blaring from across the hall. My door swooped open and that tiny little muffin I was dating walked over and hugged me. While the quickening thud of the bass from next door rattled our rib cages, she told me some inane story about how her classes were while I pregamed with Benadryl and a shot of vodka. The shot burned the fissures on my tonsils so badly I almost dropped to my knees, for the first time in college I actually couldn't drink. I grabbed my girlfriend by the hand and brought her next door, preparing to spend a night in a sleepy haze from Benadryl and bass. When we opened the door the party was a ramshackle mess. There were eight people in the apartment and ReTodded was in the middle of it dancing by himself. The door hadn't even closed and I was ecstatic, laughing at what can only be described as the dumb dance.

It's been a goal in my life to accurately describe how this beastly Italian danced because it is still burned into my memory. A steroid-filled basketball player, six foot four and well over two hundred pounds, his coordination was left on the court. When he danced, the entire room felt the thud from the rare times he actually lifted his feet and put them back down. His skull was shaped like an awkward, half-filled balloon. It was round and tapered off toward the front with a prominent Italian nose. His head moved completely separately from his body and his grin can only be described as simultaneously excited by a puppy and sad like there was a family emergency. When ReTodded nodded, he looked up and his head moved from side to side and up and down like a paint can in a stirring machine. There was little to no rhythm to it. Sometimes babies rattle their own heads and I'm not 100 percent sure ReTodded ever outgrew that stage. It looked like he was purposely trying to give himself whiplash in a controlled manic fit. The mass that held his head up was alienated completely from his arms and body. His body gently rolled back and forth while his feet stayed planted on the ground, it was controlled but off beat and the juxtaposition of a frantic noggin and a sluggish body would make anyone laugh uncontrollably. The single best part about the way my cohort danced was his arms: they had multiple personalities. One moment they were locked at a forty-five degree angle pointing up from where his elbows were sealed just beneath his rib cage, the next moment they were lifeless corpses flailing about while his shoulders did all the gyrating. When people make fun of the way white people dance, ReTodded is the poster boy . . . or the viral YouTube video.

Aside from the ogre dancing in the middle of the room, the party was a bust. Stevie Steve was behind the counter in the kitchen doing shots by his lonesome, and I suggested to my girlfriend that she partake of what he was sharing. Everyone looked a bit shocked when I explained I wasn't drinking that night, but no one pressed the issue. When it comes to college parties, I look back and understand how simple they are. As long as there are too many people and too much booze, a party is always considered outstanding. There is always some idiot dancing and people jump from one stranger to another, genuinely happy to hear the novelty of another person's life. This was not that kind of a party. Two girls, who everyone knew were going to have sex with ReTodded, sat questioning their decisions on the couch while he tried to get them to join him in the seizure. Four Fingas was chatting with the few people who were actually in the room and on good behavior for once. All in all it was so boring that I noticed my brow starting to sweat again. Not drinking lasted an hour, until I shotgunned beers to make the night more bearable.

I was still visibly sick and everyone but me was starting to notice it. They all commented I had no color in my face, and in a Benadryl-and-booze-filled cranium I kept retorting, "That just means your wallet is safe." After all nine of the people contained in the mediocrity had mentioned my coloration, I left my girlfriend's side to go into my room and see for myself. When I looked in the mirror, my lower lip rose up like it was trying to knock my top lip off my face. In front of me was a ghost, riddled with visible blue veins that raised from my skin. I literally had no color. I was translucent. But the mixture of Benadryl, two beers, and vodka had convinced me everything was going to be status quo. "If you're not having near death experiences, how are you living?" I asked myself. "I ask myself how and why we're still living every day," my reflection responded. I convinced everyone I knew I had irritable bowel syndrome so I could spend hours in the bathroom, when in fact I was taking sabbaticals from sanity and speaking to myself in the mirror. I never actually spoke back, I generally thought back. I looked in the mirror one more time and sneered, then dashed back to the party that was as lifeless as ReTodded's arms.

Re-entry was a mistake. I was still as translucent as the intentions of a man buying a sorority girl a shot. I had Benadryl in my veins but my cough was starting again. The bass vibrated my stomach and throat and I was not moving so much as swaying in a constant state of a controlled fall. My girlfriend greeted me and immediately pushed me back out of the room.

"But I wanna go in." She pushed me across the short width of the hall and back into my room.

"First, you're sick. Second, Steve just hit on me." Still to this day I wish I could say I hulked out and threw Steve across the room. I wish I could say I got angry or even went in and told Steve he betrayed my trust. Even the girliest of actions, slapping him, would have been better than what I did. I smiled, because in this sick mind the guy who slept with more girls than I did thought the girl who claimed to love me was hot. "First, I am *way* past sick. I am going to get in the shower and I am going to need as much help as possible. Second, there isn't a second. There's no way he hit on you." I let her know as I became self-aware that I was narcissistic enough to take it as a compliment, and socially oblivious enough to insult my girlfriend at the same time. I felt the hacking start again and watched my girlfriend's face turn from annoyance to concern. She walked to the shower as I coughed until my throat burned and eyes glassed over. Throwing the knob to hot, she took my clothes off and commanded me into the shower.

Fighting off a half hard-on from getting ordered around, I stepped into the shower. Being that it was a shower for handicapped students, it had a tiny lip to keep water in instead of a tub to step over, and most importantly it was long enough to lie down in. I laid down and let the scalding hot water raise goose bumps on my skin, as my girlfriend jammed an even colder piece of metal into my mouth. At this point I was slightly delusional and told her she put a butt thermometer in my mouth, so I've technically done ATM. It was not a butt thermometer, and it read 104 degrees, which is a lethal temperature when followed by a change in mental status and slurred speech. Being already crazy, the difference between me with a lethal fever and without was not drastic. I was singing in the shower then filling my mouth with water and spitting it at my girlfriend in the moments when she wasn't scolding me to swallow it.

We lowered the temperature of the shower slowly and watched my temperature go down as I laid in the extra long shower, spitting water into the air and trying to catch it in my mouth. Once I was back to a regular temperature and the realization of mortality set in, I kissed my girlfriend on the cheek and told her I was contagious. Hilarious joke, but it's an even better way to ensure sleeping alone. She wasn't actually angry, but we did agree I'd be spending the night alone to avoid the spread of infectious diseases. The only decision in life I have ever questionably stood by was spending this night alone.

It finally gets bad right. Fucking. Here.

I unlocked the door to my room and threw my wallet, keys, and phone on my desk. Low Tide's snoring was letting loose like a broken muffler and I wished she'd wrap her lips around one and inhale. Max was as dead as his girlfriend's personality. I pulled the bed sheets apart and got underneath, happy that my previous sweat had dried. It was warm and as comfortable as a mattress hundreds of students had had sex on over the years could be. The coughing began again. Like a sandstorm leaving my esophagus, it tore away at my throat. After moments of lying in bed I had to get up to vomit. I opened the door, dashed to the bathroom, and vomited with the precision that only a binge drinker could have. It slipped out of me and before a bead of sweat could drip down my brow, I was back in my bed.

Feeling momentarily better, I drifted off to sleep. But I was rudely awoken by what I thought was the sound of my roommate having sex, but was just gurgling and bubbling coming out of my upper intestinal tract, through my stomach, and out of my mouth. A wet cough clawed its way up through my throat hole and let itself out, forcing me to run out of my room again to forcefully expunge whatever fluids and solids were still being digested. This time lacking in precision, but compensating with flare as I let my arms flare out and flap pretending to be a mother bird feeding its young. This one was worse than before and I laid on the cool tile of the bathroom floor for a while, then jumped back into bed, slightly slamming the door behind me.

I drifted off yet again to the sweet white noise of a baby pig being slaughtered coming out of Low Tide's nostrils while only vomit wanted to come out of mine. I only reached half-sleep before I was gripping the sides of my mattress from fever dreams. It was torment, pus dripped into my stomach as I stewed in freezing cold pore puke. I could feel the heaving happening while I was still asleep, waking up in time to sprint half-naked to the toilet, knocking my desk with a loud thud on the way. When I got over the toilet, nothing came out. A slow trickle moved down my brow and dripped like water forming a stalactite from my nose. The ripple in the toilet from every drip made me dizzy, but a loud bang from the hallway broke me out of my haze. I stayed hypnotized by the toilet water for a little longer, and eventually got up and walked toward my room with the skill and prowess of a two-year-old who had a concussion from a living room table. When I gripped the doorframe of the bathroom, I saw that my room door had been closed.

Air pushed out in the form of a sigh as I was awash in helplessness. The door handle proved to be locked, keeping phones, blankets, shirts . . . anything a child sick and away from home would need to be comfortable, locked away. Max had done more than locked me out of my bed. He had put a barrier between solace and me that I could not break down in my weakened state. I was cold, helpless, and left alone to fend for myself in a situation that by all means was life threatening. There were no blankets in the common area and it was in the dead of winter, where no matter the amount of heat that was blasting from the vents, I felt the cold creep into my bones and linger within my marrow. Sweat still poured down my brow, dry heaves still plagued me, as I tried to cover myself in hard and unforgiving government-mandated pillows. He could sleep through Low Tide's nostrils that exuded the sound of an elephant being slowly eaten by a lioness, but after three times making minute sounds to remove sickness from my body, he locked me out while I was in a deplorable state. Sickness wracked my body. Eventually weakness took me. There was no warmth that night. There was no state of mild comfort provided by a thick comforter that let me know I'd pull through. There was only helplessness. There was only the lingering idea that I might not make it through the night as my body fought off the invading infection.

The morning came, piercing bright sun through the windows of the common area. At seven in the morning, when I awoke, my door was still locked. The barrier between me and the simple comforts of home was still present and after a night of restless sleep, I had recovered enough to feel an anger that made me feel alive again. I sat in the hallway waiting and plotting. Eventually someone would wake to relive their bladder of the previous day's ingestion. It was my burden to forcefully bear. Hours of sitting shirtless with a relentless discomfort brought my mind and body into a fight or flight mode, and before I could act on it, I had already chosen to fight. For two hours I stalked up and down the long hall. Two hours I dreamed of revenge for him making me survive a deathly fever and pay penance for poor decision making the night before. I played the situation through my mind a million times. When Max opened the door in a mid-morning haze to relive himself, I knew it was time to react. While he stepped into the bathroom to drain his bladder, I slipped into my room and opened the door to my dresser where he'd never see I was hiding.

That blond haired, entitled piece of gutter trash stepped back into the room and loafed back into his bed. Low Tide was still letting loose the noises only something low on the food chain would release while it was being mauled by an apex predator. I sat in silence, my heart thudding through a rib cage and layers of skin. It wasn't enough to stop the insanity that happens when blood pressure rises and the taste of nickel fills your mouth. I lost my humanity and let it consume me. I was thrown into a state of awareness that no words can describe. I listened to his breath, and as it lulled back into a dreamy haze I understood he was drifting off into the helpless and lovely state that I had wished for the night before. He caused the volatile and uncontrollable reaction that I was about to have. Although it was wrong, I rationalized that he had tried to kill me the previous night and it was my turn to reciprocate the lack of caring for another human being's life.

As soon as I counted less than sixty breaths per minute I knew that REM sleep would take effect, and it would take at least forty-five seconds for him to react once I was on top of him. With the grace and poise of a hunter I skulked to his bed and stared. I weighed the repercussions to my actions and came to the conclusion that Max needed to learn a lesson about how he treated other people. In a flash I was straddling him and Low Tide with a thousand yard stare.

I felt the warm skin between my fingers as my knees pinned down his sinewy arms. I was not to be thrown aside. I was not to be tossed off of him once I began my descent into berserk rage. My uncle had spent three years in the rodeo and taught me the tricks of staying in mount when faced with something that out-angered and outweighed you. Compared to a bull, Max's struggling was like a light breeze. I noticed it but I didn't think twice about it.

I kept my fingers over his esophagus and squeezed as his eyes opened and the severity of the situation overtook him. For the first time in my life I was ready to kill, I was ready to show someone else the fear they instilled in me. I bellowed, "You fucking dirt bag! You fucking fuck! I could have fucking died, but your self-righteous piece of shit mind told you to put some disgusting piece of trash over the life of your roommate?

She makes the noises of a confused farm animal and you locked me out?" I clamped down on his neck harder and watched as his eyes turned red and he helplessly thrashed about with me on top of him. Low Tide woke up. I quite enjoyed the idea of her watching the only thing that would ever care about her, that was under three hundred pounds, die. I felt vertebrae crack under the pressure I exerted with my ten fingers. The air felt like needles as I took it in and his body wailed beneath my power. "You fucking inconsiderate cunt! I could have died! I had a 104-degree fever and I was vomiting and you locked me out for no fucking reason other than yourself." He was writhing beneath me helplessly as I saw the veins in his neck and face fill with the pressure of unreleased blood.

It was in this moment that Stevie Steve saved a life. The arrogant German who had hit on my girlfriend the previous night (I later learned his majestic pick up line was, "Hey, baby, why you with Bread?") swooped in like an angel and asked me, "What the fuck are you doing, you psychopath?" He had brought clarity to a situation in which most would have been paralyzed and attempted to call the police. I unmounted Max begrudgingly, as I resurfaced from delusions and snarled at Stevie Steve, "He locked me out because I was sick." His gaze let me know I had reached an inhuman level. He forced me to put on a shirt and take a stroll through campus until I calmed down. When I reentered the apartment, Max was gone. Stevie Steve sat patiently in the hallway and offered me his room for the semester for a fee of $500.

It's funny how quickly the ability to masturbate without someone you hate in the room changes a person's attitude. When you weighed the fact that a single room was worth way more than $500, I got the better end of the deal. Stevie Steve's report card looked like Max's mouth, covered in Ds. If Stevie Steve had remembered that if one roommate kills another one, you get all As, Max would probably be six feet under with a grave stone that said, HERE LIES MAX THOM, HE WAS WORTH THE JAIL TIME. I may have been a murderer in this delusion, but my Catholic guilt still forces me to give a proper burial.

After this incident I often imagined standing over his grave and wondering what my last words for him would be, something like, "Today we bury one of God's children. Stepchildren. Lo, he did not lead a good life.

He led a life of womanizing with girls who had stinky belly buttons and never giving back to anyone because he believed he was better than all of God's creatures. It is a sad day . . . for nobody." At this point I'd crack a beer and pretend like I was going to pour it out but then say, "Gotcha," and point to the sky. I'd point to the sky because I assume all annoying white people buy their way into heaven. "Yes, I am sad to say this man-child has left the earth . . . wait, no I'm not." I'd do a little jig here then walk away from the grave.

The tension never left after the incident but Max never brought it up. I think I gained a semblance of respect for his ability to bury his emotions. Time after time he would be in the room, completely non-interactive with me, and I'd wonder if in the back of his head he thought of me as a person capable of doing the most destructive thing a person can do. In all honesty, it will always haunt me.

It's a simple lesson here. Just don't be such a dick.

You Can't Kill a Vampire with Black Mold

When I was twenty, there was an undeniable darkness inside of me that I often put in others.

My first roommate interactions were with Max, the epitome of white privilege. Max had long blond surfer hair and a body carved out of granite. He could have been an Abercrombie model in the nineties he was so in shape and I could never get over that jealousy. I spent two years in a mixed martial arts gym before college, yet Max's perfect genetics made it so that fuck rag never worked out and maintained a perfect form. Max was a pretentious asshole, which made me think he and I would get along great. But shortly after living with him, I found out he judged me and told the other roommates I was a piece of shit. We tormented each other, from the nights Max would lock me out of our room, to the time I told him to stand still as I practiced stick fighting . . . swinging sticks so close to his face he knew I was able to hurt him with anything I could grab if he pissed me off.

Max made people tense. His face muscles always constricted in such a way that let people know he thought he was better than them. When he first came to college, he never drank and let everyone know his thoughts like a vegan at a chili festival. While everyone else was relaxing and making poor decisions, he would sit in his room talking to his girlfriend on the phone or actually doing homework. But, on occasion there were nights he'd venture out with me. He wouldn't make that face that made you want to slap him so hard his entire genealogy would feel it, and one of those nights solidified me as a complete and utter mess.

Max sat perched on the hand rest of one of those cold and wonderful benches, I sat beside him as we chatted with neighbors we had never met and started to bond for the first time in our weeks of living together. I forget now what stupid conversation we were having, but at the time I know I looked at him with a sense of quiet wonder. He was amicable for the first time and it was refreshing to see him interact without pretense. I was smoking a cigarette while he stared off into the windows of our room because he was uncomfortable that I had left the door unlocked. His gut had spoken to him as he watched into our room and within minutes we were both staring back in and saying, "What the holy fuck?"

Our door crept open and a tiny brunette peered inside, making sure no one was around. She slowly stepped into our new home with calculatingly invasive footsteps. Once inside it was a whirlwind. She piled our items on the kitchen counter. We watched her run in and out of our rooms through the windows that faced the benches where we sat. Surprisingly fast, in moments we had been robbed and were too slow to react as it happened. Once it sunk in what was actually happening, we both laughed until we sobbed, on those beautiful benches we took stock of what the stranger had stolen from us. A scented candle I had bought for the kitchen to cover up the stench from our kitchen sink, which constantly held dishes we were too lazy to put into the dish washer; a box of tissues that were used to clean up from masturbation more than runny noses; and a few articles of clothing that I had left strewn about because I was running in them and they were filled with too much stench to enter our room. Instead of a call to action, our guts told us we'd be able to find this girl because she was too fucked up not to make more mistakes that night, and our guts were right.

Max and I were lying in our respective beds when our instincts proved true. The day we moved in, Max had taken the far corner and we had placed two closets in between us to give the illusion of privacy. My bed was right at the entrance of the room. I was mid-sentence when something pounced on me like everyone on ribs at a family barbeque. A curly tuft of hair is all my eyes caught before I was screaming in pain. It was only a split second; she was there then she ran out again. Max got up to give chase, while I took one look at my neck in a mirror and muttered to myself "I look like a human on Shark Week." The skin on my neck was already raised and clear imprints of a small human's teeth were outlined across me in five separate places. I felt like rawhide given to a puppy freshly teething. Tiny specks of blood were raised out of my skin just enough that anger snapped and my blood rushed to my brain and I saw a flash of white. When an Irishman sees white no good can come of it.

The scent of metal was in my nose and I instinctively threw open the door to 1B. Inside Max was yelling at a girl who could only be described as skeletal. In my anger I watched in slow motion as Max yelled something, and she responded with gibberish. Max said something else and she again responded with gibberish. He threw his hands in the air and left, it was my turn to pounce back. I stared down at the skeletal figure lying on my neighbor's couch. Her shirt was so tight her ribs showed through it. Her hair had three ties in it that were so out of place they made her hair into two brown lumps like a camel's back. When I looked into her face I saw red-rimmed eyes and she shuddered back when I walked in the room, silent and angry. When she wiped her nose a tiny speck of blood caught on her index finger, I looked at her and smiled.

"Listen, you cokehead—"

She yelled gibberish. I lunged toward her and laughed. She sunk into the couch and my eyes went wide. The throbbing from her bites raised the veins in my temples and ached with every breath. Every heartbeat forced blood into pooling bruises and I thought about murdering her for hurting me.

"Where is my shit, right fucking now."

She put both her hands under her butt and didn't break eye contact with me. She pushed up and inched sideways, keeping her front to me as if I were a wild animal. I was an animal but no amount of banging pans or bear mace would chase me away. As she went into the bathroom, the sides of my lips curled up with glee. I noticed a pair of shoes with a designer name on them and while she searched for my stuff I threw the shoes into the hallway. She retrieved a few shirts, my scented candle, and various bullshit I wouldn't have been angry about had she not bitten me. I threw it all into the hallway and screamed at her to sit down. She was obedient at this point. Cokeheads can be like dogs in more ways than one.

I kept eye contact with her as I poured a glass of water from the attached kitchen. It doesn't matter what a person has done to you, I grew up learning that every human deserved a glass of water when they needed it. I stepped back to her and when I extended a glass in friendship I was met with an atrocity of the worst kind. The bitch bit my arm. I howled, grabbed her nose and twisted. I threw the glass above her head and screamed into the possessed little cokehead's face. I kicked her bag across the room then stormed into my room. I grabbed everything in the hall, and hid her designer shoes in the top of my toilet tank.

No one in 1A did dishes besides me. They sat festering like piss bottles thrown on the side of the highway by methed-up truckers on a deadline. It had been weeks since I felt the need to clean dishes. Not only did they smell like dumpster water but a thick layer of black mold had formed along the plates at the bottom. It was floating in the shallow water, taunting me as I angrily paced, staring at the bite on my arm. I ended up staring into it . . . then I had a plan.

A wonderful, devious plan. My heart shrunk three sizes that moment, 'twas the night Bread stole bitchmas. I needed revenge. Max wandered in coyly and questioned where I had been. He was happy to have our stuff back, but his hands shook slightly as he saw me hold a glass of mold in front of my face. "No. Don't fucking do what I think you're doing. I'm out." I scooped another spoonful of black mold and smiled at Max as he left the room. I topped off the glass with rum and coke and stirred till the chunks disappeared. I imagined her gums rotting and teeth falling out in front of me, this visceral monster woman would no longer hurt anyone else. This coked-up punk had never dealt with an insane sociopath who needed revenge before. I bounded across the hall happier than a kitten playing with a dead mouse.

"Heeeyyyy," I said in the fakest and most calming voice I could. It was a voice I had learned as an intern in publicity where I needed to appease my slave masters with coffee and validation. "I think we might have had a teeny little misunderstanding, sooooo, I want you to have this." I held it in front of her and pulled it away as she greedily grabbed for it. "It's a rum and coke and it's an Irish custom to do it in my apartment. Let's head over and I'll even pour you another one." I nodded my head like a parent coercing their child into eating broccoli. It was like leading a donkey with a carrot back to my brightly lit room. As soon as we were inside I yelled, "Max come here for a second." As soon as he entered I handed her the glass and she downed it.

"Why?"

He walked back into our room as his long blond hair fell to the side and he stared at the ceiling, praying to his god that I did my best to piss off.

"How about another, one for the road? You can even take the glass." I poured it and let her run to have a coke hangover by herself. I poured several shots for me, dabbing the first one on my open bite marks, downing the rest while high fiving myself alone in the kitchen.

Two days later my phone rang and the luxurious and soft voice of a pretty girl came through. "Hi, umm, so I think you might have my shoes . . . My friend followed me back to Todd's apartment and we don't know how. It was a really fucked up night but Todd gave me your number." I ran out to the common area where we were watching soccer at noon.

"Hey. I'm putting you on speaker."

"Can I have my shoes back?"

I smiled and sat on a stool as my roommates wondered how this would play out.

"Fuck no. Fuck you. Fuck you, friend. I hid your stupid Jimmy Choos. I got bit. You get that, right? She stole from me."

"I know, but it was a really fucked up night."

"What's fucked up is you think you have zero responsibility. Bring me a thirty pack and you can have them."

Disgust is a rare face. Everything tenses up and curls in directions that a face shouldn't normally make. Twists and spirals under eyes and crows feet come out while the mouth morphs into a sideways S or a U with a gimp. I looked upon the disgusted faces of the people I lived with for a moment. While most would reconsider their actions, I hung up the phone and stared right back. I think this was a turning point in my college life. I knew I was a power hungry son of a bitch with a real hair across my ass.

Two days after the call a tall brunette left two twelve packs of Miller Lite on my counter. She explained to me her friend was really sick and she didn't have time to talk much. I handed her the shoes and asked if I could call her. Sure I had held a pair of designer shoes ransom, but that didn't mean I couldn't show her that deep down I needed someone to help me. In my defense I could have convinced her I was a fixer upper. I was a megalomaniac in this moment. My roommates looked at me with awe, as I cracked open the first beer and exhaled like I had never breathed before. I drank twenty-four beers that night, and even to this day Miller Lite has never tasted better.

This story walks a razor's edge of moral grounds. I think what we can take away is that what I did was very, very wrong. You shouldn't feed strangers black mold. That should be reserved for terrible bosses and that cousin who scratches between his toes and smells it. No one should actively try to hurt another human being. Even if medically it is almost impossible to trace something like that back to the perpetrator. Remembering the times I did things like this brings a solemn quiet to my world. I am not proud of what I did, but there is another lesson that can be learned.

Don't take shit from anyone. People who act that way are always going to act like that, even into adulthood. Sometimes you need to force a person to hit rock bottom to get them to change their life. That night a cokehead hit rock bottom when she drank a glass of mold and woke up on a stranger's couch with no context of how she got there. Another girl, who got too drunk and ended up going home with someone who would take her for granted, had several walks of shame. Both those people paid a price for taking advantage of a stranger. In my mind the girl whose shoes I stole bore just as much responsibility for not staying with an inebriated friend. Just because someone had a bad night doesn't mean they're not responsible for their own actions. Make them pay for it, but please, make sure the punishment fits the crime. Don't feed someone black mold . . . steal money from their wallet.

When it Rains it Pours, When it Snows You Pour

The usual suspects from my first two semesters were loafing about in 1A. The couch filled to the point even the armrests were taken. A large box of a chair, colored maroonish with stains from previous students, was being occupied by Steve who winked and asked people to sit on his lap. The room was comforting and warm with familiar bodies. Hot Dezzie sat at the counter, Four Fingas sat on top of the counter, and I was standing somewhere off to the side, gazing at the forged friendships and people who had come to love me. We were passing around bottles of SKYY Vodka because our hangovers had been tremendous after four days of spending every night with each other.

The Governor walked in, helped himself to a shot, and joined Four Fingas to listen to him tell stories. This was the first night Four Fingas, the only one who knew I did stand up, called me out and made me perform. After a short group of jokes that were mediocre at best, the strangest friend we had made in college joined our rag tag brigade.

A forty-year-old black man from the ghettos of Newark had become a part of our crew. He lived with The Governor and was usually non-intrusive so we always had him around. It's not like we had a choice, he was six foot seven and close to three hundred pounds, he went where he wanted, and the only thing that ever stopped him was gravity or his lungs. He was the most massive human being on the entire campus. It wasn't muscle either. When he walked into the room, his belly entered two seconds before the rest of him but he rarely talked. From foot to head, Will was a giant. He once showed us pictures of himself in the Navy when he was our age, and rubbed it in that none of us had seen the world. I can never remember him in anything but an XXL plain red T-shirt or an oversized grandpa sweater. His hands weren't appendages, they were mitts. He slowly became our group's mascot, but none of us realized there was a serious issue. There was no reasonable explanation why a man of forty years should be living on campus and hanging out with twenty somethings.

After slinging those jokes I restlessly perched on a stool, watching the rest of the usual crew, in the usual place, doing the usual things, become antsy and distracted. Conversations were hitting a lull and there wasn't enough vodka in the room to make things more interesting. (Occasionally drinking gets boring. It's a sad fact that the liquid that fuels interaction in college can prove as worthless as a communications or acting degree. Like stories in this book, sometimes a night just rambles on with no distinct reason or rhyme until the climax.) The inevitable exodus of company began, with polite thank yous and goodbyes, leaving the resident sociopaths—me, Four Fingas, Will, and The Governor—known for urinating in rooms like excited puppies to plot by themselves.

We started wasting time by spinning quarters on the table and trying to stop them while still vertical. We spun like those quarters into the throes of tossing ideas to each other:

"Let's steal lobster tails from Shoprite."

"We've got a lot of salt." They snarled at my suggestion.

"I wonder if this place has a roof?"

The Governor cocked his head to the side and smiled, "That's a very stupid question, but a very good idea."

Everyone coughed and sputtered as beers were finished in haste and the new idea raced through our minds. Then we realized we were assholes for chugging and, filling our pockets with beers, we cracked new ones. We then trudged up the nearest stairwell hoping to find a door to the roof. The first staircase yielded nothing. As lungs filled and released with effort after being beaten by cigarettes and four flights of stairs, we walked back down to the ground floor, recovered, and chose another flight. Halfway through the mountainous climb, Will stopped and ran his hand along the back of his neck, flicking wetness on the ground. "Why you dicks go down to the ground floor for? Motherfucking children. Y'all are children. I can't do this shit. We coulda walked down one flight of stairs and gotten to another staircase and you dipshits go all the way down." That wasn't the end of the rant, but if you were forced to read everything he said you'd probably make the same face as when you first saw *Django Unchained*. Will finished what could only be described as hate speech (suck it guy who wrote my foreword), and the second staircase offered no access to our heavenly goal.

We walked down a single staircase, since Will had asked so politely, and entered a hallway lined with an awful thirties-style fractal printed industrial rug and whitewashed walls. (Whitewashed walls are the least intelligent thing for college. It's like giving them a canvas. College students can't be trusted to keep their bodily fluids to themselves, never mind keep them off the walls. Why whitewash something when some half-brained stoner is just going to spill SpaghettiOs on it? Colleges, paint the apartment walls something besides white. Just ask your janitors what color the students've been smearing on the walls this year. I bet they'll tell you something awful as they thoughtfully wield broom handles.)

These whitewashed, fresh walls gave the hallway a creepy vibe under incandescent white lights, but we pushed past the creepy feeling and split up. The Governor found a stairway that had a ladder hanging down from the ceiling with a trapdoor at the top. Using my height, I jumped to the bottom rung of the ladder and pulled myself up. I couldn't push open the freezing cold metal trapdoor, so in my mind it became a gateway to Narnia. Four Fingas found the honey pot in another staircase. It was a locked door that led to the upper workings of the apartment complex.

Four Fingas popped the lock with a student ID and a butter knife he had brought just in case. Then he closed the door again, laughing, and taught all four of us how to open the door so we could cause mischief on our own. Everyone was ecstatic and began making calls to bring other people up with us. Having a space all your own that you weren't supposed to be in conjures all kinds of ideas, brilliant ideas like, "I can smoke weed in here," or, "We can throw a party in here." I could only admit this years later, but I thought of having a secret barbershop quartet.

We wove our way through narrow halls, lined with the air filtration system, and past the gigantic red pipes where the water rushed in and out of our dorms. We had yet to find an exit, but every time we picked the lock to a new door hope abounded. The first door opened and we were met with a closet filled with enough broom handles to explain why every janitor on staff always carried one. The second door revealed a place where we could pull out a layer of filtration large enough to leave a slit we could fart into and crop dust the entire apartment complex. The third and final door was the one we had waited for. As Four Fingas straightened out the butter knife that had been bent on lock after lock, we imagined the door swinging open and being rushed by trolls or finding students who had frozen to death because the door locked on them. Instead, as the door tilted on its hinges, a blast of cool night air filled the room. We breathed deep and stepped out.

The night air prickled our skin as we crossed through the doorway. The roof was immaculate, and the lowest peak nestled between two steep angled rooves. The red Spanish-style tile was at an angle to avoid ice buildup. It was steep enough to send a human sliding down, unable to get a grip. There was no yelling in celebration, just a slow hiss as we shared pocket beers and stared off to the piercing lights of the University Campus and, dimly lit behind it, the skyline of New York City.

Our normally rowdy crew sat cross-legged, staring off at the campus we had imagined to be so gigantic when going to class. We solemnly peered at it all from the top of a nine-story building that sat atop a hill. Our big world suddenly made smaller. We sat, three fingers perched upon cigarettes as embers slowly burned down to our fingertips. In the background of this man-made campus we all looked at the city, some of us imagining what life there would be like. Some of us would retreat from city life, taking up in smaller cities and small towns throughout NJ, while the dreamers imagined our potential maximized in the place that sparkled in front of us. Skyscrapers shot from the earth like obelisks to human tenacity, a hermetically-sealed wonderland of delights and heartaches. The city is where kids from NJ dream of spending their twenties, making a name for themselves in some conglomerate, and retiring with a family to our rural hometowns where we share stories of our youth until it's our own children's time to bask in its glow.

I thought of a small apartment with a bookshelf, where I'd retire to after spending my days in suits as a celebrity publicist. Invading the lives of the rich and famous while donning a costume, never letting anyone know I was from the lower-middle class. Needless to say some of us ended up in Newark, fending for our lives and commuting, where we hoped to get out of the slowly dying middle class. For the first time we were all comfortable in silence. I'll never know what went through their minds, but real friends are those you can spend moments of silence with. Will was not one of those people.

"Looks nice, can y'all spit off it or do whatever y'all wanna do? It's cold."

We had forgotten why this was a great idea. The night had turned quiet and introspective, with everyone smirking about picking locks but not saying anything to each other. I waited until everyone left to close the door, but we left cardboard in it so we'd never have to pick the lock again. Everyone in front of me, I hung back when I noticed a room we had gotten into but thought nothing of. It was the elevator room. I snuck in and stared at the pulleys and cables in amazement of the engineering. Can you tell we smoked weed on the roof yet? I stepped over the elevator shaft and looked down. It was time to go home.

Everyone retired to their rooms for the night. Some would play music while thinking about the experience we had all gone through, others would turn on pirated episodes of *Family Guy* and dream of Netflix getting a website instead of only being DVDs by mail. Others just watched Adult Swim and passed out in beanbag chairs or sitting up in bed. The night felt crisp, and the next morning, as a fresh snow fell, every single one of us had the same idea.

Being forced to go to class that day should have been considered cruel and unusual punishment. Normally going to class is droning hell for anyone. Doing it knowing there is going to be an ice storm released on you from nine stories up can cause a panic attack. The night before, we were at peace with the world because of that view. Now I was terrified of it. I'm pretty

> Stories from my ex: "One time we went up there and you climbed down the elevator shaft yelling, 'Now, I have a gun!'" Now that I'm older I would have quoted *Dead Pool* instead of *Die Hard*.

sure one of Newton's laws is if you drop two objects of different mass in a vacuum, they'll fall at the same rate. What he left out is, they'll both still fucking hurt if they land on your head. The last person to make it back to the apartments was bound to take more balls to the head than the nerdy kid in gym class.

Uneasily rocking in my class chair, I was too nervous to even sleep. My legs fired like pistons as a man from Dubai tried to teach me about international business. The only international business I cared about was pushing Aussie Mat down hills whenever possible. It became unbearable. The clock hands clicked to noon. I imagined the bodies, piling up from knockout ice ball shots, beneath the building I would have to dash into. It would be like artillery fire bombarding anyone trying to traverse the sidewalk that MSU so rarely shoveled. Facing treacherous footing, anxiety, and an enemy with the upper hand, I imagined what my father would do. I immediately stopped imagining that because he would probably would have burned down the building. Nobody hated snowball fights more than my father. In the middle of a small class, I stood up and attempted to leave. The professor stopped me and his teacher's assistant looked horrified.

"Mr. Foster, where are you going?" he placed both hands on the table he taught behind. Always cool, eloquent, and composed I mentioned the bathroom. Knowing I hadn't thought this through he retorted "Do you need your bag to go to the bathroom?"

I was dealing with a man who might have been smarter, but unlike him I had no shame. "Would you believe me if I said I had to put a tampon in?" The entire class gasped and it turned into a suffocated giggle. The TA dropped a book he was holding and the teacher smiled.

"If you're quite finished, you can sit down and stop being a disruption." A blush crept up my neck and into my cheeks as the passive, and annoying, high school version of me was about to sit down and be embarrassed. Instead, I decided to cause confusion. "Sir, this is America. We knock up underage girls, give them food stamps, and drink Bud." The back of my mind let me know we had no idea where this was going. "Sir, I respect you, I think what you're doing is amazing." *Okay we've appealed to his ego.* "But right now there is a battle going on." *Back track, there is a war going on you insensitive idiot!* "A battle for my heart." *Really? That's where this is going?* "Sir, there is a girl waiting for me and I have to go get her. As long as there are countries I can learn international business, but right now I need to learn the business of love." *I hate me. Do you hate me? I really hate us.* I tried to start a slow clap—unsuccessfully.

I have never run out of a room so fast. Later on I'd receive an email that I had to see the dean of the business school, who let me off for personal reasons. I high fived myself. I did wind sprints down the staunch hallways, making my way to a bus stop. Nothing is more humiliating than standing at a bus stop, especially when there are only two people and you came sprinting up. We stood facing forward . . , I should have said nothing. What I did say was, "So I didn't run here because I'm weird or anything." Having a school with a 3:1 female-to-male ratio meant statistically speaking, I was going to embarrass myself in from of women three times as often as I would normally. I say this because, clad in a North Face hoodie and Uggs, was a red-nosed blonde whose eyes were dark and gloomy. I had just told her I was not weird when I realized how weird that was. The bus pulled up and we both got on, and she forced me to go first.

I got off one stop before mine so I could scope the area. As expected, I could see holes in the snow where balls had been lobbed. They surrounded areas of snow where someone had clearly fallen under tommy gun-like fire of snow bullets. These bastards were mowing people down. I couldn't see or hear them up there. and I knew it was an ambush. Then . . . I realized snowballs don't hurt, I was excited to dick around with my friends, not afraid of slush. Shoulders raised and proud, I strutted into the red zone. There was no firefight, no one slinging balls down at me. I figured this story would end obviously, with them waiting until I got closer and pelting me with snowballs until I laid down and died. I walked closer to the building and looked skyward to see if anyone was there.

I stared for an extra moment, turned and headed toward the door to the building, disappointed at not being a target, thrilled that I would get to be the ambusher. Right leg first, I took a single step toward the door when a beer bottle landed in the snow four inches in front of me. Even from down on earth I could hear Four Fingas laughing hysterically, then a single ice ball crashed down from above onto my skull. Stinging cold washed over my scalp and snow dripped down the tips of my ears. For a moment there was silence. "Eat a diiiiiick," Max yelled down from above. No amount of frozen water could wash away that shame.

After getting inside and getting ready, I threw open the door to the roof where my roommates (except Max) and Will were drinking beers. Next to them was a pile of snow with buckets sitting next to it, showing how devoted they were to causing mayhem. They whipped piles of snow at me until my knees collapsed. I brought my arms up to cover my head while everyone laughed, me included. I pulled a beer from the snow pile (their makeshift cooler), and sized up the situation. Max and Frankie were the best shots and, for all intents and purposes, the only thing I had ever been able to throw was a punch.

At first I was listless and pinned myself against a wall, watching as everyone but Will smashed strangers with snowballs so compact they turned to ice. They handed me balls and I turned them down, cracking more jokes about the people they'd beaned and knocked out. Whenever they handed a snowball to me I put it down and my cheeks burned red. Frankie was in his thirties, Will was in his forties, and even Steve and Max were older than me, because I had decided to attend community college and graduate university early. Shame was something I promised myself not to feel anymore, so I picked up a snowball and everyone laughed when I threw it. "Fuck you guys," I screamed in terror, thinking the only real men I had ever bonded with had just realized I didn't know how to throw. In high school my friends played Dungeons and Dragons and did Taekwondo, we didn't throw balls. When I played backyard football, I was a lineman because I was short and fat and couldn't catch. Humiliation singed my cheeks and I tried to play it off like it was just the cold. "Fuck you, cock-guzzling jerk offs, it's not my fucking fault."

"Relax, kid," Frankie slurred, prolonging the "d." He pointed to Delta Kyle on the ground with his backpack over his head weighing him down as he tried to get out of the snow. He was slipping and falling while the weight of his schoolwork kept him down. I felt remorse until I was overjoyed that I had hit someone on the first try. We spent the day up there, drinking and pegging strangers with balls of ice. Many of our victims joined us, returning the favor to others. We remained the crew that stayed on a freezing roof ruining other people's days. Once our snow pile was gone and the beer ran out, everyone made the long walk back through the guts of the building and down the staircases to their rooms.

This was when Frankie asked me why I freaked out when I threw the first snowball. I admitted to him I spent my childhood inside reading and drawing, eventually breaking out of my shell once I boxed a bit and stopped getting picked on. At least once a week after theat, Frankie dragged Steve and I out to those benches I feel so wistfully about in front of our apartment, and we threw a football back and forth while we smoked cigarettes and drank until we couldn't throw anymore.

You can't choose your roommates. They might be atrocious alcoholics who don't know how to deal with women and always say the wrong thing. They might be smooth-operating Germans who slay Spanish women like it's their job, or they might be thirty-something vets with a drinking problem. Sometimes, those people just need someone to throw them a football. It doesn't matter that we were all assigned to each other. We had battles, we yelled, and once Fingas hit me with a beer bottle. Bonding happens in many forms and sometimes you just have to hope you're all going to open up and become friends.

Chapter 6

YOUR ROOM:

You're not at your parents anymore. I hope you remembered not to leave your porn.

That Poster is so Sick

This is my room? This is considered a room? This isn't a closet and they put two people in here? Welcome to your sanctuary. Now that you've realized you only have space for a lamp, a bed, three hoodies, a polo shirt, and a shitty roommate, you can only make this space yours with 2D objects. This is where the most important part of the college experience comes in: sick posters that show everyone who comes over how sick your life is. How else are people going to know what movies and music you like without spending hours actually sharing with people? Who needs actual bonding when you have instant gratification? Also when members of the opposite sex come over, they're totally going to see that stuff and want to rub genitals until the bed catches fire. Having a sick room means having sick posters to cover the terrible, terrible color that you're not allowed to paint over. Here are the most popular posters and why they're stupid.

Since college is a strange place where people who are still virgins interact with people who've fucked inanimate objects, I legally have to let you know, if it burns when you have sex go to the doctor. Also if you start fires by having sex, you have a really inconvenient super power.

The Kiss. Putting that picture of two girls kissing on the wall only proves one thing: you're stupid enough to pay $10.99 for lesbians kissing when you can get it for free on PornHub. Lesbian kissing is so awesome you have to put it up on your wall so everyone can see how awesome lesbian kissing is. Sorry, bros, those girls probably aren't lesbians and they probably made more off that poster than you will in your first two years after graduation. Here is the thing about this poster: no girl wants to see other girls while she's banging you. If she does she probably wants to watch porn. You should also stay with that girl during college and do weird freaky things. Let her put stuff in your holes and vice versa.

Scarface. *Scarface* is the story about a Cuban immigrant who took over the coke scene in Florida with violence and money in the eighties. Basically it's a story about the biggest asshole. If he wanted to take over the coke game in Florida, all he had to do was walk to any frat house on the FSU campus. He'd have made the same amount but without having to clean up after a chain saw. It's a story about a guy who kills someone because he has a strange obsession with his sister. Normally, stories like that in Florida involve a trailer park and bath salts. People put this poster on their wall because *Scarface* is a movie about a badass. In the end he murders hundreds of guards while getting shot himself—the main flaw in this is that real coke barons don't get caught. It's a story about a cokehead who got lucky for a while but it was short lived. Don't put this poster on your wall unless you want people to think you have a thing for your sister.

Boondock Saints. Yeah, this movie is awesome and the poster is too. You should buy at least seventeen of these posters and wish you could be Irish and a badass. Too bad you can't because real Irish people are so beaten and broken by the time we are nineteen we all have enough anger to lift a toilet and throw if off a room. This has Daryl in it, too. That's it.

Friend's Art Work You Bought. Your best friend made an awesome surrealistic painting where he hid an eye in some swirls but you promise it's super cool. Maybe a cute girl was an amazing artist and you bought a painting to try and get her to notice you (ugh, my heart). Either way, everyone who walks into your room will have an opinion and this is actually something bearable. Just make sure you say fuck it to the weird talentless stuff that was done by someone you won't talk to anymore.

Buying your friend's artwork is awesome because that twenty-five bucks you gave them pays for two of the thousands of pencils they'll need in art school.

The Unknown Band. You're so cool dude. You know of a band that no one else, except like seven hundred die-hard fans, know about. College is going to be your time, when you show people this band's awesome poster they're going to listen to the band and start following them around just like you. (*Cough,* me and The Cat Empire). Listen, no one cares about your band as much as you. So if you're going to hang this poster, don't be the weirdo who tried to bring attention to the band. You're going to be listening to a ton of different music, so there is a good chance that there will be people who like your band. Just don't force it because that's obnoxious.

Pulp Fiction. You've discovered you love Quentin Tarantino and now everyone needs to know how super edgy you are. Listen, everyone loves that guy but it's time for an update. *Django Unchained* was amazing. *Kill Bill* was amazing. Stop limiting yourself to the movie that starred Samuel L. Jackson and the guy who makes male masseuses give him hand jobs. Nothing is worse than a classic movie ruined by knowing one of the actors molests adults who are just trying to do their job.

So, now that you're not a hacky piece of garbage and your walls are covered in *Boondock Saints* posters, your room is a reflection of awesome. By avoiding all the stereotypical college posters (Keep the John Belushi one up, RIP.) you're carving a little bit of your own identity. You're saying, "Screw you world, I am different. I'm going to cover my walls in artwork, instead of boobs, and movies that will stand the test of time." You're saying, "This room makes me way more interesting than anyone else," and that should make everyone proud of you.

Popping Bottles in the . . . Bunk Beds.

One of the most important aspects of college is collecting bottles like an Asian lady in NYC. We can't forget how much each one of those bottles actually cost us, both in cash and shame. Every bottle you have is a memory of several parties, or one party, or two hours of your life depending on the amount you're able to consume. Throwing away perfectly good glass bottles that you paid between thirty and fifty dollars for is wasteful and uninventive. Not only are you supposed to proudly display all the bottles you go through in a semester, you should realize how important having those around really is.

Bottles are the perfect decoration, they're designed to look high-end and have an awesome feel to them. There's not one person on earth who's finished a bottle of Crystal Head Vodka and not kept the awesome skull bottle. There is even AK-47 Tequila that comes in a bottle so realistic a police officer would use it as an excuse to shoot a minority. I'm going to be shot someday by a police officer for that one. There are people who put highlighters in the empty bottles and fill them with water, which looks awesome under a black light. (Don't do that. Don't ever have a black light in college. Do you know how many secret stains are everywhere in college?) Try lining them up in a high place so people can see how drunk you can get. The other purpose of having empty bottles around is to show the opposite gender what your lifestyle is like. If they see bottles of Majorska around, women know your fingers probably carry yeast and men know they're about to be Eskimo Brothers with some guy named Todd. It's an important science.

Bottles are actually valuable investments in getting your dick wet or vagina filled. Since everyone in college is too drunk to be able to tell the difference between good and bad booze, a sixty-dollar bottle of Grey Goose is an investment. The trick is to buy a really expensive bottle and then every time you go to a party, refill it with a mediocre brand of the same alcohol type. Make sure you water it down too, just a tiny bit so everyone says stuff like, "That's so smooth," not, "Why aren't we getting drunk from this?" It's really important to note, make sure you only fill the bottle half or three-fourths of the way. If you're walking into a party with a "fresh" bottle every time people are going to start to notice you're full of shit. Also, it's really important when doing this you *always* share. Not leave the bottle lying around type of sharing, but walk up to a stranger and pour a shot down their throat without their permission kind of sharing. This shows how willing and able you are to have fun and makes sure everyone else is having an amazing time too. The first rule of college will always be, "Make sure you're having more fun than anyone else, and they know it." Some people say recycling is important, I say it's the key to getting laid and making new friends.

Save your sixers. Drinking a lot of beer means you can't save your bottles—too much trash is always a bad thing and there are way more beer bottles to be saved then liquor bottles. What it does mean is that you can use something other than all those shitty posters as decoration by saving the cardboard your six packs come in. Cut off the excess and save the bit with the logo. Now you can take down that awful poster of women's butts and backs painted to look like Led Zeppelin album covers and replace them with something that says you'd get the shakes if you didn't drink for forty-eight hours. This is also a fun way to challenge your roommates to drink more. Never repeat a sixer, that way you can drink their favorites and they can never have them again. It can also show you have good taste. Don't put up a Heineken sixer, even though it is an amazing beer that pretty much wrote this book.

Security is key. Let's face it, a lot of universities are in cities that aren't the safest. If you aren't worried about the drunken KEK guy having to beat a drunken TKE for harassing a girl, you're worried about who might break into your place at any moment. This is why it's wonderful to have an obscene number of empty bottles lying around. A bottle may not stop someone, but no one breaking into your dorm or causing a problem at a party is going to stick around if you start throwing bottles like you're Chris Brown when someone else fucks Rihanna.

Bottles and breakups go hand in hand. Nothing feels quite as good as smashing a bottle when you're heartbroken. Whether you're hitting it with a bat or throwing it as high and far as possible, breaking bottles helps an amazing amount during a breakup. Not only are you already going to be drinking a lot to help get over your loss, you're going to need something to do with all those bottles you have left over. Grab a mop handle and go to town on a twelve pack of something crappy. Find an alleyway and throw bottles at the walls until all your muscles hurt and you can have a breakdown. You never know when some asshole named Brittani or Bryant is going to break your heart to the point you're no longer a functioning person, so make sure you have plenty of these laying around just in case. Nothing helps you get over a bad breakup quite like breaking bottles with the local homeless people who also just want to feel better. Losing five cents a bottle in recycling isn't that much when you know it's your sanity and ability to get an erection on the line.

Empty bottles are important in college. As you can see they have a variety of uses, aside from helping you make poor decisions and wake up with strangers. Bottles are artwork, memories, self-defense, and a stepping-stone to closure. Throwing away a perfectly good bottle is like leaving a baby in a dumpster. Just because no one else can see a future for it, doesn't mean it couldn't have done more good for the world before being tossed away.

No More Heavy Petting

One of the only good things about living with parents is having a dog. They say god spelled backward is dog. Those are also people you don't want to be associating with because they're annoying. Having a pup means having unconditional love and something that wants to protect you. When you get to college, you'll soon learn that the one thing you're going to miss is having a pet around to hold and spend time with. Few things in the world feel as wonderful as having a pet. All of a sudden you're thrown into a world with problems you're not quite sure how to deal with, with no fuzz ball to curl up next to when you need it most. So naturally some of you are going to try to fill that hole in your heart with a much less adorable, and much smellier, small pet. The only problem is finding pets that you can keep in a dorm and hide from the Residential Advisers when they come to do random checks on your rooms. These are some of the animals you're going to try to keep but will inevitably die off.

Reptiles. Congratulations, you've decided to purchase a paperweight that needs a massive amount of electricity and care and gives nothing in return . . . for a decade. Why did you decide to get something that smells like crickets and has more diseases than a frat house mattress? Seriously, you idiot, if it lasts for more than six months then it's going to survive longer than your racist grandpa. Why did you do that? Reptiles have as much personality as a sixth-year senior. Now your place smells terrible no matter how often you try to do laundry and change your bedding.

Fish. They're easy to clean, don't take up much space, and pretty much leave you alone, but so do abused children and you're not ready to take care of one of those. Fish die faster than love in a college relationship. Sure you only spent three dollars on the fish, but why even bother? They swim in their own shit and eat flakes. You can't even pet a fish when you need to feel better. Fish are like having a TV that's stuck on one boring channel. Even when you have five hundred channels there's nothing to watch, so why do you want to have to feed your TV?

Gerbils. These things live about two months before you forget you hid it under your bed, or you shaved it. You don't need to bring another rodent into a dorm room; trust me, there are already hundreds of them running around you've never noticed. Keeping a gerbil in captivity is cruel . . . to all the predators that should be eating it in the wild. Sure you can pet them and play with them and they have some personality. But when it comes down to it a gerbil is like a freshman, it's new to the world and there's a 30 percent chance it's gonna drop out (die) within four weeks of being at college.

Hedgehogs. Yay, you bought something completely adorable that's also completely nocturnal. Never mind it's hard enough to sleep due to parties and stress from school, now you have to hear scampering all night too. Hedgehogs are adorable to pick up and play with until you learn that they chew up their own shit and rub it all over themselves for no reason. I know one other animal that does that and now he's a police officer.

The pets you're going to get in school are awful. There's no point. Nothing will fill the void left by a missing puppy. Dogs cuddle and are happy to see you. These other pets can't even tell the difference between food and something that came out or off of their own body. They stink, they're annoying, and if they do survive what the hell are you gonna do with them after college? Added, if you get them drunk they die, and nothing is funnier than when you accidentally get a dog drunk.

Beatrix Fodder, NaTrasha, Who Smelled of Bunnies

If college solidified anything for me, it's that I hate rabbits. Bunnies, jackrabbits, it doesn't matter what you call them, I hate them. They're the type of pet that makes children cry because they die prematurely, and never in a normal way. Anyone who had a bunny as a child will tell you the horrific story of how their rabbit got eaten by a stray cat or stepped on by their father. I even know people who tell me stories about how their bunny mysteriously disappeared one day then they learned as an adult that their parents let the bunny go into the woods (busy street). For a parent to hate something so much they're willing to bear children crying for days over it, means that it was an unbearably shitty pet.

There are tons of reasons to hate anything adorable in life, but rabbits are some of the worst animals to exist. The phrase, "fucking like bunnies," shouldn't refer to having a lot of sex, it should be used to describe people who are so stupid they have to pump out a lot of kids because they're going to have a low survival rate. Rabbits often eat their own babies. I get that occasionally dogs eat shit, but they only carry that inside them for a few hours. How stupid are rabbits that they actually feel something inside them growing for thirty days and after it comes out they immediately want it back in. Some rabbit owners claim rabbits can live up to ten years, but that's only if they survive their mother and you keep them away from anything even mildly dangerous. Most rabbits die after two years, unexpectedly, and they're too cheap of a pet for anyone to care why it happened.

They give you no reason to care for them or keep them alive. Rabbits are the type of animal that would go out for a pack of cigarettes and never come back. They're only good at running and biting, like a weird kid in kindergarten. The animal shows no affection whatsoever. It sits in your lap not to get pet, it's because it's terrified you're going to kill it. Being at the bottom of the food chain, all they think about is running and biting. You can feed the stupid animals every day and they'll still consider you a predator that wants to eat them. It's a self-fulfilling prophecy because after enough times of these little assholes doing nothing but chewing and biting you, you'll be thinking about making delicious rabbit stew.

But the worst part about rabbits is that they smell of compost, sawdust, and fear. You actually can't clean the cages every day because rabbits absolutely have to eat their own shit to survive. They can't digest everything properly so they dispel something called cecum, which is essentially a bunch of really important bacteria necessary to their stomach that evolution determined should be produced in their butts. Rabbits are the smelliest creatures, and no matter how often you clean them, the musk permeates whatever room they are in. Anything that stays in the same room as a rabbit will smell like the thick, pasty, gelatinous musk forever. It doesn't matter what goes in their room with them, it will always inevitably smell like those bastards.

So when the short Russian brick of attitude we called "NaTrasha" got bunnies because she missed having pets, we all ended up paying for it. NaTrasha lived in a room that would make a hoarder smile with glee. If cleanliness is next to godliness, NaTrasha was so disgusting she was giving Satan's unwashed asshole a rim job. Piles of clothing always sat around, dirty dishes gathered flies, and something always stuck to your shoe. When you walked in her room, she would say, "I'm sorry it's a mess, I'm such a pig." She even had the attitude of a wild boar always backed into a corner, so calling herself a pig wasn't a stretch. Actually, calling her a hoarder isn't fair, the best way to describe her smell is that of a towel you haven't washed in a year. We avoided her room like a disease because we always thought we might get one. The only way it could have gotten worse was by throwing an animal in there, which is exactly what she did.

For a while, we had no idea why NaTrasha's stink got amplified. It wasn't horrendous at first, just a lingering scent that someone might expect from a girl who still ate traditionally Russian foods. Then one day she appeared in our room to talk to us and when she left we ran to other people's rooms and swapped the pillows she sat on for clean ones. The very first moment she smelled like bunnies will always be burned into my olfactory senses. As I walked back from campus I noticed a strange hush. The weather was uncharacteristically spring-like, which meant people should have been out around the apartments throwing footballs and drinking illegally. Instead, an eerie calm washed over the compound of the six compact university sanctioned apartment/dorm buildings. It was an uncomfortable silence, so I rushed back to my room, where I could hear bellows of laughter. I stepped across the threshold and walked toward the couch where NaTrasha was sitting with Stevie Steve and Max. On my approach my eyes watered a little bit and I made eye contact with Stevie, who gave an acknowledging head nod.

My arms opened and I slowly bent forward, attempting to hug the boar on my couch. When NaTrasha's entire Russian frame moved, I got a whiff of bunny and decided to rescind my hug. While she kept her arms wide open I tried to switch to a hand shake, to no avail. I became engulfed while not hugging back. I was smoking a pack of cigarettes a day and it still stunk like Roger Rabbit if he was molested by a garbage man. I could only imagine what everyone else smelled. I hadn't showered for over a week and I ran to the bathroom to smell my own armpits to get the smell of shame and rabbits out of my body. It was the type of smell that made you worry that it's been inside of you. It was the type of smell that made me worry it would never stop being inside my apartment.

As time passed the smell of rabbits got worse. She finally admitted she missed her pets and went to a pet store to get a rabbit. Once she had informed us there was a reason for the smell, everyone laughed behind her back. I often laughed directly to her face, but that's only because stinky people are allowed to make fun of other stinky people. One afternoon, after I was no longer living with Max, I woke up hungover and bleeding from my back only to hear that horrendously cold Russian laugh coming from Max and Stevie's room. There were mumbles and then laughter, then silence. I stopped to stare at the door and cocked my head before moving on to the kitchen. This was when Stevie Steve came out to pop popcorn as I had my head crammed under the faucet trying to pump as much cold water into and all over my head as possible. They were watching the new *Rocky* and NaTrasha had invited herself over to join them. After filling my insides with as much hydration as possible, I napped again to pass the time until the headache dissipated.

An awful-smelling waft of air entered my room and I was on two feet before I was even awake. I ran over and opened my window and my door. A thick, warm breeze entered my room through a cross draft from Max and Steve's room and my taste buds immediately went into a coma. If I could visualize this smell, it would be a cotton swab wiped in someone's belly button post gym then run underneath the rotting toenail of a geriatric man. Stevie and Max sat in their room by the windows, wondering why they didn't kick her out. I asked what that smell was, and all they said was NaTrasha was sweaty. That's when we established the "NaTrasha is not allowed in sealed rooms" rule because no one wanted the room smelling like dead rabbit and Russian outdoor fish market.

I don't want to hear your shit about animal abuse in this situation. It's a god damn rabbit. If you want to get pissed about animal abuse get pissed at parents who buy those things for irresponsible kids. Rabbit's life spans are like four weeks if given to a kid. Also, as far as abuse goes the rabbit could have had a lot worse. We also didn't force it to do cocaine, we threw a rock near it and it made the decision on its own. Get pissed at the rabbit's poor childhood that turned it into a drug addict.

Eventually, as I became friends with NaTrasha's roommates, I got to see the hellion that made her smell of more shame than getting beaten up in high school. I was sitting with her lesbian roommate Kristin, who was cutting lines of cocaine in the bathroom. I politely declined the stuff. That's when we noticed the pesky wittle wabbit staring at us from down the hallway. I yelled at it and it didn't run away. I tried to scare the little fucker into leaving us alone. I even read from a website about etiquette out loud, explaining to the rabbit it was acting in poor taste. Not only did it smell, it acted like an asshole. Kristin did her lines off the back of the toilet while I drank a beer and asked inappropriate questions about lesbianism. Thanks to the cocaine, she was very open with sharing but very paranoid that NaTrasha's rabbit was loose in the common area and still staring at both of us. I told her it was probably homophobic. Rabbits are most likely very right wing in their politics, since they have so many children. Randomly, it sprinted to Kristin's feet, nipped her shoe, and ran back into the corner. Explaining that was its way of agreeing and pointing out it was homophobic. I wondered what a homophobic bunny would taste like.

Deviously grinning, Kristin took a small rock of cocaine she hadn't jammed up her nose and threw it on the ground in front of the gay-bashing rabbit. "Ever seen a rodent tweak before?" I was both petrified by the animal abuse, and entertained that something I hated was about to have a bad night. I don't consider rabbits protected pets. I consider them French food that goes well with red wine. This wasn't drugging it. We were seasoning it. I didn't think the rabbit would nibble on the rock. I've never met anyone who hates gays that wasn't also ignorant enough to think you could get AIDS from sharing cocaine. Showing its true form, the rabbit nervously hopped to the rock and began nibbling on it. I immediately felt bad and chased it into a corner of the common room. It wasn't guilt over drugging a rabbit. It was guilt from Kristin wasting perfectly good cocaine. It sat in the corner staring and it's white fur started pulsating as its breath hastened. Its eyes opened up wider than its eye sockets should have allowed. The single most hilarious thing was although rabbits naturally move their nose an annoying amount, after it ate the rock, the thing's nose and whiskers started going wild. I watched as a white rabbit fell under the effects of white rabbit.

It did not stay in the corner for very long. As soon as the cocaine reached it's blood stream, the idiotic beast ran directly at a wall. It wasn't even attempting to stop. It zigged and zagged, not like a drunk driver, more like a person avoiding bullets being fired at them by someone who makes $25,000 a year. It was sporadic and mildly beautiful. There was no attempt to avoid anything, like most right-wingers, when it was on cocaine it thought it was much more powerful than it was. It slammed its head directly into furniture and walls, as if trying to move them. Kristin laughed wholeheartedly as she watched it dive into a wall with a shuddering crack resonating from its head. "Someone had better get this thing a helmet. Not only does it stink, it's got no depth perception," she cackled. All at once it stopped. Its heart rate was still visible thumping through its entire body. It stared at us, then jumped in a vertical leap that would make a boarder guard shoot first and ask questions later. Its eyes shone with fear as it soared upward. Kicking its legs out, then flailing like it was running midair.

It was a five-foot vertical jump, impossible for a domesticated rabbit. When gravity took hold of it again, it continued flailing on its way back down to earth. While Kristin and I exclaimed, "Holy Shit," like we had just seen a UFO, the rabbit landed like a cat, and dashed into NaTrasha's room again. I've always been partial to free-range food, so I hoped that it was running off to overdose so I could bake it with fennel. Instead we heard crashes and the sound of toppling dishes. An upside down pot came hovering into the room and I knew the rabbit underneath it was coked out worse than Drake after someone says something mean to him.

Again, the little Whitney Houston impressionist jumped into the air, soaring up and up like a World War II fighter jet, shining in the glow of florescent light as it flew toward it. Now it was a glistening pot running around but inside the rabbit was getting covered with the crusted-on noodles NaTrasha had left inside it. When it landed there were two thuds this time: one of the black-and-white coked up hare, and the other when the pot fell on top of it. The rabbit did not move after the pot fell on it. I asked Kristin how much longer it would be coked out for, she informed me eight or nine hours. I began biting my fingernails and fidgeting in my seat. The rabbit had not moved for several minutes and I was out of questions about lesbianism. She wiped her nose, and I got up and hugged her good-bye.

As I left, NaTrasha was stepping out of the elevator, so I beelined it for the stairs and walked down remorsefully. I thought I had witnessed the death of a friend's pet. Granted, it was a homophobic pet, but still I

Hey are you Drake? Not a huge fan but I know people who are!

Drake is hard to draw as a stick figure

Why me?

imagined NaTrasha shedding a single tear as she lifted the pot and found a white corpse with black spots. Just because something is a homophobe doesn't mean it should be dead. It just means it should be put into a reeducation camp of some sort, and forced to work its aggression out while helping the nation produce goods and become a nation of economic prosperity. I hugged a stranger smoking in the stairwell and let a tear or two roll onto their filthy smelling hoodie. Awful smells just reminded me of NaTrasha at this point, so I took a drag of the stranger's cigarette and gave it back.

It took me three days to forget what had happened with the rabbit. It took me three weeks to find out what happened to the rabbit. Turns out, getting the bunny coked up was a rather regular occurrence. After three more weeks of the bunny, NaTrasha's roommates held an emergency meeting. It was Kristin, NaTrasha, another girl, and a girl who once got drunk and told me she wanted to be a shoe designer. (Four months after she told me that I watched her get hit by a bus so hard she went flying out of her shoes. She was completely fine, but I wondered if she might come up with some genius accident-proof shoes. I think she might be a heroin addict now.) Those roommates banded together and made NaTrasha send the cocaine-addicted bunny back to the pet store. I imagine the interaction at least once a year.

"Ma'am, this bunny is sniffing a lot and keeps eying up my jewelry."

"That's because you sold me a rabbit addicted to cocaine, you let an addict into my household."

"Ma'am, this isn't a state adoption agency, nothing we place in your home would be addicted to anything upon purchase."

"Well, how would it get addicted to cocaine?"

The cashier holds the bunny in his arms and looks into its eyes, "Who hurt you?"

The bunny then bites his hand. He drops it and snaps its neck.

"I am not refunding you for a dead bunny."

Several days after returning the bunny to the pet store, NaTrasha came back with a ferret. I have always loved ferrets . . . I will always hate NaTrasha. Well, her smell at least.

Owning a pet in college is a responsibility not everyone is going to be ready for. Most people I know who get dogs in college end up with an awful asshole of a dog who tries to watch them have sex. Other people who get pets make sure the animals become their parents' responsibility as soon as they are done with college, much like kids who get pregnant too soon. Owning a pet in school is an awful plan. It seems like a great idea at the time, until you realize pet-friendly apartments cost three times what a normal apartment costs in the real world and you can't go drinking until 2:00 a.m. without walking it or feeding it first. Get something like a bug or a turtle. I'm pretty sure those animals don't have souls so it's fine if they die.

LSDeez Nuts

LSD is a powerful and sometimes unpredictable drug. The government considered it a schedule one drug, which means it carries some of the heaviest penalties by law for being caught with it. It can cause you to act out and do completely crazy things when taken in high enough doses. It is used by assholes, who listen to terrible bands like Phish and The Grateful Dead, and every single person on earth should do it at least twice in their life. You shouldn't do LSD thinking you're going to come to some great realization or epiphany, you should do it to realize how fucking stupid people actually were in the sixties. They thought this fueled creativity and would change the world, maaaan. When you take LSD, you realize the people whose parents loved it in the sixties were the same people who idiotically convinced us college was going to get us a job and the housing bubble would never burst. Thanks, LSD and shitty music, for the politics and idiocy of the people who raised the millennial generation.

Older generations say we have no work ethic and are addicted to the computer. When was the last time they actually talked to their kids instead of playing Bejeweled at the kitchen table? Taking LSD will remind you how feeble minded anyone who took this garbage seriously is. Even Ken Kesey, the guy who ran the Kool-Aid Acid Tests (written about in Tom Wolfe's *The Electric Kool-Aid Acid Test*), wrote *One Flew Over The Cuckoo's Nest* while on peyote not LSD. LSD is a distraction, LSD is a shallow, meaningless high where strange electricity shoots up your spine and the universe rotates in your stomach and brain. LSD makes the world seem alien and strange and, sometimes, untrustworthy. While everyone will tell you that LSD is some amazing life-altering trip, let's not forget those are usually the people who want you to do it with them. I've done LSD at least thirty times in my life, and I'd like those hours back to do mushrooms instead.

I was not a just a dabbler in LSD. Take this advice wholeheartedly. It comes from a man who once did five hits and managed to witness a Santeria ritual in Coney Island, walk in on a heroin addict shooting up in a public bathroom stall, travel across Brooklyn to Bay Ridge and watch Staten Island losers try to have public sex with their girls along the Hudson River under an impromptu fireworks show, and still go on a successful date while he was coming down. LSD is a shit drug, a shit drug that it is your patriotic duty to pump into your spinal column on at least two occasions.

Why should you do LSD twice in your life? Once because you're bored and with a group of really trustworthy friends, and another because you are bored and alone and need to figure out how mentally strong you actually are. If you aren't an idiot, LSD will make you see melty faces and fractals, giggle non-stop, and then get bored.

Hunter S. Thompson once said, "LSD isn't a drug you find, it's a drug that finds you." Granted that is true, but it also comes from a guy who shot himself in the fucking face. That man is part of the reason why I write, but he lost credibility when he was killed by a piece of lead instead of an overdose or a pissed off politician. LSD found me. I had read *Fear and Loathing in Las Vegas,* like every good college student, but I was still completely unprepared for the strange world of hallucinogenic distractions that LSD was about to open for me.

Thursday nights were the party nights at Montclair State University. Many students went to class, smoked weed in their car, then went home on any other day. It was a stereotypical commuter school filled with sad pricks who drove home nights and weekends because they would never outgrow their high school friends. Thursday nights were never quiet so on the rare occasion I was not invited to anything (people actually showed up to Facebook invitations then) a brown paper bag filled with beer and a stroll was all it took.

On one such brisk November evening, I meandered up and down the same dimly lit street, a gentle slope upward that leveled off at the top. At its peak you were met by a haunting, shabby set of row homes. They were the corpses of the old university. Every other building was made of bleached stucco with burgundy tops, the Clove Road apartments sat like a rotting log parallel to the street. They were outlined with crappy wood paneling of an indistinguishable yet drab color. Some windows had cracks in them, some had students doing crack in them. They were rumored to be haunted, but I have a feeling that was started by the faculty as an excuse for terrible upkeep and weird noises. The muffled sounds of "Soulja Boy" wafted through the air and caught my eardrum, which was hungry for mayhem. I was holding a forty, and I cracked it open.

I followed the notes up a sidewalk and through a door. I was thinking I'd be entering music blasting, strangers meeting, adrenaline pumping, looking for people to throw tiny white balls at slightly larger cups. I was met by a few guys laughing and dancing in a corner, who didn't even acknowledge my existence. I walked directly into the first room I found. This was where the music was coming from. I was still expecting a party only to be met with a dude face down in his bed, smoke still coming out of his bong. I wondered how no one had noticed me yet, and if I was this much of a ninja, I had to steal something to remember this by. Sitting on top of this passed out stoner's desk was an eighth of marijuana and a few pieces of angel food cake. A secret love of mine is the crusty outside baked parts of angel food cake, and I imagined this was sent from home. I was more than happy to steal delicious cake and something to smoke that would make it even better.

As I left the room, one of the guys stopped dancing. For a moment, he locked eyes with me. We held glares and the fear was overwhelming. I could talk my way out of a normal apartment, but I wasn't sure how I'd explain the cake. He smiled, waved, and said, "Hey, Kev," then went back to dancing like a skeleton attached to marionette strings. I walked out of the apartment with a forty in one hand and cake in the other. It was still a perfectly good night for a walking beer so I went back to my empty apartment, rolled a joint with the stolen weed, put the cake in the fridge, and went to finish my beer under some dim lights and questionable legality.

There is nothing else to tell from that night, it ended in a sleepy haze of drunkenness as I returned to my bed . . . my entire apartment empty besides me. The night was wasted, which gave me an itch to make the weekend more successful. Stevie Steve, Max, and Frankie were still gone on Saturday morning. I poured sugar and maple syrup into heated water and made simple syrup, which I drizzled over the angel food cake that sat next to slightly undercooked bacon on a cheap porcelain plate. I remember wondering how I could make an entire Saturday memorable, how I could make up for an uneventful Thursday and Friday night. I inhaled some stolen weed, ate the stolen angel food cake, and sat on my couch at 10:00 a.m. I flicked on my PlayStation 2, and chose my usual character, Lee, on Tekken Tag. A million rounds passed as I played the only video game I was ever successful at, until I started to notice how uncomfortable everything felt. It wasn't a quick change; slowly the room I had gotten to know so well became strange and alien to me. Objects I had gotten used to glared at me with an unfamiliar menace I had never felt before.

LSD does not make you say, "Maaaan," and talk about the vibes. Your personality does that. If you are prone to douchebaggery, then that's exactly who you will be on acid. If you ponder life and think about it in ways that would make the average person look at you like you're a moron, that is what LSD will be like for you. I am a realist. I explore the facets of everyday, boring monotony and wonder at their implications. That is what drove my first LSD trip, the overwhelming curse of seeing things for what they are.

Everything was uncomfortable, everything was out of place and, although I was sitting on a couch, the room was starting to move. When I was eighteen I went on a deep-sea fishing trip that left me vomiting into the ocean. I was considered good luck because wherever I had vomited someone would catch an oversized fluke that was within legal size to keep and devour. This high felt similar but the desire to vomit was not there. I had no idea what was going on when the acid had started to take control of my body. I wanted to yell and scream and go to the nurse's office but as sparks shot up my spine and I felt a mini universe swirl in my belly, the fact that I had somehow been drugged was apparent. The saving grace came from a documentary I had watched at seventeen with a friend of mine who once choked me out in gym class after he had drank too much cough syrup.

People on drugs often speak about their "mind's eye," which makes it intolerable to speak to them, and all credibility they have gets thrown out the window. Think back to being a child for a moment, to when you actually played pretend. Those moments when you were fighting fake soldiers or playing with an empty cup you imagined filled with tea. Give it a moment as you read this. Stop stopping yourself from seeing it in front of you. Let go of those moments when you stop yourself from imagining things and really try to see something in front of you. As a kid, you never actually saw those things in front of you, but you believed they were there. That, readers, is the correct way of explaining "the mind's eye" in a way that's not fucking abhorrent or layered in so much idiosyncratic spirituality that no one can take it seriously.

For a moment I lost my ability to play Tekken Tag and I remembered a documentary where Alice Cooper explained someone had hit him with a cake while he was on stage, and a smile worked its way across his face when he said he ate the cake. He laughed and explained it was stupid to eat that cake because in those days, people would put LSD in anything. The memory mixed with the lingering taste of maple syrup between my teeth helped me to recognize I had taken an unknown amount of LSD. Giddiness filled me. LSD had found me the way Hunter had explained and I had no idea how much I had been dosed. I thought about the adventure I was about to have and anything positive that would linger in my brain. The one thing that my naive self could remember was that on a drug trip, staying positive and realizing it was just a drug was always the most important thing.

Most people do LSD for the first time with friends at a concert or where they can feel like part of a collective group of people. I was abjectly alone and feeling a rushing tide of emotions and alienation rushing through my brain and into my eyes. The day became hazy and I cannot remember all of it, as drugs are known to do. There was a desire to explore campus and be outside, but at the front of my mind was the fact I was playing Tekken and fighting a character that was a devil. A stupid, stupid meaning came across this. I wondered why I had become so attached to a simple video game where people worked down each other's health bars by pressing O, X, triangle, and square in the correct order against a program that responded to your actions mindlessly. I was an extremely offensive player regularly but all of a sudden, facing an opponent that was my demons, I played defensively and tried to pick my opponent a part. There was more strategy than I had ever felt. I knew I would never win against Devil, but I still played and was enthralled in a way I had not been before. Time after time I hit continue as it became harder and harder to play against the final boss. After what felt like hours of playing, I put my controller down. Thinking about the bigger meaning of what had happened, I stepped back into my room and realized how fucking stupid putting a deeper meaning to the game had been.

"I am a fucking idiot. I was not battling my demons, I was battling a game," I mumbled to myself as I ripped a hit from a prepacked glass piece. "I guess I should try doing something someone from the sixties might do." I said this as the cheap linoleum floor became a tide of spiraling fractals, those shapes became a kind and caring fractal pattern that stopped the motion sickness I had been feeling. I was knee deep in the mathematics of the real world and for a moment I believed it. Then I thought, "It's just drugs," and did like any male in the sixties would do: I turned on football and didn't talk for a while. The feelings running up my spine were shocking my entire nervous system, pulse upon pulse of brilliant humanity and life started in my tailbone and shot up to behind my ears. I thought, *How the fuck were those guys in that apartment dancing?* I inhaled and reminded myself it was just the drugs, and suddenly I was no longer in mathematics but standing alone in the middle of my room like a fucking loser.

I stared at the posters on our walls. Stereotypical two girls kissing, *Boondock Saints*, *Pulp Fiction*, and Led Zeppelin posters . . . *Fuck ourselves,* echoed through my brain. I realized there were businesses making millions of dollars off petty posters like this. I had seen these time and time again in everyone else's rooms. As I tore the posters off the walls I thought, *I want to work for those shitty companies. I want to make something watered down and relatable.* But years later I still find my writing terribly unrelatable, to the point where I thank those who hate-read this book. Something about feeling cookie cutter at the time when others would have been inspired to make a change or have a creative thought made me laugh. Then I laughed more. I didn't stop. Not for at least twenty-five minutes. I laughed beyond what was funny, it was like my face was stuck on repeat for a bit, my eyes teared up and throat dried out and after I was done laughing I thought, *That wasn't even funny.* Which made me legitimately laugh for forty-five seconds.

When I looked around, the air seemed thinner. It's strange to try to explain but there was a certain distant and medical feeling about my room that once felt like home. A marketing professor once explained that new vs. old is a strange concept. When does a house become a home? When does a treasured item start to gather dust? He made us try to pinpoint when something new turns to something old, and when something old might become new again. Instead of getting a C, I should have just written, "LSD," and hoped for the grading curve to save me. It would have made more sense than the garbage I had written.

I stared at my bed for a long time. The wrinkles in the sheets wove together like smoke tendrils from a cigarette and gyrated with themselves. I felt my heart rate drop and my eyes dry up from forgetting to blink while I gazed into the sheets. Strange thoughts filled my head as dark blue sheets undulated smoke spirits all jutting from head to toe of the bed. Those wrinkles morphed into infinity symbols and my limbs froze unwillingly. It was entrancing and then I poured myself out of my own body and looked back. I was staring at myself, standing over a bed next to a pile of torn down posters and I thought, *What a fucking loser, who stares at a bed for an hour because he thinks he sees infinity symbols that are trying to tell him something.* That's when I stopped staring and said out loud, "These fucking wrinkles gyrate more in my bed than I ever have." I closed my eyes and exhaled realizing it still wasn't dark yet, but those fucking wrinkles wouldn't stop gyrating. They went from beautiful to an annoying reminder I had been on LSD for hours and was getting bored of it. I flipped my mattress to stop the sheets from moving and immediately wished I hadn't.

In every acid trip there is what's known as a "peak," where your trip comes to a climax and then you're miserable for hours trying to sleep or function afterward. It's when the effects of the drug are at their maximum and you lose the world you live in for a while. It's what most drug users have a hunger for that can never be quenched. The first time I peaked was after hours of wandering my room, then looking at the underside of a mattress that hundreds of college students had dumped fluids, food, and cigarettes on since it was brought into existence. As LSD sparkled up my spine and into my eyes the swirling strange floral pattern swam from one side of the mattress to the other. The background was the fabric but on the foreground was a splattering of bits of human and garbage that only a crime scene detective could appreciate. The very, very first time I peaked on acid, I was forced to think about the life of a college mattress. I think people who are awful in this life are reincarnated as college mattresses.

This was by far, the stupidest thing I have ever thought. This sequence of thoughts will make you, the reader, put down this book and wonder how I managed to graduate college and write a book. After being violently pulled from the ground, dumped into a vat, and made molten, the ore it takes to make a mattress is dumped into a mold then bent and twisted into a box with springs, then a fabric that was made by a seven-fingered prepubescent worker is wrapped around the interior framework and behold: A mattress is born.

Its first thoughts are probably, *Wow, I exist, this is wonderful. What's my purpose in life? I am a mattress? People are going to do what to me? Oh god. I hate you world.* As it's having these first thoughts, a giant robot is pounding into it one hundred times in two minutes for quality testing. As the mattress struggles to accept its place in the world, it's thrown into a dark truck then shipped to docks. As it passes from the truck to a container, it sees the ocean for the first time. *Gasp, what is that? This world is strange and wonderful. Look at that vast space and how huge these things that move across it are. Things aren't going to be so bad.* Until it gets shipped to a confined space with hundreds of other mattresses similar to itself all trying desperately to differentiate themselves in the cramped space. It tries to communicate with the other mattresses in the container but always finds itself falling flat. Then it sits and sits in the container for what feels like forever. Again as it's pulled from a container to a truck it sees another ocean. *Dear lord,* the mattress convinces itself that all the horribleness is worth it if for just a moment it can escape and see the ocean. It's transported to a school where it's eventually thrown into a cold, concrete room where other people's lives come and go in front of it.

The mattress now spends the rest of its life being a spot where hoodie-wearing loafs of college students lie on it, bang on it, burn it, and stain it. The very first time intercourse is had on the mattress it's shocked, it's sad, and doesn't understand why it's being abused. It wonders why it was brought into existence and slowly comes to accept this is it's life now. As cigarettes get dropped on it and, after bar fights, students bleed through the sheets down onto it, it slowly and assuredly becomes numb. The college mattress gets used to the abuse and accepts it as the inevitable and inescapable future. It dreams of the two times it saw the ocean. It lays . . . alone . . . as students come in and out and in and out until eventually it is replaced. The last time the mattress sees the ocean is when it's tossed overboard and slowly sinks to the bottom. It falls and it falls and accepts the cold numbness from the depths of the ocean. It stares upward into the darkness and finally it is free. The college mattress has the saddest life. It's the unsung hero of the college experience, where 60 percent of lives are spent and it's taken for granted then thrown away.

Now as the reader if you just said, "That's a statement about life," perhaps you shouldn't ever do LSD. You might be one of those people who assign meaning to worthless events. If you are a person who read that and, like I did as I snapped out of it, said, "What the hell was that garbage?" LSD is probably a great drug for you. It's those kinds of people who do LSD and look at the world for what's actually going on and learn something from it. They then immediately say "Eh . . . it's just drugs." That's the saddest part about all drugs other than mushrooms. When they're done and over with you can always just say, "That was just the drugs."

After the peak of a drug comes the lulling and obscene notion of coming down. It's like having a small cup of ice cream after you've already eaten all the toppings. It's still ice cream, but it's lost all of the best parts. It's a trudge through how you felt when you first took the drug, but it's not as wonderful as coming up. There's not much solace, there is only the nag of your body wishing for sleep but a vibrant, annoying mindfuck of a rainbow kaleido-scope under your eyelids is left to hang around, making closing your eyes near unbearable.

I ventured out of my room through a window. It was just around nightfall and the few people who stuck around that weekend were outside smoking whatever they pleased and drinking beer in an attempt to see who was still around. Everyone always met at those benches. I noticed faces that would normally be filled with comfort and smiled as they melted a little and their eyes grew and shrunk in front of me.

"Hey everyone. How's your night . . . I think I did LSD this morning and I thought a lot about a mattress."

Only on LSD would someone say something so stupid in front of a crowd that was already intoxicated themselves. For the next few hours, people jazz fingered in front of me and yelled, attempting to fuck with my brain. I don't know that any single sentence I could have uttered would be worse than what I had told people.

As I craved sleep and food (but still couldn't bear to ingest it), I watched flashes in the sky as people did their best to freak me the fuck out. All I could think was, *This is what you get when you steal, Bread.*

Someone once said a life unexamined is not worth living. Doing LSD will make you do just that. You will examine grass, you will examine social interaction, you will look and think of things a little differently for a few hours. It's an escape from how awful the world is. If you are smart it will not inspire you to change the world like the idiots in the sixties, it will just make you look at it a little bit differently. Don't let the ghost of Steve Jobs confuse you—only geniuses take LSD and create life-changing things. LSD is the television of drugs, a shallow high that occasionally makes you think, but mainly makes you veg out or have stupid and meaningless notions.

Instead, understand that taking LSD alone will force you to look at yourself and how you interact with the world you live in. An LSD trip is not what everyone claims it to be; most of the time there is no out-of-body experience, there are no bicycles turning into elephants or what the media portrays it as. LSD is a drug that will make the normal world strange again when alone. LSD is a drug that, with a group of friends, will make you all laugh and speak like cavemen who are just discovering that sometimes rocks look different. You will cry and laugh and dance. Mainly LSD makes you realize we are all just brains surrounded by skulls that are so influenced by other, easily manipulated organs that nothing you believe after doing it will ever be set in stone.

Chapter 7

POT

Are you high? I think I'm high

POT IS FOR WINNERS

Pot is essential in college, it just is. It always has been. People used to smoke pot and arrange sit-ins and demonstrations. Now we smoke pot, sit in, and demonstrate how to make a gravity bong.

I'm writing this as riots are happening in Baltimore, and I want one moment in this entire book to be frank and honest and share a hope with my readers. You fuckers really do have the power to change everything. To drop the bullshit you're caught up in, put down your phones for a minute, and stop posting narcissistic selfies. You're the generation with Bitcoin and Anonymous, you understand the technology that could take down the systematic oppression of your fellow man. My generation got fucked over economically; we're struggling to make ends meet and dealing with mental problems that the generation before instilled in us. You're the assholes who can really change the world if you're smart enough to get into the system, become cops, become economists, become whatever you need to be, and don't get caught in the rat race. What the fuck are we doing? You have all the tools at your disposal. Get pissed off at the world you live in and burn it down. Stop supporting assholes who do nothing for society like the Kardashians and Kanye. You have so much to be angry about and you're wasting time getting offended by petty shit. Look for the real problems; look at our banking systems, our governments, even our systems of education. They're corrupt and useless. Please, please change the world because you're the last hope.

Pot isn't a drug anymore. It's a flower that has encouraged generations back to the dawn of civilization to be creative and inventive and make the world slightly better. Now it's used to get more followers on Instagram. Pot was a creative plant, an artist's plant, a lover's plant. Now idiots with knuckle tattoos are posting pictures of how much of it they have, hoping idiots with daddy issues will not use a condom with them. It's actually far more common in the corporate world than most people think as well. When it boils down to it, plenty of people from every background smoke pot, some people are just more vocal about it. Smoking pot is essential to college, from the occasional indulger to the daily smoke stack. Pot breathes a little more life into the world, as it brings a little more death to your lungs. It raises metabolism, helps people see things more vividly, kills pain, lowers anxiety, and most of all makes sure you have a kick ass time no matter what you're doing.

Pot leads to adventures, when it's your first time doing it. Nothing else makes standing in line feel like an epic journey. Most colleges are surrounded by cities that are absolutely deplorable, so getting high and wandering around these cesspools is more entertaining and way less petrifying than doing it sober. Getting stoned makes you wonder why you never spoke to the crackheads before, because maybe they have valuable life advice to give after they're done spitting at you and yelling at themselves. Those guys aren't muggers. We're all just part of a global consciousness. Pot lessens your instinct for danger, which is amazing when you realize you're adventuring in a city that's more dangerous than Mordor because now people have guns.

Pot gives you instant friendships. Pledging a frat means paying $60–$100 in dues every month to make sure you have friends. Pot costs $20 and a smile; additionally, pot friends won't drag their balls over your forehead if you pass out with your shoes on. Nothing brings two people closer together at a party than sneaking off to be antisocial and smoke a little flower. Pot makes you feel like you and your smoking buddies are Bonnie and Clyde against the drinkers, but instead of tommy guns and bank robberies you're eating your roommate's hummus after the Hot Pockets are gone. Sharing a joint is like making out with someone who has herpes—sometimes that shit is for life. Once you've shared weed with someone, they're friends with you for at least the rest of college.

Late night visitation to the post-party smoking room provides ideas that expand your mind and obliterates any chance you had at glaucoma. Stoned people are willing to share the stupidest thoughts that you'll over-think to the point they sound like Aristotle. Did Mike just say that unpaid internships are the equivalent to today's version of sharecropping? *Damn, that reminds me I need a job, I'll apply after one more round of Assassin's Creed online.* There is no better way to pass your elective classes than a stoned conversation about women's literature with a girl who hasn't washed her hoodie since she was a freshman. Carl Sagan and Neil Degrasse Tyson smoked weed, they explored space, and are a number one Google keyword search. Sure, weed isn't going to give you the ability to do math, but if you get high enough you might be able to think in numbers.

Music in college can be terrible, unless you're listening to The Cat Empire. (Seriously, I just want them to invite me to a show for free or give me backstage passes and a hug.) College is a time when you're going to discover new music because you have the free time. Pot is a wonder drug that makes you think bands like Phish are amazing when you're missing out on actually great bands like Dead Man's Bones. Pot is the only drug on earth that will make Florence and the Machine bearable for three hours after you've discovered Alabama Shakes, Devendra Banhart, and Gogol Bordello. It's this wonderful little plant that makes it so you don't want to murder your roommate when they decide to play Something Corporate and Jack Johnson. If you're not constantly searching for new music, you should have to donate your ears to the homeless. It's not that homeless people are deaf; they just need something to gnaw on if you're not going to use them.

Previously, music separated people. Now that you're in college, it brings everyone together. Stoners have their pulse on great music, as long as you avoid The Grateful Dead and Phish. Hanging out in the smoker's room means taking turns with your iPods and seeing what everyone has to offer. In one night you can learn about underground rap from everyone's hometowns or ska music you didn't know people still made. After college you'll still be listening to the albums you had back then and saying, "Do you remember when we sat in the smoking room and listened to this stuff?" Your lack of memories now become your memories for a lifetime.

You can actually sleep! Seriously, in school it's incredibly difficult to sleep when there is so much shit going on. Why sleep when there are after-after-parties and the chance to meet someone as drunk as you and slap organs together so loud it sounds like someone dropped deli meat into a tub of cottage cheese. If you're not releasing hormones your roommate has locked you out while they're doing it and you're on the couch. If it's not sex then it's finals and papers or because someone got a new type of beer. Pot also helps you to come down from all the ADHD medicine you're abusing to get through your classes. It's a wonderful little herb meant to make you not give a shit enough to get a decent night's sleep when all the odds are against you ever getting a good night's sleep again.

Pot lets you see things for how they actually are. It makes great movies better and mediocre movies even worse. A good sativa distances you from the social situations you're in and lets you see people for who they are. If pot is a gateway drug, it's a gateway to realizing that half the people you're surrounded by are actually douche bags who don't actually care about you. Nothing will make you more disgusted by people than smoking a joint and listening to them speak when they're clearly full of shit. It also spaces you out and breeds enough creativity to make you much, much funnier than you ever could be without.

Pot is a lovely flower. It's a fantastic flower, a plant, a weed; it's not a big deal. We've legalized it in a shit load of states because everyone is realizing that nobody wants it illegal anymore. If more people smoked pot in college, I can guarantee you crime would go down on campuses and there would actually be a lower college drop out rate. Fuck it, have a college-sponsored dispensary that sells sativas that make you good at math and hybrids that make philosophy bearable. Pot makes college better because pot pretty much makes everything better.

I Totally Inhaled

All right high schoolers and late bloomers, this one is for you. The first time you smoke weed you're gonna be annoying as shit to those around you. I had been stealing green from my brothers for most of my adolescence, but the first time I really smoked was in high school, on Halloween, with people way cooler than me. I ended up eating all my Halloween candy and getting way too aggressive with women way out of my league. Honestly, I was a complete douche bag when I was stoned the first time. It was embarrassing and it wasn't pretty waking up covered in Butterfingers. Fun sized just means it'll get caught in every crevice you have. Smoking for the first time you could end up melting into a couch playing video games and watching movies, or eating everything in your kitchen. Most likely you'll go right to PornHub and get chaffing. It's common so don't feel too shitty about being annoying your first time. It's when you're annoying after the first time that even stoners start to get pissed. So since you're new to the best thing in the world, here are some basic things to avoid saying and doing so you don't give stoners a bad name.

Don't post naked pictures of yourself, or pictures of you smoking, on the Internet.

You know who smokes weed? Everyone smokes weed. So it's obnoxious to show the world how much weed you have or how often you smoke. Smoking weed doesn't make you awesome, and most of the idiots who post pictures of themselves smoking all the time have girlfriends who will bang anything they think has money. I don't know why but there are dozens of girls who think it's so hot to post pictures half-naked smoking weed. You know what's awesome? The half-naked pictures, not the weed. Why clutter up the image, why post them to the Internet at all? We understand that maybe your dad wasn't there as much as he should have been but don't look for attention that way, and send those pictures directly to someone you can friend zone and torment the rest of his life.

Stop and read this carefully. If you ever say, "Are you high? I think I'm high," everyone around you has the right to hurt you with whatever is hard and in reach. Here's an easy way to figure out if you're high: Does boring shit seem less boring? Are you a little bit hungry? Does the idea of standing in a line both petrify and give you anxiety? Is time passing weird? Then congratulations, you inhaled properly and you're stoned. There is no need to ask anyone else if they're stoned too. Everyone is just going to think you're a needy prick if you utter those words. Most of the time, when people smoke for the first time and talk, it's hilarious, and the only way you could ruin it would be to say, "Are you high? I'm high."

Bongs and pieces are a one-way street. If you're new to pot, the simple mechanics of a carb and slide while inhaling may be completely alien. Or every single person is stupid the first time they smoke weed. Why no one is ever able to hold a lighter, inhale, and slide their first time goes to show you that we haven't come far from cavemen poking at animals with sticks to see if they're delicious. Bongs, pieces, pipes, trainwrecks, bubblers, dabs, all of these devices may look like they're out of a science lab, but they're really simple. The first rule is never blow into any of these unless you want everyone to hate you. You're going to cough, so take smaller hits more frequently so you don't blow into the piece. If you do, the weed shoots everywhere. Not only are you annoying for losing weed, you're annoying because that ember burns the shit out of whatever it touches. The only reason you should ever start a fire when you're high is because you forgot you were cooking Ellio's when another episode of *Game Of Thrones* came on.

Look at your bank account. If you can't afford another eighth then "corner" your fucking weed. If you have people over sharing, "corner" your fucking weed. No matter fucking what, "corner" your fucking weed. Nothing is more douche-baggy than someone who doesn't understand you don't burn the entire bowl at once. You inhale tiny little bits and work your way out. Not only does this make weed last longer, but it makes weed last longer. That's it, you're out to make your weed last as long as possible, and if you can't do this simple little trick than please quit smoking and get a sleeve caught in a paper shredder. It doubles the amount of weed you have and it's polite so that others don't complain about ash pulling through after the first hit. Weed is about sharing and having a great time and a burnt throat is only something you should get because of too many Fireball shots.

Don't panic. Some people don't like weed, and that's totally chill, bro. But if you get too high and start to freak out, the best option is to lay somewhere quiet and put on a movie you've already seen. You don't want to freak like a fourteen-year-old girl who just realized she gained five pounds. You're just smoking weed, not doing black tar heroin. Unless you're smoking weed as you come off black tar heroin. If that's the case, thank you for buying this book and kudos for still reading while being a heroin addict. Some people get paranoid and anxious when they smoke. The trick is to give up. It's that easy. You know how you acted when you realized you failed a test and there was nothing to do about it? I don't because I'm not a failure, but I can imagine it's the same feeling. Try thinking about what your dad did with his dreams when he had you—that's the level of giving up you need to do.

Not surprisingly, most weed smokers are patient and caring individuals, but these novice mistakes will really bum everyone out. Not only are you going to ruin people's nights making these mistakes, you're going to catch an endless amount of shit from other smokers. Which is scary because smoking weed makes you funnier so the insults will be even better. If someone is kind enough to share weed with you and you blow it out or talk about how high you think you are, they're within their rights to explain to you in depth the awful things they want to do to you at that moment. Now that you have some insight, the only things that will give away how much of a novice you are are those tar-free lungs.

Holy Shit, They had Weed. (Originally published on Brobible.com)

So you're completely out and it will be a week until your dealer picks up. You've contacted all your friends and no one has any they can spare and only the lonely stoner kid is willing to smoke you out. You've noticed waffles don't taste as good and all of a sudden The History Channel is boring again. How many times can a single person watch a show about Nazis sober? In fact, you're so sober that Republicans make sense. Well, there is hope in the world because these are the four places that always have weed. Remember stoners, when visiting these places look like a normal member of society; everyone is more willing to sell to an average person, not someone in a Phish T-shirt who is trying too hard.

Basketball Courts. Try filling up a backpack with a twelve pack of beer and putting on some neon Nikes. Shoot around for a bit and listen to the conversations going on around you. The trick in this situation is to go for the high schoolers. High school guys, like high school girls, will do anything for beer. Find a chubby kid or a weird one who's not shooting hoops along with his friend, then listen until they talk about drinking or pot, which should only take ten minutes. Once you hear that it's go time, roll your ball over to their court and mention you heard them talk about pot. Offer them the backpack in exchange for a gram or two, and you become a hero. The trick is to come off like an older brother and not an adult they're going to call a faggot then call the cops on. Congratulations, you just bought a gram for a $12.99 pack of Milwaukee's Best.

Kitchens. Anyone who's never worked in a kitchen has lost out on one of the most fun and depressing parties you can be a part of. Kitchens are like White Snake videos in the eighties. Cooks are notorious for doing lines of cocaine to keep them going during fourteen-hour shifts working a fryer. At the end of the night the wait staff and line cooks chug bottles of wine like old Italian women who just found out they're going to be grandmas before they die. For pot, the dishwashers are the guys you're looking for. Light up a cigarette and hang out where the bikes are chained up and bring a bilingual friend. You're going to overpay, so be prepared to be shorted on weight and over-charged, but these guys have a ten-person family to feed. The best part about buying weed here is smoking in the parking lot then walking back into the restaurant, Simba can go eat an air dick, that's the real circle of life.

The Internet. There aren't specific websites to go to (there totally are), but spend some time on social media and make friends with someone from Colorado or California. The lovely part about the US postal service is that they're currently overworked and barely check packages. Sure, it might take a few more days than hanging out at a basketball court, but there is little to no chance you'll end up having to tell your neighbors you're now a Megan's Law-abiding citizen. They can send you brownies, candies, and muffins that will make you happier than the care packages your mom sent sophomore year.

Open Mics. What happens when a bunch of shitty performers get together to perform terribly together? A lot of smoking pot to make themselves feel better after bombing. Go on the Internet and look for some open mics in your area. Spend five minutes writing something that tricks people into thinking you're creative. Spend two minutes on stage doing your slam poetry or song, and then ask while you're on stage if anyone has pot. At first everyone will look shocked but then the artists will flock to you to try and make money so they can eat Chef Boyardee tonight.

Moldy Weed and Gin's Quesadilla

"What the fuck is this?" My pulse raced and heart started beating out of my chest. "Who the fuck did this?" A million excuses filled my head. "Seriously what the ever loving shit is this?" I stayed silent as Gin pulled the quesadilla she had been looking forward to eating from the fridge.

"Well, what happened was . . ." I stared at her trying not to giggle. Not only was I immature about it, I channeled the voice of my cuzzo and black friend Amber and spoke like I was in Newark.

Selling weed in college isn't as profitable as everyone imagines. For the few months Beer Clause attempted to sell weed, he probably never made more than seventy-five dollars. Adding to his amazingness as a roommate was the fact that for a while he always had a supply of bargain-basement pot. You could imagine the stalks hanging upside down on the clearance rack when he went to purchase it. I always thought of him walking into his dealer's house and asking if the guy honored coupons. His weed had the consistency of a stale cookie that a senile grandmother would make.

It was dry, crumbly, and it always had shit in it that didn't belong there. It was less marijuana and more dry kindling that someone would use to start a forest fire.

I never really had to buy weed during this time, because Beer Clause more often than not gave me his garbage weed for free. The worst part about being twenty-one is the entire world can, and will, take advantage of you around every corner. Beer Clause had the worst dealer in the world, who always fucked him over. His weed was like a box of cereal in the 90s, because to short Beer Clause on weight, there was always a surprise hidden inside. In an effort to make a profit, his dealer would hide toys and other items inside the drugs, like a nineties cereal box, so the weight was always much less than what Beer Clause thought he was purchasing. Whenever he brought back a new batch, I'd anxiously wait to find what was hidden inside.

Beer Clause's weed days were hilarious because, while I was laughing hysterically, he'd be livid. Instead of finding a new dealer, he'd always check his weed and manage to be outsmarted. The very first time it happened, I was uncontrollable. He reached into his weed and pulled out Chuckie Cheese tokens. "Maybe he's trying to get you to sell to kids," I cracked, while staring into his upset face. I was stoned enough to wonder out loud, "Why the fuck did your weed dealer use those tokens?" I remembered being a poor kid and whenever we went to Chuckie Cheese's everyone else had handfuls of tokens, while I got a meager eight and was forced to watch other kids play video games while I played hide and seek in the ball pit. "Dude, give those to me, they're like two bucks a piece. You could probably get kids to do some fucked up stuff for Chuckie Cheese tokens."

I was already stoned so I kept wondering out loud, "What if he was trying to hide those tokens from his kids?" I imagined the guy telling his imaginary kids they couldn't go to Chuckie Cheese's because he lost all the tokens. "Sorry kids, Daddy wanted to take you, but I accidentally sold your tokens in some weed to a college student."

His wife would be yelling at him, "You *always do this*, stop hiding their toys in the pot!" They'd be heartbroken then, in public service announcement style, a little caption would come up that said, 'Drugs Hurt Your Loved Ones.'" I was laughing hysterically at Beer Clause's misfortune.

"This dude does it so the weight is off. He can't make more than an extra eighty dollars from me."

"That's what you get for buying weed with a coupon."

"It's not that funny."

"It's fuckin funny man, why don't you get a new dealer."

The next time Beer Clause came back with pot, he opened the bag and pennies fell out of it. The familiar face of disappointment struck him and the all-too hilarious situation had me cracking jokes at him again. "In his defense you probably just made money." He stared blankly at me. "Aw, man," I couldn't stop myself, "do you think those were leftover pennies from Halloween?" He actually laughed at that remark and acknowledged it was funny.

"I hate Jamaicans." He went back toward his room.

I yelled, "I guess not a single one of those is lucky, huh? You're gonna need it trying to sell that shit weed." I cracked myself up. Beer Clause was too busy being sad to appreciate it. The bank must have hated that guy; I imagined on the first of the month he cashed his welfare check and got pennies. That's the type of guy who should have been teaching business classes.

Beer Clause was a very smart guy, but it was clear he had no idea the getting fucked would never stop. Other objects included washers, car lug nuts, and screws. I imagined his dealer had an old car he was slowly dismantling and putting in his weed after Beer Clause didn't say anything about the pennies. Every time a new piece of hardware came in I thought, *Knew they hated him at the bank.* The final straw in Beer Clause's drug empire was when a half-pound of weed came out of the bag, soaking wet. That was the Jamaican man finally saying, "Seriously, fuck yourself." I was admittedly disappointed at this surprise too. It's one thing to give Happy Meal toys. It was another to give my friend the middle finger. We thought everything was ruined, which it really was . . . that didn't stop Beer Clause though, and soon every window was open and the smell of dank weed was permeating the outdoors from our dorm apartment.

Outside stank so badly strangers came to 1A asking to buy weed. Beer Clause happily obliged, passing off the wet weed to idiot strangers. In just a few hours he had sold most of it, the remainder of which he left out overnight. A few warm nights passed and Beer Clause had left his weed rewrapped in a plastic bag, until one day he threw the remainder at me and said, "Smoke away." I hadn't smoked much at this point in my life, so I rolled a tin foil pipe and looked at what he had given me. It looked like terrible weed or exceptional cheese. There was a fine black mold growing over the outside of the nugs. I gandered for a moment then whispered, "If black mold is good enough for a cokehead, it's good enough for me," as I placed it on the tin foil and inhaled the Alzheimer-creating smoke.

In moments, I was higher than I ever had been in my life. There wasn't the usual cleanliness to the high, it was muddy and faded. I wasn't completely sure where I was. I fumbled with simple tasks, and didn't go to class because I knew I wouldn't be able to walk soon. It was the worst kind of body high—dry mouthed and slovenly. My body had become alien to me. It was frightening to lose control from a simple flowered bud. I stumbled to the couch and fell *into* it. I melted down into the cushions, staring at the ceiling. This is where I gained the life-long habit of staring at ceilings whenever I become distressed.

The high lulled and roared and waved and I stood like a slab of granite against it. I was an immovable object against the rolling tide of THC and mold. As the waves broke and the high lessened, I got hungry. I was starving, my stomach burned like it did when I was a kid coming home from school to an empty house and having to make food for myself. I rolled into a fetal position momentarily then got up and walked over to the refrigerator.

"You didn't even eat the entire thing. You only ate the middle of it. Did you think I didn't notice?" Hell has no fury like a roommate's girlfriend. "Did you fuck my quesadilla? I could have eaten around where your shit mouth was on my food, but instead you tried to cover it up."

In my high daze, I had thought moving sour cream and salsa to the middle where I had made mouth love to her quesadilla would hide my shame eating.

"You didn't even use restaurant salsa . . . you took the salsa from the *back* of the fridge and dumped it in the middle. How old is that jar?"

Honestly, I wasn't even trying to make excuses at this point. Every college student has a jar of salsa in the back of the fridge.

"Gin, I'll give you money."

"Fuck your money like you fucked my quesadilla."

I turned to Chris for help but he was too busy standing behind her, looking solemn.

"Gin, I'll give you money for it. I'm going to put it in your purse."

"That's fucking offensive. That's more offensive than what you did to my food."

Gin walked into her room and threw the quesadilla in the trash. Chris sat down on the couch. I got up and took it out of the garbage. "Fucking moldy weed. This is Beer Clause's fault, not mine," I explained to him as I took another bite from the quesadilla.

"Really, dude?" He looked exasperated watching me chew. He stood up and went back into his room.

"I'm not letting it go to waste and I'm putting money in her bag!"

As he strode down the hallway after Gin, he yelled, "Money won't buy your dignity back."

It was a flaky flour tortilla, perfectly browned in oil, stuffed with Monterey Jack, cheddar, and amazingly spiced chicken. Even cold, the cheese oozed and the spices in the chicken tingled the tip and outside edges of my taste buds. The aftertaste was slightly spicy but the sour cream and house-made salsa from the restaurant cooled the taste buds when the heat was too much. I ate every last bit of it. Every tempting and delicious morsel of the Mexican delight, I devoured it all alone. Who needs dignity when you have perfectly made Mexican food?

If you look at this story there is one major moral that stands out: always have a pot dealer as a roommate. It's fantastic, no one ever gets hurt, and even if you still have to pay for the weed sometimes you get Chuckie Cheese tokens. I destroyed an eleven-year-old at Artic Thunder and taught her life isn't always fair. A roommate who deals pot is a lazy person's dream. You get to be so lazy that even thinking about doing anything is too much work. The other moral is try to have a roommate who works in a restaurant.

Ginny and my roommate aren't together anymore so he's not pissed and I got to eat delicious Mexican food with no repercussions.

Recipes

Sometimes you need to get high in places where smoking is frowned upon. Sometimes you want to get high but you don't feel like screwing up your lungs. Sometimes you just want to rocket to outer space. This is easiest to do through the ingesting of THC instead of smoking it. The two easiest things to make are THC-infused oil and vodka. I'm not condoning the use of these substances, purely for legal reasons, but I will let you in on the easiest ways to make them in a dorm or apartment setting.

CannOil (Cannabis Oil): This is not a professional recipe, but it works on a hot plate and tastes bearable enough you can throw some spices in and dip bread in it if you can't make anything else. Most people make this out to be some crazy procedure but really, it's not. First, open your windows, spray Febreze, and put wet towels over everyone's faces. Slowly smother them to death. Leave no witnesses.

All you need is about three grams of marijuana and five cups of oil. This is going to be rocket fuel so use sparingly.

1. Grind up your weed. Now grind it again. Now grind it again. Now grind it again. Seriously, the finer it is the easier this is going to be.
2. Preheat your oil. You want it just before the boiling point, before bubbles form. You don't want to burn the weed you put in until the very, very end. If you burn the weed it smells and you'll get caught. This is going to stink anyway, which is why most of the time I used an old camp stove and did this in a parking lot at night.
3. Get a bunch of ice water and put it in a container big enough to put your oil pan in.
4. Once the oil is hot, put your ground up weed in it. Some directions will tell you to heat it for an hour, but this is college and there are people who will fuck you over if you get caught. I cut it down to thirty minutes.

5. Keep the oil hot and stir constantly without letting the oil boil at all. If it gets too hot, dip the pan in the cold water and keep going. You'll be working on a time crunch before someone smells and tells. After about thirty minutes of this, slap the heat on high for about a minute. Burn the weed a little tiny bit while stirring constantly.
6. Take the pan off the heat and leave it on a windowsill or somewhere it can air out for another half hour or so. Don't cool it down before this. Let it stay in a safe place.

You now have weed oil you can use to make whatever the fuck you want. It was that easy. Sure, there are more effective ways but this shit will still get you high and not caught.

Weed Vodka: This stuff really messes with you and it's kind of complex. The first thing you have to do is release the CO_2 attached to the THCA particle and blah, blah, blah. I passed Organic Chemistry in high school. Basically, for a high-proof solution you gotta make the THC come out in a different form. So get a pizza stone and heat the oven to about two hundred degrees. You're gonna bake your weed for forty-five minutes. Stir it and make sure everything cooks evenly. Don't let it get hotter or you're gonna burn off the THC and ruin everything. You can even use stems for this because those also have THCA that can be converted. When it comes out, the weed should be slightly burned and slightly stinking. This is a good thing.

Now the easy part! Put about ten grams worth of this decarboxylated weed into 750 mL of the highest proof vodka you can find. Throw it in a mason jar in a dark place and shake it once a day for seven days. Put in in the freezer for one of those days. After that waiting period, boil some water and throw your mason jar in it with the top removed. This boils off some of the booze. It should look like iced tea. Now drink up, you slag. Share the bottle with as many people as you can because this gets a party going.

Chapter 9

DRUGS

Fractals aren't just for nerds anymore

HOLY SHIT AM I IN A BOOK?

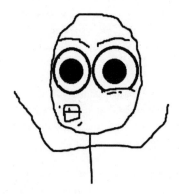

Drugs on Campus

I know we've had a ton of fun so far in this book. We've talked about roommates and strangling strangers and a whole bunch of really atrocious stuff under the guise of humor. This is where I ruin our rapport. So unless you want to hear some preachy bullshit, just skip to the story at the end of this chapter or the article on ADHD medicine. Those are fucking hilarious.

Okay, did the idiots leave? I think they're gone. I assume the only people left are the kids who play Magic the Gathering. It's okay, guys, because when it comes down to it, the real world sucks as bad as school did. It never gets better. So on campus you're going to have a buffet of different substances that are readily available, if you know a white guy with dreads. Some of this stuff is fun and a lot of it is actually terrible and addictive and you might lose a friend or two to it. So if you're curious about hard drugs (anything that's not pot, acid, or mushrooms), let me tell you how stupid they all are and why you shouldn't actually do them.

Cocaine. I hate cocaine. I hate cocaine. The only thing that's good about cocaine is the crippling depression that lasts for days after you do it. It's great because you deserve to be depressed for doing one of the most obnoxious drugs on earth. Wanna know what it's like to be on cocaine? Imagine liking yourself. Imagine thinking everyone wants to hear your every thought because it's so important. Now mix that with the ability to drink without feeling drunk. That's cocaine, only douche bags like it because only douche bags want to do something that makes you feel self-important. Cocaine is a performance-enhancing drug. If you want to drink for days you have to be truly devoted, unless you take cocaine, which makes a bender really easy. If you do cocaine with other people, get ready to hear about their amazing guitar or whatever thing they do really, really well for hours. It's obnoxiously addictive and really doesn't do that much other than make you want more.

Crack. Seriously, if you're on a college campus where there is crack you should just move off-campus. I've never done crack because I'm not an idiot, but it was once described to me as twenty minutes of orgasming from a unicorn jerking you off and your parents telling you they love you. I don't know about any of you, but my parents have told me they love me enough and unicorns have hooves, which just kind of makes me feel uncomfortable.

Peyote. Okay, admittedly, I cannot say this one is that bad. I say it's a hard drug because peyote trips last way fucking longer than anything else I've ever experienced in my life. Imagine mushrooms but instead of hallucinations you're in a completely different world where everything is made of energy and it flows in and out of all of us. Yea, pretty stupid in my mind. It was a twenty-four-hour trip and, after six hours, I wanted to tear my own face off to make it go away. Once I got comfortable and walked around, I saw annoying animals that wanted me to get back in touch with Mother Nature. Fuck you, Mother Nature. You've made literally thousands of creatures we've had to hunt because they're so good at killing humans.

Heroin. I'm not saying you should do heroin, but I will say some of the most creative and successful people on earth have done heroine. Heroin is like floating in a pool that's a little bit warmer than the air, while drunk on good gin. I've actually been jealous of heroin addicts since I was a teen. They're the simplest organisms on earth. For me to be happy, I have to sit in front of a computer for a year and write a book and, when I'm finally finished, I'll be happy for a few moments before starting to think about what I have to do next. For a heroin addict to be happy, all they have to do is find some heroin. Nothing else really matters to them. You have to suck a dick to get heroin? Well, they don't have a whole ton of shame left to bother them. They've boiled their lives down to the simplest and easiest thing in the world, and I constantly think, *I'm not good enough to be happy like a heroin addict.* I have to go to counseling. If a heroin addict has a problem, they just do more heroin. So . . . I guess don't do heroin . . . cause you'll die at twenty-seven and be a creative genius, or something. Heroin is bad though. You'll have to suck dicks for it. Not even healthy clean dicks, you'll have to suck dicks that you see and you think, *That should have been treated a long time ago.*

Molly/Ecstasy. Molly will make you think everything is great until you wake up in some guy named Trent's flat apartment. First thing you see when you wake up is broken candy jewelry and his tribal tattoo. And, whether you're a girl or a guy he'll talk about how, "hawt the finguring" was. Molly will make you think laser lights are amazing and you'll find you think words like "Deep House" are socially acceptable. When doctors discovered ecstasy creates huge holes in your brain, they were right. Holes that go directly into the part of your brain that normally regulates the part that tells you not to say things like, "On fleek," or willingly taking a drug called "Miley Cyrus." Don't do E or Molly, not because they're incredibly bad for you, but because you're going to sound so stupid only ravers will want to hang out with you.

Nitrous. *Waaaahhhhhh, uuuuuuhhhhhh, waaaaaaaahhhhhh, uuuuuhhhhh, waaaaaahhhhhuuuu. Womf, womf, womf, womf. Waaaaahhhhh uuuuuhhhh.* That's literally the only effect. It makes you hear an annoying noise and your eyes go weird and you stop thinking for forty-five seconds. Nitrous gives you a slight bit of euphoria and then you're back to realizing whatever situation you're in is stupid. Be an adult, and don't do nitrous. Huff paint thinner instead. Don't do either of those things.

Pain Killers. Read on for more information on this one. These fuckers are so bad that I devoted an entire story to them. They ruin lives and are incredibly addictive. Kicking these is one of the worst things you will ever feel.

Xanax. If forty-year-old housewives mix a drug with white wine (with ice in it), you know it has to be good. There is a pill out there specifically designed to make the people who gave up on all their dreams and will never be appreciated happy. It can make anyone happy. The problem is it also makes you very, very stupid. Not like Molly stupid, but legitimately can't string a sentence together or make coherent thoughts anymore stupid. A few people I've known abused Xanax for more than a couple of months, and not only were they twelve IQ points short, but they got married and had a kid. That's the stupidest downside to any drug.

Speed/Angel Dust. You're never going to purposefully do this drug unless you're hanging out with bikers in the seventies. However, there were two instances when weed I bought really cheap as a freshman was laced with the stuff. Sure, I could be angry that I smoked something that made me climb under a bed sweating and thinking about murdering everyone on the third floor of a Rutgers dormitory, but really I can't be pissed because normally it costs extra. Be really careful after you've accidentally had this. It's pretty much meth and meth plays for keeps.

Drugs get glamorized in society, then the negative side effects get blown out of proportion. Yes, they are cripplingly addictive and they ruin lives. If you're an average person with no problems that might not happen to you, but these drugs will always make you look like a douche bag. They're awful and watching people succumb to them can really can break your heart. But what's even worse is knowing there is nothing you can do for most addicts. I tried to make this article seem light and not preachy, but really don't bother with this shit. It's garbage and will never do you any good . . . except for heroin.

Are we there yet? Avoiding a Bad Trip

I've spouted some pretentious bullshit in this book so far. I recognize that, but this might be the worst and saddest yet. However, you need this article more that a frat boy needs an HPV vaccine. Experimenting with drugs can be bearable and even fun sometimes, but doing it in the wrong situation can leave you in a worse position than a finance major in a Women's Studies class. If you're going to do hallucinogens you should do them correctly. This isn't an essay to encourage you to be a filthy hippy. It's to make sure you don't jump through a window because you decided to ingest a stupid little substance. Drugs that make you trip can be good or bad, depending on the situation you're in and the people you're with. Taking them on a whim is dumb as shit, but since you bought a book called *Dude, Bro,* written by me, it's safe to assume you might be a kid who had to take non-credit courses to be on the same level as normal college kids. So if you randomly decide to take a drug, chances are your first experience with the stuff is going to be absolutely terrible. Instead let me be your guide. Yep, that was it. That's the most pretentious thing I've ever said. It's a good thing I'm legally obligated to finish this book, but as soon as it's done I'm going to think about it.

The first rule is: be with people you like. Do it with your good friends or by yourself. Being around people you like, and don't feel the need to always talk around, is the best. During your trip you might want to be quiet for a while and other times you're going to want to be louder than a vegan's speech when eating with a non-vegan. You need to be with people you aren't self-conscious around. You also need to really like these people. Not a little bit, a lot. When you're balls deep into a trip, you're going to be hyperaware of the people around you. If they bother you in the slightest, you're going to feel like a kid who wears a Weezer shirt in high school trying to sit at the cool kids table. If you're with people you don't like, you're going to end up sitting in a corner thinking about why you even hang out with them. When you're doing it with a friend you like, you'll wonder why their eyes are getting all big, meh, it doesn't matter because now I'm thinking about birds. Fuck you falcons, you have no idea how awesome you are. Fucking talons and amazing eyesight and all you do is float around and eat small mammals. You don't even know how awesome flying is, you sky predator.

Also make sure you have a whole bunch of weed. Weed calms you down and helps with nausea. A lot of hallucinogens will fuck with your stomach and vision, which means some of you might get seasick. A healthy amount of pot is good because before your trip you want to be calm and settled and after your trip you might not be able to sleep for hours. Watching *Fraggle Rock* after their hair stops being really emotion-inducing and the plotlines aren't as intense is going to take some pot to make it bearable again until you can go to sleep. Also, smoking weed during helps keep a trip mellow or helps you come down if you're peaking too heavily.

Make sure you're happy. Hallucination and depression aren't great when mixed together. You don't have to be rainbow-painted unicorns getting laid while eating Nutella pancakes happy, but if you've cried in the past twenty-four hours it might not be the best time. To get in a better mood, try going to a place in nature where there is no one around. Pick up a small rock, look at it deeply. Examine a leaf. Try looking around you and seeing nobody. This will make any single person happy enough to do mushrooms or peyote. The only thing to ever guarantee happiness is not interacting with other people for a while. Other things that could make you happy include showering after the seventh day of laying in bed sad, listening to Morrissey, or not cutting yourself for once. The lovely thing about drugs, like mushrooms, is that if you take them while you're happy you'll change your life for the better afterward.

Think about your life for a while first. I once went to Jamaica completely alone and spent a day thinking about my life before spending three days on 'shrooms. Oh, and they're completely legal, organically grown, and ethically harvested there, so future employers can't frown upon this. If I hadn't spent some time being introspective and figuring out what I wanted to think about, those eight hours (that accidentally turned into days) would have been horrifying. I came to some wonderful realizations about my life and actually got back on the straight and narrow after that. If you have some self-actualization before mushrooms, you'll see nature twice as green, movies twice as good, and people twice as funny during.

Remember at all times, you're just on drugs. Most hallucinogens aren't lethal. So if you think you're about to have a bad trip and die, just remember you're an idiot because you're on drugs. If you start seeing demons and bad stuff, well that could happen, don't freak out. Just remember you're an idiot because you're on drugs. Keeping that in your head is the single most important thing. No matter what insane thing just happened, you're on drugs and it probably wasn't as insane as you imaged. Always take a deep breath and remember the drug's effect will end soon enough and you'll never ever want to take it again.

Cell phones off. If you have anything going on in your phone that's more important than the awesomeness that's happening around you, find a new place to be. Phones are risky because you never know what a little bit of bad news or a call from your parents might do. Hearing your mom or dad's voice when you're screwed up can send you into a shame spiral, so turn your phone off. Even if the trip lasts for eight hours and something bad does happen, you can't deal with it when you're on drugs.

Have a notepad and pen. Not only is it nice to have something to do when you're in space, it's important to have a place to write down your thoughts and what you're seeing when you can. This isn't for some spiritual reason, it's because you're going to think really stupid things. Let me show you an excerpt from my paper in Jamaica: "So, Challenger was a satellite that got turned around and take a picture of Earth and remind us how worthless we are on a small blue dot. Carl Sagan invented the first selfie to remind us every time we take one we should feel insignificant." That seems brilliant when you're hallucinating, but when you're sober that shit is the stupidest and funniest garbage ever. Sometimes you might even want to draw pictures, but trust me, when you're sober you're going to want to throw those out.

It should seem like common sense, to anyone with half a brain, to Google this stuff beforehand. The problem is most people end up taking these drugs at a concert and hiding in their tent for hours, or freaking out because there are too many laser lights. Drugs like these are usually more proactive than negative the first time you take them, so make sure you've set yourself up for success. Remember, you want to come out of this a slightly better person, not some spaced-out hippy. Enjoy these responsibly and not too often or else you'll start to think Chemtrails are real and politicians are lizards.

The Pros and Cons of Coke: I'm Sorry the Last Article Wasn't Funny

Cocaine is a magical powder that screws with everyone's brain worse than a bad relationship, a little white substance sold by bikers and white guys with popped collars changes lives. What is commonly a great party drug that makes everyone want to have sex easily turns into a crippling addiction that lands you in one of those religious rehabilitation centers. A little booger sugar never hurt anyone, but a lot of it makes people do gross stuff with other dudes in public restrooms. The media celebrates cocaine with movies, hit TV shows, and doing it at any board meeting or industry party. Cocaine is the drug version of a Yin Yang . . . if you snorted Yin Yangs off a mirror. There are pros and cons of cocaine usage. Here are but a few.

Pro: Snorting a line of cocaine while sober makes you work harder than a child factory worker. Two lines of this stimulant could make accounting interesting. The only reason it's a drug loved by people in finance is because it hides that they're math nerds.

Con: Sinus sugar makes you talk more than your coworkers when you bring up that Karen never makes more coffee. All of a sudden a little blanca bite makes you think everyone loves every word coming out of your mouth, when in reality they just want to stuff something in there.

Pro: People will have sex *for* cocaine and have sex *because* of cocaine. For some reason blow goes right to the genitals. You can only think about running and banging. People have done sexual things for cocaine that would make the Pope break doctrine and kill himself.

Con: Guys can't always get it up. Nothing like sharing an 8-ball with someone who wants to unclog your urethra like a double bypass and looking like a half-cooked Ramen noodle. Mentally you're all about it but circulatory wise, you'd need twenty-five Viagra to even consider getting it up.

Pro: It's a short high. Sorry, hippies, not everyone has five to eight hours to blow exploring other states of consciousness. Sometimes people just want to get fucked up for an hour or two.

Con: It's a short high, which means halfway through a great night you're thinking, *Shit, I need more cocaine.* Then when you get more cocaine you think, *I need more cocaine.*

Pro: It makes everyone think you have money. Belushi bloat is a status drug. It shows you have income to waste on something that everyone knows is a complete waste. Doing cocaine is like setting your money on fire, but surprisingly more socially acceptable.

Con: The hardest part about cocaine is opening the bag. It's a super easy drug that takes nothing more than a key or a pinky to do. The hardest part about cocaine is that it's midnight, you're drunk, and it comes in the tiniest bag ever. Trying to separate the plastic after it's been warming up in your pocket for two hours is harder than your dick will be able to get.

Pro: Cocaine makes people talk about themselves, which means you can find out secrets—deep, dark secrets that you'd never hear without a big dose of devil dandruff. Having dirt on people is what builds long-term friendships, because they have to. Nothing motivates someone to come to your birthday party quite like knowing that thing they did to a homeless guy when they were seventeen.

Con: Coke dealers are even flakier than pot dealers. While potheads run late because they have no perception of time, coke dealers are even later because they're off being scum bags. If a coke dealer tells you they'll be there in thirty minutes, it's going to be two hours because, inevitably, the people who pay in sexual favors always come first.

Pro: It doesn't matter that you already drank a bottle of whiskey, that's called pre-gaeming when you have party powder. You'll be yelling, "Yaaaa Yoooo," at the top of your lungs once you're sober enough to keep the party going. Snort a few lines and it's time for another drink at the Pablo Esco-bar.

Con: The only reason to do cocaine is to do more cocaine. It's not a drug that you do a few grams of and call it quits. Cocaine makes you think everyone is going to party until 4:00 a.m., and makes you sad when everyone else is in bed by 2:00 a.m. But, you know what makes you feel better about everyone going to bed? More cocaine. By the end of the night you're covered in it like it was glitter at a strip club.

The Solar System is Actually a Spiraling Orbit that is Being Thrown at Massive Speeds Away from a Singular Point on Our Holy Shit: ADHD Meds, What Actually Happens

Between papers and finals, student's workloads are packed tighter than the arteries of someone who works at Arby's. The crippling amount of information students have to retain is making them resort to taking pills meant to treat ADHD. Taking ADHD medicine is steroids for nerds, but with weirder side effects. It will make you get all your work done, but it could also make you count the amount of tiles in your ceiling. ADHD meds can help you succeed, but they also make your heart race like the first time you saw a clown. Here is a better understanding of what actually happens when you take ADHD pills.

Lists: The moment ADHD medicine hits, you're going to make a list like a Buzzfeed editor looking for Facebook likes. Step one on your list is to write a list. Step two is to finish everything on that list before the world stops moving slower than normal. Step thirteen on the list is to find out if you've developed bullet time superpowers or not. ADHD medicine sends your brain into a frenzy of productivity while making your body content with sitting in the same place for two days. All of a sudden you're going to remember that time you forgot to call your best friend when you were ten, find him on Facebook, and apologize about that, directly after you finish a paper and reorganize your fridge.

OCD: You thought you were OCD because you washed your hands a lot and got a little anxious when you didn't make your bed? ADHD meds are going to make it so you have to count every single stitch on the arm of your couch before you're allowed to drink water again. If you don't have a million things to do, OCD comes out in full force on ADHD pills. You're about to be awake for twenty-four hours, so it's hard to stay productive when you finish work at a pace a Japanese iPhone builder is jealous of. ADHD pills are medical-grade speed. In one night you can learn everything about the economics of guns vs. butter, or you could end up feeling like your teeth are itchy and you should adopt a dog.

Food: You may find that food is disgusting. Who came up with the idea of putting other animals' flesh in a bacteria-filled hole, grinding it with external bone structures, and swallowing it down into an acid pit? Why do we do this in public? ADHD meds will cut your appetite down to that of a thirteen-year-old girl before a school dance. Even looking at food can be absolutely disgusting. You'll realize that mac and cheese is gross because it's nothing but chemicals, which is ironic because you just ingested a bunch of chemicals.

Social Anxiety: ADHD pills make listening to other people difficult. You want to be learning or running or scratching or anything that's not waiting for someone to finish a stupid story about their aunt. Sure, you can't help but focus on every detail of the story, but it doesn't mean you want to be there. Your anxiety level goes through the roof when on these pills in a large public space, it's not fun interacting. You'll find yourself asking questions like someone who has had thirty concussions, while thinking about how you could be cleaning your place instead. People are boring to begin with, so adding a drug that speeds everything up makes them boring faster.

Why is DollaBill Blue?

Cookie Dough was a fat, lazy, Italian piece of shit and that's why I named him Cookie Dough. The man we once stuffed in the elevator while we robbed apartments was a worthless dickhead with no aspirations to do better in life. For the longest time, I hated him. Whenever he came to the apartment he brought cocaine to lure in unsuspecting college women with self-esteem issues. Everything about him was hateable from the overly man-icured eyebrows and overly tanned skin to his idiotic diction, which left the room stinking of ignorance. His gut hung slightly beyond his belt and was usually covered by an Armani T-shirt that did his slovenly body no justice.

Behind every human being there is the story of how they got there. One drunken night, while my eyes pierced through the layers of fat and self-hatred, he showed that he still had an amazing heart. For a while in college there was a steady stream of eighty-mg Oxycontin coming into the apartment. I had avoided them since the beginning but eventually Cookie Dough rolled up a fifty and convinced me to snort one. Fingas was in his room with his girlfriend at the time screaming about something or another while she continuously told him he was a jerk off, leaving Cookie Dough and I alone in our addictions and vices. After snorting a pill and feeling a lulling calm wash over my body, I was hooked on painkillers. They got rid of all my anger. While my blood pressure was down and I wasn't grinding the filter of a cigarette between my teeth, he let me in.

"It helps, don't it?" He put a hand on my shoulder as I pulled the bill out of my nose and handed it back. I was already feeling goofy and calm, my legs and arms were working but everything had slowed down.

"I'm not in pain so I wouldn't call this help."

"Pain happens to more than the body. You should see my dad."

Seeing a real moment happening, I was scared and tried to lighten the situation, "Why, is he single?"

"He's dying. He can't even swallow these anymore. We have bottles and bottles of these. I should sell them."

"Dude, he's dying?"

"For a while . . . losing to cancer," and he started nodding off and asked for a beer before continuing, "his throat cancer is so bad he's on liquid now."

My initial hate for Cookie Dough was replaced with hate for myself. I had so erroneously judged someone I thought was an awful prick without realizing he may be going through some shit. I watched as he took a sip from his beer, popped another painkiller, and nodded off. Acknowledging this was his way of coping didn't make me like him more, but it made me hate him less. When he nodded off there was a peace to him I rarely saw when he was awake and causing problems.

Although I was just hit with a realization that his life may be terrible, not once did that stop me from stealing from him. I took a handful of the painkillers and put the top back on the bottle. I left the room to smoke a cigarette and when I returned, Four Fingas, his girl, and Cookie Dough had left. It became a sad night, a night when regretting all the time I spent judging him was only worsened by drinking alone, hoping a roommate would join me. Soon I nodded off on the couch to painkiller dreams filled with monkeys and surrealism. Painkiller sleep is a strange and wondrous thing until you realize there is a good chance you won't wake up from it.

A few weeks later I was sitting on the couch, which now smelled like a dirty water puddle. I had done them with people once and we all just sat around watching TV, which seemed like a waste of time. I had dispersed the painkillers among my friends because it wasn't really my thing, one of which being a new friend The Governor introduced as DollaBill. He

PSU, Van Wilder, Animal House, Accepted, Undeclared. This is your homework.

had gotten through law school, or medical school, or some form of really intense math masters and ended up being a bum for a while compared to what he was capable of. He showed us pictures of his family, who were a cookie-cutter family of people who've made a name for themselves. I guess Bill just wasn't ready for it. He and I snorted painkillers once together and he managed to stay awake and keep drinking for hours. They were like cocaine to his circulatory system, or meth to anyone in Indiana, they kept him awake for hours. Once they were in his system he'd talk complex audio logarithms or medical anatomy, then we'd sit for hours talking about science and weed. All of a sudden he went from DollaBill to Dolla Dolla Bills y'all. By far the man was a tank for the stuff.

So it was no surprise when he came back to campus, he immediately looked for me. Finding me alone on the couch he turned into my new pale friend, with his backward hat, always inviting himself over. He helped himself to a seat on the couch and stroked his auburn goatee with fingers that were never meant to do manual labor. Being that he was in his late thirties, he dressed like a character in *PSU* and was easy to imagine out on the lawn at a Dave Matthews concert.

"It's impolite to sit down and not bring over a beer." He got back up, grabbed beers, and sat back down next to me in silence. I got up and walked over to the counter, being a passive aggressive dickhead. I'd never ask for money for those actions, but I'm never below holding someone's time hostage. We exchanged the usual quippy back and forth where a lot was said while nothing was actually being said. The Governor joined us and as we got drunker our dumb brute sides showed themselves.

Like hormone-filled primates, drunk and bored, we shadowboxed. Whenever it was a few of us guys someone always asked me to show them how to break a finger or twist a joint up, or even sometimes tossing someone in the process. Most of the time a kid named Alex CarDouchey picked a fight with me, which always ended up with him on the ground after being thrown and people pulling me off of him as I put him in a Kimora or smacked him until he said uncle. Tonight it was drunken jerks bouncing on the balls of their feet dodging punches that would never connect. The entire dance showed how unevolved young humans could be. We pounded beers and listened to DollaBill talk about his most recent shenanigans in his own town. The Governor left to go play Fight Night after a few lost rounds in shadow-boxing and DollaBill kept yammering on about getting older.

"Sure, I'm gonna be in school forever. I want to stay here. I beat The Governor's test scores and rub it in his face. I teach other people in my class this stuff."

With two fingers I tipped the bottle lip and poured beer into myself.

"Want my pain killers?"

"How fucking long was it going to take you?" His credit card was already in his hand ready to crush the pills before I even had them out.

"Cheers dude. Here's to you and here's to me and, if we should ever disagree, fuck you and here's to me." We tapped beers and I threw the remaining pills on the counter. He rolled a dollar bill and snorted two of the four left. Almost as soon as he had the pills, he was back to hanging out with The Governor. When he left, I sat in a quiet room filled with bottles. I looked at my reflection in some glass.

"Am I his dealer?"

"If you are, you sure are an asshole for keeping him waiting so long."

"I'm awful as a dealer."

"You're awful as a person too but you just keep trying."

"Are you saying I should try to be a good drug dealer? That's awful advice."

"I don't even know what I'm saying."

"That's the story of our life."

I looked up from the bottle and made sure no one saw me talking to myself. I always left the blinds open because occasionally guests would come over to the window or wave for me to come outside. My conversations with myself remained a secret, but I heard crashing from The Governors room. Either a game of Fight Night got intense or someone was falling over things. I wanted no part of it either way, it had been a rough few days of drinking and a night off was in order to scheme up something new to fight college boredom away.

Soon that boredom kicked in, when no good schemes came to mind, and I sat on my phone looking for drinking buddies. After a few shower beers and peeing in Max's shampoo bottle, I decided to lay on the couch and enjoy HBO, something I was never privileged enough to have. Some late night comedy special made me dream of some day making people laugh, especially while I was under the influence. I started to write in my secret joke book, until The Governor burst in my room. "I need to learn to lock that thing."

"What's up mother fucker, still drinking?" I held a beer up so he could see it and nodded. DollaBill burst into the room, "What's up mother fucker, still drinking?"

My brow lowered, "Did you guys plan that?" DollaBill walked over to my fridge and helped himself to a beer. "I've only got a few left." He cracked the top and drank it anyway.

They were a nightmare of social interaction, sporadic and spontaneous, jumping from one story to another then they made plans and never did them. The whole scene in my room looked like something a coked-up art school student would pass off as a movie.

"So let's call people and get a party in here."

"DollaBill, I have four beers left."

"I'll call my girl and have her bring up some beer, she's only an hour and a half away."

"Wait, you're dating someone?"

"Wait, let's go on campus and see what's going on."

"I'm not in the mood for a freshman party, and DollaBill is already calling his girlfriend."

"Do you have any instruments?" The Governor didn't play music, and DollaBill's conversation with his girlfriend was in the background.

"Do you have any instruments?"

"I know its late, that's why I'm calling. Empty the fridge and come up."

"No dude, no instruments."

"So blast music and keep the windows open. I want to see you."

"Then play some music, 'Fuck You I'm Drunk,' play that and we'll finish the beers."

"I only have four left."

"How late is it, shit is that late?"

"Fine, I'll play some music."

I went to grab my laptop, walking past DollaBill.

"It's 3:00 a.m., we should be asleep," he mouthed at me while covering his phone.

"I don't sleep much dude," I retrieved my laptop and put on "Fuck You I'm Drunk" as per the insistent request.

"You're right we're going to bed."

"What are you guys gonna do?"

When DollaBill came back and sat down, he immediately dozed off. It was like he was dating the voice of reason and she often won.

"This is insane man, even for me," The Governor was still wide-awake, so we put on Fight Night and he destroyed me. After a few rounds, the silence coming from Bill was bothersome. I cocked my head and out of the corner of my eye I noticed DollaBill was the color of a body found in a glacier. "Holy shit dude, he's blue." The Governor looked at him and laughed.

"He's breathin', he'll be fine." He got up and shook DollaBill so violently that he woke from what looked like a coma. "You're blue. You need to stay awake and breathe."

The veins in my forearms bulged as I freaked out, "He's the color of a knockoff Barney. He's almost Grimace. How is this fine? He's *blue*. Humans aren't fucking blue."

"I'm fine. You're not supposed to drink when you take painkillers is all. My blood pressure is down so my circulation sucks." My face had to have been white. "It happens occasionally." He was blue, and everyone was fine.

Anti-drug commercials and ads miss the ball. They're fucking stupid. For painkillers they show kids stealing prescriptions from Grandpa's medicine cabinet then taking them and dying on the couch. That's basically telling kids, "Fuck your grandpa, this shit feels so good people are willing to die for it." You don't even get painkillers from you grandparents, all you get is Lipitor, Viagra, and the Prozac he takes because he hates that his daughter settled for your dad. You normally get painkillers from some white kid named Kyle, who has tribal tats and fingers questionably aged girls in his studio apartment. If not him then a doctor who prescribes you ninety-mg Oxycontin because he's getting closer to a Pfizer-sponsored golf vacation. Leave the elderly alone, they're not stupid enough to leave that stuff lying around, they take their pills exactly as is prescribed out of fear of death.

The newest one just shows a kid in a hoodie popping handfuls of painkillers and standing in a pool, a hallway, and playing video games, but not in that order. As his mom calls him down for dinner, he doesn't answer and she finds him dead in his room. Then he says, "They said prescriptions were safe. They lied." First off, what type of a mother makes dinner for her kid but doesn't notice he's been standing fully dressed in a pool? Then he takes handfuls of pills blaming other people for not knowing it's unsafe. Swallowing that many of anything that sized at once is dangerous, painkiller or not. You can't blame lack of knowing on someone else. Ask any human being in the world and they know anything that makes you happier is probably shit for you.

If you want to create an effective ad about addiction, show them my buddy blue as fuck and acting like nothing is wrong. If you want people to stop abusing painkillers show them DollaBill trying to chug a gallon of room-temperature water to flush his system, saying, "No, it's no big deal I do this all the time," as if that made it less sad. That would show addiction better than some kid in a 30 Seconds To Mars T-shirt overdosing on his grandpa's expired pain meds. Bill was blue and had water coming out of his mouth. The slogan would be, "Looking like a inbred Water type Pokemon: That's My Anti-Drug." Most the time painkillers just make you pass out, so just show a kid getting yelled at for being late with a bunch of garbage written on his face. That will at least teach them to be responsible enough to set and alarm and look in a mirror. Adulthood just means knowing how to manage your vices.

So a blue DollaBill—he was sad as well—a blue, blue DollaBill went back with The Governor to his quarters to make sure he stayed alive and I was left alone, staring at the space where they once were. I just saw the effects of painkillers and it made me want a Xanax. The whole night turned me off from doing them more than a few times afterward. Heroin has needles to stop you from doing it. Painkillers only have a childproof cap. There's no horrific ending to this story where he was rushed off to the hospital. He eventually got his shit together and lived regretting all the time he wasted on those stupid things.

What we can take away from this is a simple lesson: if you or someone you know has an addiction problem, don't lend them money. Don't talk to them. Tell them they're the devil. If someone you love has an addiction problem, stop loving them. If that's too hard try chasing them away with rocks. That's what I should have done. Chased him away with rocks because then my night would have been easier, and when it comes to others' addictions, it's best to make it all about yourself.

I could have left it there and let you wonder if I was serious or not. Take painkillers responsibly, they're the most addictive thing on earth—besides soda. Addiction is shitty and you act like a scrotum until everyone gets sick of you. Although you may not see immediate repercussions, they'll hit. Don't be blue. No one likes a blue scrotum. Experiment safely.

CHAPTER 10

PARTIES

Let's get so drunk we make life-altering mistakes

The Best Party

Parties—where you get laid, where you get drunk, where a common strain of herpes gets passed around, the place that makes you question yourself, and where you always make the wrong decision when it comes to decision-making time. Parties are an important part of having traumatic experiences to help form you into an adult. They're where you shave your head into a mohawk and are too stubborn to grow out said mohawk afterward. Parties help you realize exactly who you don't want to be. A good party leaves all those who attended sore and questioning their own lives. That's why you want to show everyone you're the man who can do this. But converting a dorm room where you have five square feet of space into a party room is going to take some work.

Remove everything valuable. You have friends right? Put everything breakable and valuable into their cell. This gives room for extra oxygen in a space where that's an honest fear. Not only does this help make some room, it ensures none of your stuff gets stolen. That's always the biggest bummer, when karma gets you back for all the stealing and destruction you've caused over the years when someone decides to jack your laptop. Stealing a laptop is like stealing someone's identity. Yeah, it may seem like it's filled with meaningless shit to you, but it means something to someone else. Hide anything breakable too. The problem with drunk kids is that they'll find something you didn't think was breakable and they'll manage to fuck it up. This also includes any bottles that you were saving for special occasions, because at 3:00 a.m. everything will feel like a special occasion.

Fuck furniture. Seriously, take your beds and stack them, throw a small dresser on top of the desk, and move your closets together. Play Tetris with it and make the most room possible. If your bed isn't disgusting and has nice sheets, turn that into a couch. It's about creating space with what little you have. If you can't stack the furniture turn it into something else. A wheeled desk cabinet makes a great rolling chair. A freestanding closet is the perfect place to hide a half keg. The top bunk makes for a great bar. If it's in your room it must serve an alternative purpose, this includes turning the bathtub you share with your neighbors, as well as the sink, into an ice bucket for beer. In fact, anything you can get is now a cooler.

Cheap, light beer is the golden rule. Yes, this stuff tastes like piss water, but no one shares their sixer of a good IPA. Don't supply the obnoxious beer. Supply the, "Great at 2:00 a.m. when we're out of everything else," beer. This is a party, so it's more important that everyone has several beers than it is to have good beers. If you're hosting a good enough party no one will be able to taste it anyway. After ten hours of drinking, it's the only thing you can put in you because it almost immediately comes right out. You won't even have time to finish an entire beer before you have to piss again by 8:00 a.m. The goal is quantity not quality. The American higher education system is about excess because in the US we don't believe in taking a year off and getting worldly after high school. Straight to college you go so you'll come out engrained into the work force, so enjoy college way too much because it's the last time you'll have freedom or happiness. Drink cheap, large quantities of beer.

A foreign friend helps make a great party. Nothing starts a conversation quite like a friend who speaks a little differently than the rest of us. It leads to amazing conversations like, "Where are you from?" and, "Say 'Fuck' in your language." You'd be incredibly surprised how not sarcastic that statement is. It should seem completely outrageous but seriously, people love asking those two questions to anyone foreign in college. It honestly does keep the night going because people forget and constantly ask the foreign friend to repeat himself. He'll be completely frustrated the entire party until he gets laid. if he's a dude. If she's a girl, she'll be disgusted and pass out alone after all the creepy attention.

Bottles and more bottles. Yeah, it seems expensive and unobtainable unless you've read the chapter about your room. Mixers go faster than the booze, so make sure you have gallons of soda and anything annoyingly fruity people could possibly ask for. Stealing a case of Red Bull from somewhere is suggested, but only if you do it wearing a GoPro and drinking a Red Bull. Then it's not theft, it's sponsorship. Getting people drunk, and quickly, is the best way to keep them around. A seemingly endless supply of bottles of liquor is sure to keep people interested for hours.

Entertainment. This one is crucial. If you're going to have people over to drink, you're going to need things for them to do while drinking. This is why you have a few essentials at all times: shot glasses and quarters, Cards Against Humanity, and music. I also suggest Jenga, but only if you write insane things on the tiles that the person who pulls it has to do. If tons of people show up to your party, music choice is key. Stick to fast-paced rock or dubstep, whatever shit college kids are listening to now, but make sure you have classics people will obnoxiously sing along to when they need a second wind. When the party starts dying down, give everyone a second wind with a classic that every single person on earth will try to sing along to. Quarters is the perfect game when there isn't enough room for Beer Pong. Finally if everything blows and only ten people show up, rock out some Cards Against Humanity and everyone should drink till they pass out.

Meth . . . too far?

Methamphetamine is the only way to guarantee visitors at your party will actually become your friends. Slip it in everyone's drinks, throw piles of it in their faces, put it into a humidifier and get everyone cranked up. Not only will this guarantee a great and addictive time, you're all going to end up accessories to the crime someone is bound to commit. Getting people addicted to meth means they'll always have to come back to you to get their fix. Remember, after getting them addicted, never loan them money or drugs. They pay like everyone else because otherwise you're being an enabler and good friends aren't enablers.

Spot the Jackass: The People You Find at College Parties

College parties are awesome at first. There are so many cool, new people. Everyone came from somewhere and it's interesting. You have no idea how jaded you're going to get yet. Life is still new and you have hopes and dreams you want to share with the world. Everyone is still new and interesting and wants to share the stuff they like with other people, hoping they'll like it too. After a few more years of going to parties, you're going to start to notice some of the same characters showing up, it will still be okay and sometimes fun but eventually you are going to get sick of the same-old college bullshit. But before that happens, look forward to seeing some of these characters at every party.

Too High Guy: You see that person in the group with a big smile, who's nodding intently at everything said? That person is stoned. On the outside, they're playing everything perfect and seem really likeable. On the inside, they're probably thinking about a funny movie or having a crippling social anxiety attack. They probably don't smoke often and someone offered some weed to pregame and now they regret it. If you see this person at a party, rub your hand down their cheek and say, "You're never going back." If they are the Too High Guy their face will drop and they'll wonder what that means. If they don't freak, they might be a genuinely nice person who's interested in others. In that case your choices are run or murder, because genuinely happy and nice people are petrifying.

Everybody Like Me: He's the chattiest and nicest guy at the party, he slings quips like they are beers, and everyone likes him. He's chatted with everyone at the party and as it gets later, random groups pull him in for a while and ask about his night. He might even say something slightly offensive but not in bad taste. He's got a case of the "Everyone needs to like Me"s. Maybe he wasn't cool in high school or maybe he's an emotionally unsympathetic, emotional sightseer who comes into your life, makes you his best friend, and then leaves once he's bored of you. Who cares, because he just quoted that movie we all recently saw.

The Acoustic Guitar: This human has been talked about and made fun of for decades. Everyone knows that no one likes the person who brings an acoustic guitar, so it takes a special kind of douche bag to actually bring one to a party in 2015. Is he doing it ironically? That's just as stupid because there is still an acoustic guitar at the party. The only time an acoustic guitar is okay is when it's on a stage or on YouTube; it's never acceptable anywhere else. Anyone who still does this gets all their strings broken then strangled with them.

How did they get here? They have a slightly glazed over and they staring at their phone a lot. They may pace or come in and out of the party. Either way, it's clear they have no idea how they got there. Are they at the wrong party? Did they invite someone who didn't show up? Are they going to make awkward small talk or explain why they're alone? This is the most fun person at the party to talk to. Screw with them a bit and enjoy it because they'd rather talk to you than trying to talk to anyone else.

Introvert: They're the type of person who doesn't like most college parties because there is no dog to play with. Now they're in college and trying to interact with others. This person is the incredibly awkward one at the party; watch as they manage to make entire groups of people find an excuse to be somewhere else. They open their mouth and suddenly everyone is willing to help clean up and end the party after they utter three sentences. Try to be nice to this person, because if they ever get out of their parents' basement, they might end up being successful.

The Jackass: A case of the try-too-hards and a dash of narcissism keep this twat going at parties. He's flirted with every girl and made sure everyone at the party knows how funny he thinks he is. This guy is usually the saddest guy there. He thinks he's being charming, but really, he's kind of a jackass. When you stop and think about his life, it's a pretty shallow and meaningless one. He's so concerned with others' opinions of him that his personality is lacking and he has no idea who he actually is. There're no jokes about this guy, because he is the joke.

Old Guy: He's way out of college but maybe his girlfriend just broke up with him, or maybe he realized his life has gotten monotonous and he misses college. Whatever the reason, eventually you're going to see the guy who's way too old to be at a college party. You'll be able to spot him easily, he'll be the pathetic one trying to hit on freshman girls or the guy sitting away from where it's loud realizing he's too old for this shit. Whether we like it or not, eventually every single man will end up being the Old Guy at the party at some point.

Impressionists: Murder should be legal for a lot of reasons. There are way too many people on earth and we're slowly destroying the planet, and because there are people who do impressions at parties. We aren't talking about people who do silly voices and the occasional character. Generally those people know they're a douche. But Impressions Guy thinks he's talented. Being the Impressions Guy at the party is like being the car jumping guy on YouTube—secretly everyone wants to see both of you get hurt.

Someone's little sibling: This was a personal favorite. When someone brings their little brother or sister to a party, it's their responsibility to make sure you don't do anything stupid to them. There is zero responsibility on anyone but the older sibling, so grab the little one and run off like an idiot to cause problems. There are few things that feel better in life than getting someone drunk or stoned for their first time. In the monotony of college, a little sibling is a way to guarantee a great night. Everything that has become routine and stupid by senior year is still fun to this little snot rag, so give him a night his sibling is gonna have to explain to Mom and Dad.

Where do I know you from? You're going to go out . . . a lot. Too much. You're going to realize that every night you stay in is a night that was wasted because you could have been doing something extraordinary. All the fun stuff happens when you aren't there. This is when the "Where Do I Know

You From" happens. You're going to meet tons of different people, have meaningful and in depth conversations with them, then forget who they are entirely. Months later you may run across each other and all you'll be able to think is, *Where the fuck is that person from?* You could have made out with them, banged them, or just heard their life story but neither one of you will be able to put a finger on how you know each other.

ICING: BRING IT BACK LIKE A ZAMBONI (My first article on Brobible.com)

A few summers ago, a bored genius frat bro invented icing. Using only a hidden Smirnoff Ice, he was able to humiliate his friends while at the same time giving them diabetes. Icing was the best way to show your bros that you care about them enough to think of amazing ways to humiliate them. Icing showed that you took the time to think about how much you secretly hate your friends, and plan the perfect time to humiliate them in front of their peers and hot chicks at the party. Icing was the pinnacle of socially acceptable douchebaggery. Icing was one of the greatest running gags that died out; planking is also gone and no one does the Dougie anymore, it's time that the Ice Age comes back.

Icing could make you the single-handed hero at any college party. There was nothing better than watching the douchebag who was picking fights and getting too aggressive with women get on his knees and chug fermented diabetes. Instead of getting in a brawl with him and his friends that ruins everyone's time at the party, icing that dude over and over again until he puked whitish grey carbonated water and everyone laughed at him was the best. Knowing that tomorrow he might be at risk of losing his foot and his head would feel worse than his social skills was even better. It removed the problem at the party while still making everyone feel like they're having a great time.

The perfectly timed icing could ruin your friend's night. Everyone gets way too drunk on occasion; it's never a good look. So icing a friend who's already super drunk was always hilarious. There is nothing more entertaining than watching someone who can barely walk try to get on their knees and chug. He's going to fall over, he's going to scrape his hands, and tomorrow the front of his shirt is going to be stickier than a sorority girl's stomach the first week she gets a boyfriend. If you're lucky he's going to puke everywhere and be drunk enough that he tells you he loves you, make sure you get it on camera and blackmail him for a thirty pack.

Icing was the best running gag that frats ever invented. It came in waves. The first few icings were always funny and got a good, *"Oooohhh,"* out of everyone watching. The simple act of watching a friend do something miserable could make the afternoon more enjoyable. The problem was after the fifteenth to twentieth icing, it got a bit boring and repetitious, and even those watching didn't enjoy it anymore. But those who were really devoted got to see the wave come back. Somewhere after the twentieth icing of the night a new wave hits the onlookers and the people doing it. It was no longer a gag, it was a test of endurance. Double icing turned into chugging competitions and, there, becomes a serious love for getting iced.

It only took two dollars and sixteen ounces of liquid to make or break a night. Icing could make you a bigger hero than Young Hercules or ruin a friend's night like a breakup text. Icing showed devotion to making your friends want revenge on you, and sometimes turned into a bonding moment like throwing a baseball at a neighbor with your Dad. Al Gore is wrong, it's time we say fuck global warming and bring back the Ice Age.

The Six Best New Drinking Games You Should Never Play

Drinking inside gets boring. Let's admit it. Even if there are a lot of people around and there's conversation, eventually people get bored. As soon as beating kids became illegal, heavy drinkers needed something to fill up the extra time so drinking games were invented. You can only dance for so long. Back in the day people drank to take out aggression, so they threw pointy things at boards and darts was invented, and once people realized that game was stupid they invented pool. Pool is still awesome, but then someone realized you could play games that forced you to drink much faster. Yeah, we all love Beer Pong, flip cup, and quarters but aren't those getting a little old too? The people who are too good at Beer Pong get annoying and everyone gets way too excited over flip cup, so I've invented a few new games that add the thrill back to drinking.

Windows: Binge drinking isn't dangerous enough anymore. Oh sure, there are a thousand ways to die from being an idiot while binge drinking, but you can always add one more! Play Windows. It's just as dangerous and it's completely legal. Everyone sits with one leg out a window and one leg in, all in different rooms. The name of the game is to drink as fast as possible. Everyone grabs a thirty pack, and after you drink a beer you throw it out the window and keep track of who gets the biggest pile, bonus points for hitting cars. There's actually no point system whatsoever, the winner is the last person to stop drinking while they're hanging out a window.

Grapes of Wrath: This one needs a bonfire. Everyone gets a bottle of wine and sits around the open flame. Everyone has their bottle of wine open and ready to chug, because someone now throws a handful of bullets into the open fire. There's no winner in this one, just everyone avoiding getting shot. Not only is this a great way to get Instagrams with your friends (#22caliber, #StacyLost) it's also a great way to tell if your friend has problems with depression. I bet your friend who lives in a garage drinks wine the slowest! This is a great party to play at the end of the night when you want everyone to leave.

Of Mice and Men Lenny Dies edition: A twist on a new classic. Instead of sitting around a fire, sit around a circular table with a bag of heroin and a needle in the middle. Loser gets a life-crippling addiction! I bet your friend who lives in a garage *always* loses.

Rock Paper Scissors: A twist on a classic. Just throw a bunch of rocks, paper, and scissors at each other. Sure, hoarding rocks and scissors all day is tough, but worth it. If having scissors whiz by your head doesn't drive to you drink, you're a good person or a complete idiot. So is anyone who throws paper.

Slap Cup: You slap the cup out of someone's hand and then they drink it off the floor. It's a great game because it fills time and risks the players getting hepatitis. Ebola is the least of your worries if you play this game! Just make sure you're playing with solo cups—you don't want to have to pull broken glass out of some girl named Stacy's gums.

Mousetrap: Every time you set a mousetrap, take a shot! This game is great because setting mousetraps when you're drunk is the funniest thing I've ever thought of. Not only do you set mousetraps, but then you get to place them all over the house. Two points for every mousetrap you set, ten for any that get set off on your friends. If you set off a trap, you also have to do a shot. Try placing mousetraps in spots you'll forget once you sober up. Then as people get snapped the game lasts for a week! Everyone also lives in crippling anxiety!

Cards Against Maturity: Everyone takes a few Cards Against Humanity. Throughout the night everyone has to scream what's on their card loud enough for strangers to hear it. One point for everyone who hears it, ten points if you whisper it into a non-player's ear.

Old drinking games get boring. It's time to make things more risky. Yes, I am legally saying you should never play any of these games (Except for Cards Against Maturity), but so do TV shows that show people filming themselves doing this stuff. Next time someone suggests boring old flip cup, call them a loser and slap the cup out of their hand. Bring your party to the next level and try playing some real drinking games.

Dear Millennials, I'm Going to Repeat Myself. Knock it Off.

Millennials are the technology-addicted, pseudo-political generation that was told there are no losers. It doesn't matter that big and small business are both fighting for their dollar or what Mom and Dad told them, they are losers. Millennials are smart enough to run a proxy to hide their purchase of Dogecoin, but most of the time aren't smart enough to realize that making a mix tape will always get you a sexual favor. We've all heard the term Millennials as a compliment, but guess what, you can still learn from the generation before you. These are the things all Millennials can learn from Gen X and early members of their own generation, Gen Y.

Cheap Beer: That craft beer isn't going to impress anyone because you could only afford to buy a six pack. The only thing going in your mouth is going to be that microbrew if you don't learn to share. Yes, cheap beer tastes like crap, but something Millennials need to learn is quantity beats quality. Drinking games were invented to bring strangers together and you can't play those with a triple hoppy IPA reserve. Learn to drink garbage so that everyone can get drunk and make friends. Besides, thanks to your ironic drinking, the price of PBR has gone up, so now you're stuck with crappier beer. Who says it's always the previous generation that messes things up for the next one?

YouTube Doesn't Belong At Parties: You have iPads, iPods, and four thousand songs in fifteen different file formats. Take a little extra time and put together a decent playlist, or let the awkward friend you don't want talking to girls man the music. Sitting around waiting for a YouTube playlist or a new viral video to buffer is not only boring, it makes you look like an idiot for not preloading it. Try blasting Wu Tang clan then Com Truise; not only does it keep everyone happy, eventually it makes people dance.

Online Friends Aren't Friends Until You Meet: We live in the social media era. This author, for one, has made a great deal of friends from Twitter. Just because you talk to that person via Kik, Skype, or DMs everyday, doesn't mean they're your real friend. Real friends not only confide in each other verbally, but they meet up too. The show *CatFish* was invented for a reason. Until you've met @Pizzakylee, @rightc0ast, @Erinxx, @Nick_Turco, @bieoe, or @JustinWRoot they aren't your friend, they're a possible identity thief. @MollyMoonDance isn't your friend. She's just some girl who shows you her tits every now and again. @Nickgodd is just some guy who sends you Snapchats about what he's drinking. @AbbyDraper isn't your friend, she's just some girl you only follow because she followed you and writes for the Huffington Post. You probably don't even know what gender @ Bindzbrain actually is. It's hard to escape social media when it refreshes with something new and interesting every four minutes but it's complete shit and most of those people will turn their back on you.

So get the fuck off your phone when you're at a party because these people could become your actual friends. Seriously, something terrible could happen tomorrow and they might be the ones to help you through it. Throw your phone into a lake or stream or just into your pocket because it's expensive.

This Party is Dorm-ant

When I moved into my dorm/apartment I had more bottles than an Asian lady who picks recycling. The previous summer I had accumulated so many full bottles from parties I crashed to fuel me for a month. When you're not old enough to buy liquor, you'll find any excuse to steal it. This was how I was planning on making immediate friends. I ventured from my room to wander the halls with a bottle of vodka and a bottle of whiskey. There was still a strangeness to the hallways that weren't quite home yet. For most of college I didn't wear shoes, so a tepid September evening left the ground cool beneath my toes, yet the surrounding air was warm like a hug from a close friend. I stepped bit by bit into the courtyard for the very first time, sipping from the whiskey. At Montclair when you stared into the sky there were no stars to wish on, wishes weren't as good as hard work. I stopped for a moment and inhaled self-dependence then exhaled thinking about never having to check in with family again. This was a time for scheming; I raised both bottles to the sky in a toast then drained them into my mouth at once. I looked at the benches for the first time, shiny and new, that still had green life around them because we hadn't stomped it out yet. I didn't know at this point that it would all become home. I poured both bottles into my mouth again, and when I brought my head back down to swallow, a little pygmy man was standing in front of me smiling. "I like the way you drink." He was a jungle man like myself, even more wild looking. The only clothing he had on was a pair of super-tight jean shorts that were cut too high around his thighs and a hemp necklace around a thick Cro-Magnon neck. His filthy long hair passed for blond and he smiled harder than anyone I've ever met. His knees were so battle worn that over the caps he had, "Crash," and, "Burn," forever imprinted in the skin and a single thick black line wrapped around each of his ankles. "I like the way you drink, come on." As he turned, I noticed "666" tattooed right where his underwear was sagging down to.

He went inside for a moment, I handed him the whiskey and said we couldn't share a bottle without at least knowing each other's names. He went by Asshole because it sounded like his last name. We swigged the whiskey and he told me to wait right here. He ran like Tarzan, light on his bare feet and his chest puffed out. When he returned he brought with him a girl who could have been a Suicide Girl she was so pretty, and a girl who looked like she would probably commit suicide. Asshole didn't introduce us so I held out the bottles, offering them booze.

Girls usually made me an asshole or a church mouse. I couldn't hold eye contact with Suicide Girl very well while the other one was like a car crash you actually didn't want to look at. Asshole had my sense of humor. He was throwing rocks at the garbage can yelling, "I'm bored," when I started chatting with other people. They dragged me down the sidewalk and into another one of the apartment buildings. I was promised a party that would kick ass for which I was helping supply the booze. The elevator ride was demure and awkward, and when the door opened Asshole called us faggots. The Suicide Girl grabbed me by the wrist and said, "Has anyone ever asked you why you're so aggressive?" As I wondered what type of passive man she was into, Asshole grabbed my other wrist pulled me into the party.

It was like walking into a carnival of alt kids whose parents never controlled the way they looked. I wanted to yell, "Someone pierce me and hand me a band T-shirt, I want to be underground too!" A blonde with overly straightened hair and too much eyeliner was walking on tables screaming, "Yeah you're sexual. You're sexual and hot, you're like s'hot!" She began dancing and telling everyone to join her. Tattoos may have covered her skin but nothing could hide her bigger issues. The only thing stranger to me than her look was how she could climb onto a table wearing those heels and a skirt. "We're all s'hot!" As soon as she yelled it, drunken alt kids rushed over to the table she was on to do shots.

In front of me was a couch flipped on its side so it could act as a table, along with chairs and several small coffee tables strewn about, all topped with bodies. I knew I admired the party goers, but it was obnoxious for them to put themselves on pedestals. A kind-faced, leather-clad kid strolled over smiling at me and Asshole. They laughed upon seeing each other then embraced so aggressively that a thud sounded when their chests hit. This sent shivers up my spine, when he came over to me with arms outstretched I stuck a hand out, "Sorry, I'm not quick to bond."

As soon as I gripped his hand, I forced a deliberate and non-reactive poker face. I realized why he hugged everyone once my five fingers wrapped around his three. He took no notice of my interior freak out. After the handshake, when everyone's back was turned I looked at my hand. I thought I deserved a thank you. I'm sure a number of people in the world have probably stared at him or asked about it, butt I just shook it. How about something more than a smile? How about a pat on the back and a, "Thank you," for treating him like a normal person? Everyone deserves to be treated normally, but we don't have to think that way. I deserve at least an extra shake as a means of recognizing I didn't act like a dickhead.

For anyone who's upset at the above, he cheated on his girlfriend a bunch I later found out. Just because you've got a deformity doesn't mean you're not an asshole.

Being a bro at an alternative party should have been alienating, instead they were welcoming. Later, I stared into the bathroom mirror, disappointed in my own judgments. Clothing and music didn't alienate us the way it did in community college. Here, everyone threw tables then danced on them. Proving this fact, a table flew across the room, immediately another kid—who looked like Portland had cum on him—fixed the table upright and started dancing on it. Asshole, who'd run off and come back, smiled at me while stalking closer. "Hey Asshole, is the floor lava?" His head turned and when he faced me again, a wild belly laugh came out of him. It carried through the room and resonated like an animal roar.

"If it's not lava, it has AIDS," he scoped the entire scene. Hipsters awash in denim and no-name band shirts danced on chairs, couches, tables . . . essentially no two feet were touching the floors anymore.

"I think the floor has super AIDS," I lifted one leg off of it. He squinted his eyes and pulled the pretend noose that was around his neck.

"Can we go somewhere without AIDS?"

Asshole wrangled Suicide Girl and suicide girl by screaming, "I'm worried about all the AIDS here." He strong-armed everyone I had met before the apartment party and forced us back down onto the sidewalks. "Asshole, that was my first party of my life while I wasn't living at home," I let him know. He tied his hair back into a ponytail and stared down at the ground. He rolled a rock in circles between his big toe and the sidewalk.

"Sorry you got AIDS at the first college party." Both girls looked like they could commit suicide now.

"Asshole, if there was any way I wanted to get AIDS, it was through you," I retorted then all of us wanted to commit suicide after that joke.

Asshole dragged us through several apartments, and I dragged him through a bottle of whiskey. We ended up in Suicide Girl's room. It was amazing, because it lacked any sense of being a girl's dorm. From what I had seen in pictures, girls' dorms had shit on the walls, nice blankets on the couches, and a homey feel. At some point the vodka had disappeared, but I had a hunch when all of a sudden the one girl had perked up and didn't look like she wanted to commit suicide anymore she had downed it. From behind me I heard, "You're not ugly in a really fucked up way." I felt fingers fumbling with my shoulders, trying to massage while also trying to pull me down to her height. "I don't pee the bed when I drink anymore," Suicidal-looking girl whispered into my ear while also shouting. Now I had become the one in the room wanting to commit suicide. The pretty suicide and the real suicide threw their arms over each other's shoulders and walked back toward the bedroom.

"Hey, you didn't bang her?" Asshole said in a tone of complete amazement.

"Yeah, thank god I lost my V-card or else I might have."

"That's awful, she's a sweet girl."

"Really?" I was amazed by the compliment.

"Nope, just bored." I laughed at Asshole's quickness.

"What are we waiting for?"

"Just because you're dying from AIDS doesn't mean we need to rush."

"I'm not actually dying of AIDS," I reminded him.

"How do you know that?"

"Actually, I got tested."

"What was her name?" When he said it, I didn't understand his joke at first.

"Asshole, stop being an asshole."

"You only get tested when a girl wants to know you're clean or when you think a girl wasn't clean."

"I can't even argue that." He was right and my faced showed it.

Pretty Suicide Girl walked quietly back into the kitchen. We got shooed out while she put an index finger across her lips. After standing in her kitchen for a moment, her door opened again as she made an escape, shushing us the entire time. I was fixing for a cigarette and to get home. As soon as my pack was in the open, Asshole took it and dashed up the flight of outdoor stairs leading to my complex and out of sight. "Don't chase him, he comes back." Her lips were cherry, moving softly but with purpose in front of her pale skin. "So, why are you so aggressive?" I squinted at her and a right angle formed in my neck. "See? Aggressive. Why do you exaggerate things?" While my mouth made noises still trying to find words, she sighed and started up the steps herself. I threw a rock at a window as soon as she was out of view only to hear a distance voice say, "Aggressive." A million curse words fell out of my mouth, but none made a sound. I started up the stairs, at the top was home, Alice Paul building. 1A was so close. I was met by Asshole with my cigarettes, and Suicide Girl who had bummed one.

Others around the court yard and benches near 1A knew Asshole and he left Suicide Girl and me to ourselves so he could go mingle (horrify new people).

"I didn't realize I was aggressive. I'll think about it." She didn't smile or laugh or react at all. She just smoked her cigarette and looked straight through me. "So, could we hang out again after tonight?"

She finally smirked, "No thanks." I continued talking to her, knowing full well we had become nothing but a means to pass time. I curtseyed and thanked her for a fine evening, in my best attempt to be charming and funny. She just cocked her head, which let me know I was trying too hard.

I found Asshole to say goodnight. He whispered in my ear, "Dude, she's only sixteen. She graduated high school crazy early and is an absolute painting child prodigy, but mostly she's sixteen."

"Why did I waste so much time? Why didn't you tell me?" I was furious.

"Because . . . I'm an Asshole."

Some people in college are just assholes. You have to learn to box them up and put them in the right cubbyhole. Not everyone you meet is going to be a wonderful person, but they will show you a wonderful fucking time if you're open to it. Do I still talk to Asshole? Occasionally, because we all need a friend who reminds us we're not as bad as them.

Now that I'm done making fun of a friend, the real lesson to be learned here is that booze is a great equalizer. If we got all the leaders of all the countries that hate each other in a room together and got them blindingly drunk for two days, we'd have a few dead heads of state, but more peace would probably come out of it than death. We're all so open in college and that's probably due to aggressive drinking to the point of self-hatred. If you can carry that kind of openness into the world, you're probably not going to work at a bank.

The Shortest Story in This Book

During my third week of college everyone was still gone pretty often and I was left to my own devices. I was drinking more than any other human being on earth. My size and stubbornness made me want to out-drink everyone, even when there was no competition. I walked into a stranger's apartment and we all finished my bottle of vodka. Then I went back to my apartment and finished another bottle of vodka. I went to bed and woke up refreshed and clearheaded until I found out it was Wednesday and I had been drinking on a Sunday. Years later a friend from college said, "Do you remember drinking yourself into a coma?"

I replied, "If I remembered that, it wouldn't have been a coma." That's the story about the time I drank myself into a coma.

There is no moral to this story. I just wanted everyone to know my actions probably shouldn't ever be mimicked. I drank way too much and acted way too stupid but at least I learned my limits for when I reached adulthood.

The Best Frat Party Ever

Sitting in the middle of Newark, New Jersey, is a ramshackle row house wedged between an abandoned red-brick warehouse, whose ceiling is slowly collapsing (learned that the hard way), and another home that I never visited but was as ramshackle as the rest of the block. College engineers repaired the porch time after time then painted it with the crest of the frat KEK. When you entered the door, you were met with more paraphernalia and "found" objects on the walls than one could imagine. Straight ahead and to the right was a room that held a projector to blast movies during the late-night hours. A few steps past that, you ventured down a cramped hallway, to the right the skeleton of a wall separated the hallway from the custom-made Beer Pong table. Creeping behind both those rooms was the greatest thing any frat house could have: a bar. The bar at KEK was legendary because the masterpiece was a hundred years old. The wood was dark and worn smooth from years of college-aged greasy palms. Thick, hand carved, and ornate, it took up half the room lined with wood paneling just as old. Across the top of the bar room, on handmade shelves, were old beer cans and bottles from the frat boys of previous generations. Not one had been cleaned in a century. The room stunk sticky sweet because cheap beer was engrained into the wood of the floor.

The bar at KEK was not to be taken without reverence, nor were the fine brothers who inhabited that space for the two years I visited when I needed a vacation from MSU. I watched the brothers early on and appreciated that they let my antics happen. There was no reason guys who drank on par with me and got better grades should still want me around. The Brothers of KEK remain superheroes in my mind. Gobe Itchka. Gobe brought me into the hall of heroes, who became some of the most resourceful and intelligent engineers and architects post-graduation. Men Ayn Rand would have loved, and not just for their efficient, Catholic-sounding sex.

One day a year these men throw the greatest and most legendary party I had ever been to. It was all the drunken wet dream of any college-faring man. The KEK Beach Party is and forever will be the greatest spectacle of college debauchery ever to grace a campus. If the Romans had mixed their feasts with the Colosseum battles that was the KEK beach party. The preparation itself was back breaking. The homoerotic pledges, sweating and lifting together, would heft bag after bag of sand into the bar room. It took them hours, being directed where to take the loads by older men. In the end not only would the bar room be filled, but it spilled into the hallways and Beer Pong rooms. The most stunning aspect of this was they filled their entire backyard with sand as well. They kept it minimalistic; the backyard adorned with tiki lamps and a bonfire to warm even in the crisp New Jersey night air. As women entered, they were adorned with leis and adored to get laid. The decorations were the incredible college-aged bodies that entered into the house to ruin what they had.

A college-aged body is a beautiful and wondrous thing. I don't just say that because of my former fondness for dating twenty-one-year-olds until I was twenty-five. It's the only machine on earth that takes a pounding every night and still looks shiny and new in the morning. While in college, you can ingest thousands of calories worth of booze and with minimal effort maintain a perfect six pack. Those in college who don't take advantage of this are slovenly, but probably amazing at Nintendo 64.

The Beach Party meant having a beach body out of season. There was a subtle danger to how drunk everyone got, because most spent two days without eating to prepare and there was more punch than the ATF should allow.

One misty Beach Party night I entered the house pre-party, greeted by Gobe Itchka. A smaller man, he still gave a hearty hug with an open hand slap on the back. He had been a friend since my freshman year of high school. As always they watched as the pledges finished the touches on the party, but when I entered the bar area, they greeted me with an ice luge. A solid block of ice so perfectly drilled a human could put their mouth on it and not feel the booze sliding into them. Never empty handed, I forked over the handle of Canadian Club and we all tried her out. Gobe, like always, directed me to the second floor. Up the back staircase from the bar, it went to a simple kitchen with four burners and enough dirty dishes in the sink to start an Ebola outbreak. The top of the steps weren't guard-railed on both sides, so after drinking it was a perilous thought to fly over the balcony. They almost always had the stairs blocked off with cabinets, but I'm sure it wouldn't stop a determined drunk. On four stolen restaurant benches and a frat-made table in the kitchen sat a few brothers smoking weed and cigarettes while telling the story of Johnny 2x4 (I hope some day they allow me to ghost write a book for them). Handle in hand, I passed it around and everyone took a swig. This was always the peace of the night before the insanity. There was tension in the air as soon as the first group arrived to the party. It's strange how in college you can spend hours doing absolutely nothing and it's still the most fun you can have.

Hours droned by and slowly the sexiest party of the year started to bloom. Low cut bikinis and high cut swim trunks cycled in the door. In droves, short shorts with tiny neon strings popping over the top forced the mind into the gutter and curb stomped it until it stayed down. Bikinis, strappy once pieces, and even the occasional feminist in underwear spouting, "It's the same thing as a bikini, why is there a difference?" filled the rooms. Sexuality was on display, but so was drunken behavior, almost immediately. I felt all of this happening the floor below me, waiting for the girls who were friends with the frat to join us in the kitchen.

As much as I wanted to stay when they arrived, it was my time to book it downstairs with the rest of the civilians. KEK is famous for a lot of things, but my favorite in the world was none other than the famous OIP. It was how real men started their parties; it was more than a beer bong. It was Excalibur. Upon mentioning it at the bar, the ritualistic removing of the sword from the stone happened. They waved it in front of you. The OIP was a foot and a half of PVC pipe topping what can only be described as the nozzle to a high-pressure fire hose. You didn't drink the OIP, you survived it. A full pitcher was dumped into the PVC tubing, the gravity from the liquid swirling, and it blasted itself into you. The most difficult thing about the OIP was its weight. The metal from the fire hose, which came down to a fine point with a flattened tip, pressed against your teeth. If balanced wrong or not held up properly, the OIP chipped more teeth than a hockey player in the eighties.

I waded through bodies, all shorter than mine, as they stared up and watched the wretched word "OIP" come out of my mouth. As soon as it was said, everyone chanted it. OIP, OIP, OIP, OIP. The house shook as the Red Sea of scantily clad underclassmen let me through. The bartender was a dark haired Italian whose last name sounded like a frozen cake brand. His weasely smile widened as he chanted OIP and stood on the bar filling the monster. His body was that of an average person but he always had the shoulders of a fatty. He held the OIP and filled it as I placed myself under it. The beer forced itself directly into my esophagus, seeming to bypass the mouth entirely and go directly down the throat as everyone in the house yelled. A full minute of chugging it took, but, after thirty seconds dizziness set in and it was torture. My stomach expanded and eyes watered as the rest of the beer forced itself down. After finishing it, the OIP was removed and everyone screamed and cheered then immediately stopped caring. Then the next person stepped up and the ritual began again.

A pitcher's worth of undigested beer loafed and swished in my belly, adding a weight and gravity to maneuvering through a packed and half-naked crowd. The bar always got stifling hot but the exit to the backyard blasted a refreshing breeze through the house. KEK's backyard was a wonderland of danger, an oasis in Newark. The left side was walled off in brick from the warehouse and the four stories of their frat house blocked the noise from echoing into the street. On the right, behind sound-dampening ratty bushes, was the ramshackle backyard to the ramshackle house next door. The far back was always dark and I never saw what was behind it. I stepped down into my Shangri La. To the right there was a random drop into a BBQ area and a retaining wall where college kids mingled looking up and smoking cigarettes.

As per the usual, I fell directly off the retaining wall and slammed into the paving stones under it. A multitude of hands groped at different parts of my body raising me back to my feet and a few people even asked if I was okay. I thanked most of those who helped me back up, hand shakes and hugs for all. There was pressure in my back and I spun to react only to take a step back at who was smiling at me. "Where's my hug?" She was absolutely adorable. The mixture of brunette and blonde hair curling just below her ears wasn't perfectly manicured like the other women at the party. She was naturally adorable, two cigarettes behind each ear and piercing eyes that made my knees shake with nerves. I've always had a thing for girls with cheekbones and butt dimples and she fit the type. Her defined features and slightly upturned nose left her just imperfect enough to care about. The best part about her was the perky B-Cup that forced itself upon me while I was still in my own head checking her out. She hugged me, slightly gyrating as she did it, clearly trying to mess with my head. At this point in my life, I was getting self-esteem but my motto was still, "More than a B, she's not interested in me." So finding a perfectly adorable girl who was perky and made a move on me first was like God coming down from the heavens to give me a hand job.

"You're gonna have to help me up, I just fell again." Her eyes met mine and we held them there for a minute.

"Hey. I thought we were gonna kiss if I gave you cigarettes." A random dude cut in to completely ruin my momentum. She broke our stare and turned around to give a TKE shirt the finger.

She apologized to me, "This guy just keeps giving me cigarettes thinking I'm going to make out with him." She pulled a pack out of her pocket and showed me.

"Hey, I thought we were gonna make out if I gave you cigarettes." This time he was holding four cigarettes toward the sky, perched between his thumb and four fingers.

I reached over her and took one from him, then lit the remaining three on fire still in his hand. Brushing her off to the side, I lit my own off the flaming bunch. "Hey, buddy, I think you should quit while you're ahead."

"My name is Leah."

"Nice to meet you, Leah. You know, it's so weird, I was planning on wearing the same bikini but decided against it."

"Hey I thought you were going to give me a kiss if I gave you cigarettes." TKE was relentless.

"How about I give you a kiss for a cigarette?" I licked my lips and pouted them at him.

"I gave her a pack of cigarettes."

"Are we in prison? I gave her the greatest gift of all, laughter." I hated myself again after saying it.

A pack of cigarettes flew from behind my shoulder and hit the douche in his face. He bent down to get them then walked away.

"You're stupid and it's cute." She put her arms around my neck, got on her tippy toes, and kissed me—a sweet tiny little peck on the lips. Her head pulled away and she opened her eyes and her face gleamed. When her heels touched the ground again, she put her hands over her lips and kept looking up at me. I finally noticed a pink string from a pair of bikini bottoms popping out from her super short cut-offs. I pulled two cigarettes out of my pack and lit them both.

"You both are fucking weird for each other," the voice came from behind Leah. "You fell downstairs, almost got in a fight because Leah my slut-bag friend was gonna kiss a guy for cigarettes, she kissed you, and the entire time you were saying by far the cheapest things I've ever heard. It all ends with you handing her a cigarette after she kissed you. You're all insane." The infamous cock block came in the form of her roommate, Sam. The unlikeliest of candidates for a block, Sam wasn't bad herself. Button nosed and hourglass framed, the only thing she lacked compared to Leah was perfect hair and two inches. Sam was darker skinned, darker eyed, but redder lipped. "Leah, you could have had thirty cigarettes instead of one."

"Now, you'll have two beers though." I kissed both their hands like an idiot and excused myself to the bar.

Wading back through the ocean of people who hadn't been outside, the bar room smelled like the aftermath of a locker-room orgy. The top layer of sand was becoming a slurry from spilled beer and spit. It sank between the toes and in the spaces between the sandals and feet. At the bar, fat-shouldered Nick Carvel was serving beer like some frantic coked up monkey, arms swinging as beer was served at a speed that would shame professionals. While waiting I was chatting with another KEK brother, who's hard to describe as anything but average. His hair was cut short in accordance with fashion trends in the late nineties. His skin was a strange olive tone that if you looked at twice you'd assume he was paler than he was. Chris Boring was always a source of silliness without mayhem. His mouth hung slightly open with a wide grin on an overly trustworthy face. Attempting to speak was difficult with the overwhelming sounds of beach music mixed with punk rock.

"Did you hear that?" I asked him.

"I can't hear anything." His voice was monotone.

"There it is again."

"I can't hear anything." He became repetitive.

"How do you not hear that noise?"

"I can't hear anything." The same boring answer from Chris Boring.

"Why did your parents put you in that special school?" I started fucking with him.

"I can't hear anything."

"Why do you talk with a funny voice? You seriously don't hear this noise?"

"I can't hear anything," he paused. "I don't know if you've noticed but some dude is flicking your head."

"Oh, that explains it."

"I can't hear anything; someone is flicking your head."

My fingers dug into my hand and I clenched as tight as my bones allowed. My nose flared and I spun around just in time for an index finger to land right between my eyebrows. "Are you serious? Is this a fucking joke?" Again a finger hit between my eyebrows and I saw a TKE shirt in front of me, but instead of a face there was a target. I lurched back to telegraph a right-handed punch, so a quick left'd surprise him. When my arms should have been moving forward they weren't.

"Fight outside," Chris Booooring had control of my arm and let it go. "Don't be stupid here, be stupid outside." Like a child I explained to the TKE we'd have to fight outside. He walked in front of me while I stayed back doing my best not to spill the three beers I refused to leave behind. I precariously held them over everyone's heads repeating, "I'm sorry," as I drenched half-dressed men and women grinding like animals against each other's body parts. Seeing me having a problem, target TKE held the door open for me so I could put my beers down on a bench.

"All right, fucker," I said, then instantaneously the desire to fight was gone. Playing out in front of us was an eighties action movie. A rail crackled and splintered as a KEK brother with fiery red hair tackled someone off the porch and broke the balcony. There was yelling, a crash, and more splinters. Three other brothers were smashing at someone who was too old to come to a frat party and too high to feel how badly they were getting their ass kicked.

"We gotta find somewhere else to fight." TKE laughed. We sat staring into the beatings that were happening on the street and toasted with the beer that was previously for Leah and Sam. Two guys and five women in head-to-toe Hollister walked through the fighting and stepped up onto the porch. "Five a head for the guys, ladies, I'm too preoccupied to get you laid." They placed ten bucks in my hand and went inside. The red-headed frat brother got back up from the fall, "Hey, Bread." I tossed him the ten bucks. He thanked me then barreled head first toward the guy who was holding his three brothers off with the power of crack.

"Makes you realize win, lose, or draw fighting looks hilarious when no one knows what they're doing." TKE and I tapped beers.

"I guess we're not fighting?" he questioned me.

"I guess we could just spit on each other?"

"What?" TKE looked confused.

"Yeah . . . that'd be weird right?"

He leaned in, not to kiss me, but to stare at me and wonder how strange I actually was. He rotated the door handle and insisted I go in first. In moments the crowds changed at KEK, it was constantly abuzz with people aimlessly wandering to see who was upstairs or downstairs or even who's up next on the pong table. The bar and pong tables were always where the most people crowded, while those looking to talk to strangers got drunk in the kitchen or outside in constant rotation. I had lost Leah and Sam to the natural ebb and flow of a party, so I went searching for Gobe Itchka to tell him about the fight that went on outside.

Up the stairs to the kitchen, I stared over the sea of heads, boobs, and butts. Gobe was cooking Ramen, in his own little world. He added soy and hot sauce to the broth as I apologized for accidentally groping everyone on my way over to him. Being awkward and tall meant there wasn't a genital in sight that I didn't accidentally brush against with some part of my body. "Sorry I didn't mean to touch your balls . . . Excuse me, your tits are in my way . . . Sorry about touching your butt, bro . . . Is that Man-mel toe?"

After I successfully molested half the kitchen crowd, Gobe was now in front of me finishing his Ramen. With a laser focus he was creating food more so than cooking it. "Dude, this is a sex crowd, it's a crowd made for sex. You could accidentally be inside someone it's so cramped with so little clothing." Steam rose from the bowl as the Ramen slid in from the pot. "I already got two girls pregnant, are you happy now?" Gobe purposely tried to drive me insane with back handed responses. A forceful scowl, my lips crept up and brow furrowed. It's annoying when someone is smarter than you to the point where their sarcasm is too heavy. "Besides, that guy doesn't like The Cat Empire." He pointed at a stranger and made the accusation so I'd leave him alone.

The Cat Empire is an Australian band that was the sound track to college. I had discovered them off LimeWire, in a post-Napster time when figuring out how to not pay for something took forever. Not only are they an amazing band, none of them died on an island where 87 percent of the animals are poisonous and the ozone gave up on them because they like being outside too much. I think anyone who moves from Australia to another country should be awarded a medal for figuring out their home country is a floating death trap. The Cat Empire was the up-tempo Spanish and ska mixture that made every day seem sunny and every beer taste cooler. Gobe nodded to a kid sitting on a stolen bench by himself. "Hey, you don't like The Cat Empire?" he cocked his head. He rolled his eyes and pointed to himself. "Heard them, don't do anything for me."

"What does that even mean, they don't do anything for you? What does something for you?"

"The Moody Blues," Stranger told me.

"Look, you probably love jam bands too. The only people who music like that 'does something for' are assholes who take drugs too seriously in an annoying way, or people who put out an album with two different bands in high school. Everyone loves The Moody Blues but only jerks rub it in." Gobe laughed at my rage towards a stranger.

"No, The Moody Blues is way more talented than The Cat Empire."

"This is an insane comparison. You probably think Jim Morrison was a god too?"

"Of course he is!" stranger the his hands in the air, to show he really did care.

"He was also kind of an asshole. Can we all admit this? Yeah, he put out great tunes but was it worth him always being a dick? If a talented person stops acting entitled do we even consider them talented? The Cat Empire makes people enjoy life, and they're not assholes. This is stupid." I kept getting more upset and Gobe kept enjoying me being a dick.

"Are you saying The Cat Empire is better than The Doors or The Moody Blues?" Strange dude proposed this question while intently staring at me.

"I'm saying you're a dickhead making a dickhead argument. Just like something for liking it."

"No one knows who they are, you're a hipster." He sighed after telling me.

"Put The Cat Empire on now and everyone will dance and have a fucking awesome butthole time. We're all gonna put babies in each other."

"But, what I like is time—"

"Nope, I give up, this is stupid. I respect your right to be wrong." I started to walk away.

"The Doo—"

"Okay, blah, blah." I yelled back while flipping him off.

Gobe was gone. That muskrat scrambled away somewhere after learning assholes love to argue with assholes. I opened the fridge and took from his twelve pack, and also took someone's left over dumplings. Stumbling past the kitchen, step by arduous step, I made my way to a hallway that housed a stairwell up to a top floor with rooms and a secret window exit onto the warehouse roof, along with Gobe's room. In a stupor I tried to open it but was defeated. Shaking the handle did nothing to open it. After beads of sweat prickled across my hairline and down my lower back, air became a precious commodity in the dingy stairwell I was climbing to get to the roof. Every time someone exhaled I could feel the pressure. I was officially too intoxicated. The steps were more like Dutch ladders—one wrong step and your kneecap was ricocheting off the walls. I crawled up them as others easily stepped down, asking if I was okay. "Fine, fine, just need a cigarette . . . I'm really thirsty, can I get those beers you're holding?"

Passing the last stair on the case, directly to the left was the open window and plywood bridge to the warehouse roof. That roof was a sweet haven of cool air and rooftop drinking. The only obstacle was a four-foot window frame that I had to fit six feet and five inches through after drinking enough beer to make me forget how much beer I'd had. I crumpled like a Honda after someone drank too much sangria at a quinceañera and forced myself through the hole. Fresh, wonderful, awful, terrible Newark air blew across my face. It wasn't great but it was better than what 250 college kids crammed into a house were exhaling. With freshly acquired beers in hand, my neck tilted as I wondered, looking into the night sky. "That's a really nice . . . star . . . one star in Newark." My ankle popped as I sat cross-legged, alone and panting for fresh air, "This fucking ankle, Fucking Delta Kyle." One star splattered and spun into a billion stars as the spins overtook me. With a thud I was on my back and staring at the one star as it spun around in a clouded night sky. "Drunk, drunk, you're drunk," as the only light dashed across the sky and plummeted toward me. A brunette waft of hair entered my view and soon some brunette followed and then a tiny upturned nose stuck out from the ball of hair. "Hi again." I felt a sweet wet taste on my mouth and a tongue pull my lips apart before I knew what was happening.

"Holy shit, I have beer."

"You're still stupid and it's cute." I was shocked to see Leah blocking my view of the single star in the sky. "I'm gonna sit here." She was prettier than I remembered, but I was also drunker than I was when I met her. She curled into my armpit, the pressure from her head on my collarbone was obnoxiously comfortable. "Tell me something about you." Her fingernails danced across my chest as she moved in closer to me and pulled my wrist until my arm wrapped around her for warmth.

I stared up into the universe while she stared at my poker face, trying to discern what I was thinking and feeling while I was quiet. "It's a single star, Newark is shit. North Jersey is shit." She kissed my neck, nibbled at my ear. "It's awful here, I hope I never live here. One star." She kept kissing my neck and running her hands from my collarbones downward. "One fucking star. You know there are millions upon millions of them. Billions and in Newark, New Jersey, you can only see one." She got on top of me, put her hands on my chest, and pressed down with her hips, trying to feel something through layers of clothing. "Leah, we're too drunk, I'm too drunk." Shock ripped her once turned-on face into a crumpled and confused look of slight dismay. "I'm wasted. I could try really hard and fuck you with a half-limp dick and then try to convince you how good it was, or we can just get slightly less drunk and have sex tomorrow."

"What if I don't like you tomorrow?" she pressed her hips down onto my junk.

"If we had sex tonight you definitely wouldn't like me tomorrow, so I'm gonna try to avoid the shame." Her hands went under my chin, and she dragged my head to the side.

"You're kind stupid, kinda smart, and it's cute." We made out again and things gradually progressed. After a few minutes of dry humping on an old warehouse roof, our luck gave out and so did a support beam. My penis still in my pants, she lifted herself up and slammed her hips down onto my pelvis. A shock of joy and of shock riddled my nervous system.

I felt the support from the ceiling start to give under us. A splintering noise shot across the warehouse beams, the noise of rustic metallic supports giving way, moaning like a whale in the ocean. It was heard in KEK and across the street. Suddenly I was engulfed by a hole, as Leah looked down and freaked out. I felt like Indian Bones, "Leah, if we fall do not fall on my penis. *Please do not fall on my penis!*" I felt the hole widen, instead of just my pelvis falling in, now my abs were holding Leah and me above a second story fall. "Get off me, you have to get off me. Please oh god, please stop trying to have sex with me. I'm too young to die and I don't want to die banging some stranger in Newark." She looked down at me slightly petrified. "Please. Please don't look at me while we're about to sex-die. Please stop holding eye contact, I don't even know you." Her horrified look got snarled after those words.

Finally the curvaceous cock block, Sam, came dashing along faster than I thought girls of her shape could move. While my ankles dug down into the crumbling tar and asphalt and my fingers grasped for dear life, Sam pulled Leah off of me. I was still half-hard and dangling over an open chasm (it really wasn't as big as I'm making it out to be). "Oh thank you, Sam." I rolled and rolled until my middle was on a solid surface again. "Sam, that hole could have killed me."

"Did you just say she'd give you a disease?" Sam misunderstood.

"No I meant *that* hole could have killed me." I pointed at the hole in the warehouse roof.

"Leah deserves better than being called a hole."

"Yeah, I deserve better than being called a hole." Leah was getting progressively less cute.

"Ladies, I meant that hole, the one that crumpled under us when you got on top of me. I'm offensive but this one time I'm being serious. *That* hole could have killed me."

"Stop calling her a hole." Sam was getting more and more aggressive.

"I literally mean that hole. The huge hole, the one I stopped Leah from falling in."

Sam's hands moved before her mouth did. Her speech was slurred and she walked around like she had left her balance at home for the evening. "You're not a hole, Leah."

"No one is a hole. A hole is a hole you a-holes." I pointed to the hole I had just rolled out off. The tar and asphalt sunk down, the hole in the middle of the depression. It was an almost impossible hole to see at night. Sam didn't believe it. Not only did I almost fall down it while being dry humped, it was clear others would fall into it to.

"Okay, you're not a hole but I don't want to be near this hole at night." Abandoning the potential hook up, I meandered back toward the window hole. "Careful, there is a hole out there," I let passing strangers know. "Safe enough."

Being back inside the house, confronted with sweltering heat and pheromones like predators at an African watering hole, was intoxicating. I weaseled my way through the parade of sculpted torsos, jutting hip bones, thigh gaps, and voices so high pitched you knew they were aiming to marry rich. Not a soul was dancing anymore. The party had shattered to one billion sub-conversations like shards of a mirror. The party was fragmented; being really drunk I didn't realize everyone was talking and trying to get laid. I crept over to the bar and asked for a specific song to play and for a few beers.

"Hello Hello" by none other than The Cat Empire sent shivers through the house as people started mingling and being active again. The song's uplifting and addictive horns made hips move instinctually. A seductive voice controlled the crowd, forcing heads to bop in rhythm to a keyboard accompaniment. This was party music. The slacking party was back to a dull roar. My eyes were drying out, gunk forming at the sides, and a dull headache was starting to thump in the front of my brain.

Finding my way back to the kitchen, awash with the smells and fluids of other partygoers, I decided to retire. The fanfare of sexy bodies was now replaced with binge drinking guts. The spilled beer left most people looking sticker than a public toilet seat. The sexuality on the roof drained from college bodies to college corpses. The bar sand smelled like someone had taken a litter box, filled it with ashtrays, then blended it, and put it between someone's post-workout ass cheeks. The smell climbed the walls and the stairs, forcing its way into the pores of people in the kitchen.

There is no way to make a "What's that smell?" face sexual, so the illusion of the party was dying off late in the evening. My legs ached, my head was painful, and it was time to lay down and enjoy some spins. Gobes's couch was flirting with me and I wanted to be on top of it. Unlike earlier, his door was open but the room was empty. It was a perfect space for a frat-house sleeping situation. To the right was a bright, open window that a homemade bar was in front of and next to it was a stolen coke-vending cooler, filled to the brim with beer. To the right of the doorway was the dusty, fluid stained couch I'd be calling a bed. It was drab, lumpy, and covered in cat hair. The problem with binge drinking is always waking up. It's never just the hangover, it's playing "Where in the world am I?" It didn't matter to me the amount of seed and hops and possibly even bugs were on the couch, if I knew where I was waking up. Falling onto the gray beast, my feet still peeked out at the end and into the doorway. Lying down, the beds of the other men who lived in the room became more obvious. Two loft beds were installed just above the closets an in-room sink below them.

Each bed was curtained off from the rest of the room. This allowed the illusion of privacy instead of the true nature of the environment, they were cocks roosting in the rafters. Sleep was starting to hit, it lulled in, and I felt myself plunge into the depths. Immediately my body was shocked back awake. "I hate it when that happens."

"What?"

Gobe moved the curtain slightly and stuck his head out from behind, grinning ear to ear. I looked up and pulled a half-broken joint out of my swim trunks pocket. He slid the curtain back more, and that's when it was my time to make a "What is that smell" face.

"It smells like oysters and old lunch meat up there."

"Shut up." He pulled the curtain back over the space of his bed.

"I'm smoking this weed to cover up that stink. I don't even want to get high . . . yes I do."

"Shut up."

I dozed back off into sleep for a while. The haze of purple haze and beer was wonderfully dreamy, until a kitten prowled on top of me. Flexing its claws on my chest, the tiny needles forced me awake and to a horrifying sound. The rancorous noise of two human beings beating hipbones together and the stench of unkempt college sex were worse than any nightmare I could have. The screaming and squealing from whomever Gobe had lured into his most likely unwashed bed was a mixture of joy and terrible, terrible animal slaughter. Every few moments I'd hear a low mutter of something from him, but minute by minute more of her cacophony of sexual sadness was leaving an imprint in my brain. I can never forget how the sound of them having sex resembled punching cottage cheese while slamming two freshly roasted hams together.

I laid paralyzed, one part of me rooting for him, the other part hoping he survived what sounded like the murdering of farm animals. After every few thrusts the curtain would waft down the smells of what was occurring. It was a nightmare. The image of Gobe masturbating with two thawed cod filets, while covered in fermenting fruit juice was burned into my retinas. I could hold back vomit pretty skillfully by this point, but my training was being tested. The odor from his bed was so unnatural that in the 1800s he would have been burned at the stake for producing it. Gobe had to have been fucking a garbage man's glove—sorry, sanitation engineer. I imagine most of my readers have dads who do that for a living.

It was a smell that took over the room like a giant waking up. It filled every crack and crevasse and I wondered what cracks and crevasses were being filled to create the smell. I closed my eyes hard and tried to sleep while my ears and nose were being molested. It was nerve-racking, I was stoned and feeling like I was being nerve gassed. The smell got sour and finally the sound of two people drowning in maple syrup came from behind the curtain. Everything hushed.

"Is the sacrifice over?" I blurted out.

"It had been a while, I needed that." Gobe looked refreshed.

"Hey lady who had sex with my friend, is he as terrible as I imagined?"

Her voice was sweet and cute, when she wasn't making the noises of a horse getting impregnated. "He's wonderful."

"You're not just saying that to make yourself feel better for sleeping with him are you? I know that's how I felt after sleeping with him." I patted myself on the back for this comment.

"You're not very funny." She groaned.

"Neither is all the hepatitis floating around the room now." The curtains swayed momentarily.

"You know I'm still here, Bread, right?" Until he chimed in I had honestly forgotten Gobe was in the room for a moment because I was proud of how funny I was.

"You're my friend, of course I know you're here; I'd never say this behind your back . . . Hey, did you guys remember to Purell?"

When they stopped responding, I stopped joking. A quick turn facing the wall and a pillow over my head, provided a break from the utter disgust that I was forced to hear. The condensation buildup in my pillow face fortress stunk of beer and cigarettes; not surprisingly, it was a much more welcome smell. When I woke up she was gone and Gobe bought breakfast. We sat hung over recollecting the night before. I hadn't the nerve to ask whether he had grabbed a stray animal off the street.

Sometimes it's better to have secrets between friends. We don't need to know everything about each other. There is a time and a place for a friend and listening to him have sex isn't one of them.

Getting Rainbow Drunk

When I was in college my drinking had gotten so bad all I wanted to do was entice members of the opposite sex to come do it with me. Not to have sex or take advantage of them; just to have someone around who wanted to talk about something besides pussy and video games. This is when I started to make mixed drinks and learn how to bartend in my own apartment. I'd go out and buy fruit and mixers, make drinks, and sit in my room sad and alone for hours. That's also when I learned the two secret recipes that brought me to the next level of drinking. The kind of drinking that other people have no other choice but to join in on because it's so colorful and weird it's like eating Niki Minaj's butthole.

Skittles Vodka: This is easy as shit and anyone who can't figure this out on their own is an idiot. Separate a bag of Skittles by color. Do *not* make racist jokes about separating Skittles. It's stupid and every single person does it. Now get some cheap containers from the dollar store, Mason jars are best, or even those beer bottles with the weird air-proof cap. Fill it about a quarter of the way with vodka then kill yourself. Once you've been reincarnated as a real man with drinking problems, put all the Skittles of each color in the Mason jars then fill that shit with Everclear. How my liver ever withstood this beating I'll never know. In a standard-sized Mason jar you only have to fill the bottom with the Skittles, don't use all of them. Now, the secret I always used: Make sure the lid is on tight and put all your filled Mason jars in the dishwasher. Stop it every now and again to shake them, but something about the hot water bath melts the Skittles super quick. When they come out of the dishwasher, wipe them off and throw them in the fridge overnight. The next day, strain the excess stuff that floats out with a strainer. Anyone who says to use a coffee filter has never cleaned up a counter top filled with sweet Skittle Everclear. Coffee filters suck at straining.

If you don't have a dishwasher, you're not shit out of luck. Just throw the Skittles in and leave them in a cabinet for two or three days, shaking them every few hours. It tastes the same but it's not as cool as putting it in a dishwasher. Also don't put soap in the dishwasher when you do this, you twats.

Vodka Gummy Bears: Sometimes, after a night of screaming at a show or a party, your throat gets sore and dumping vodka down it feels like swallowing fiberglass. Sometimes you get mono and you can't drink or move . . . or stay awake for more than three hours at a time. How are you supposed to drink on those occasions? Mono will force you to detox if you can't figure out how to imbibe booze while you have a massive fever and dehydration. What's a devoted partier supposed to do? Not drinking is not an option. Butt funneling is the funniest pairing of words, besides dick cleavage, but it will kill you if you actually do it. That's where vodka (Everclear) comes into play. Throw a bag of gummies into a plastic container with some Everclear, and put it in the fridge for about eighteen hours. When they come out they've mutated like an X-ray technician from the 1900s. Every single gummy bear will have absorbed about two grams of booze. These little sons of bitches taste just like normal gummy bears so it's important that you eat as many as possible. They say drink responsibly but no one ever says eat responsibly. It's candy that gets you drunk. It will be beloved by the children or drunk white college girls you're trying to lure into your van.

Chapter 11

DARES:

Not the type that keep you off drugs

Dares are Essential

It was one in the eve and the darkness had its chilly and clammy claws in the spines and underbellies of all the would-be scholars of Montclair State University. Corpse paint and Behemoth T-shirts reigned supreme over the guys in polo shirts and normal clothes. 'Twas a slow evening of cheer and merriment, however 'twas getting to the point in the eve when young men tested feats of strength. A man by the name of Metal Steve had wormed his way into the intoxicated crowd wearing a suit of armor. The whiskey had been running deep in everyone's bellies when one man proclaimed, "Hey, Steve, can we try punching you while you wear armor?" We lined up and one warrior after another pounded Steve's armor only to have knuckles cracked and merriment dampened. Then a warrior stepped up to swing, he bashed Steve with the might of Thor and Loki combined, denting the armor. The party went insane and five people gave him shots. Seriously, the story of that night still gets told in the annoying old timey manner I just wrote it.

The whole idea of a dare is obscene. "I dare you," is the same as saying, "I know doing this is so stupid it probably goes against evolution itself but . . . totally do it." We have a special sentence in the English language that's a verbal warning saying, "Don't do this unless I say that special phrase." This fact is what makes dares become legend. It's something that everyone knows is dangerous and stupid, but you're all filled with hormones and freedom from no supervision. You can do whatever you want, you're paying ten grand a semester to be out on your own, that's why any time a dare comes up you have to do it. I know, this is going to get me sued but my editor dared me to put this article in the book.

Ninety percent of the time people wimp out on dares. They make a big stink about how they're totally going to do it then they don't and no one is surprised. It's like a peacock shaking its feathers at you. It's making a big show out of nothing to hide its lack of aggressiveness. The most badass people on earth are the ones who don't even say yes or no, they just do whatever the dare was. What's even better about that is if you do it immediately, without thinking, no one has time to film it. A legendary dare is never filmed, it's told as a story that mutates and changes over time as people add and remove. What starts off as the story about that time you jumped off a roof into a bush turns into that time you jumped off a roof and landed perfectly as the story evolves. Filming a dare ruins the legend when a really good dare is a story that will be told every single time you're all together.

Dares bring people together, even those who aren't a part of it. Everyone wants to feel like they were a part of something amazing. So when you pull off a ridiculous dare, everyone will write themselves into the story somehow. They'll emphasize how they pushed you to do it or brag about how insane it was to watch. Doing a dare brings a group of friend closer, like going to a strip club or committing a double homicide. The people who will stick together are the people who have dirt on each other. A dare that is humiliating to the person who did it and those who watched it guarantees that a group will stay together for the entire four years of college. If they don't stay together, everyone will be too afraid that the dare story will get around in a non-flattering manner.

Most importantly dares are important because they are fucking silly. Dares show you don't take life too seriously and you're not afraid of a little embarrassment. We're getting to a stage in life when everyone is so worried about being inclusive and exclusive, or offending and defending, and worrying about what we have to say that a simple little dare is a self-hating and dangerous way to make everyone loosen up a little bit.

Chris's Portuguese Flamer

Average days can become days of college legend if you're willing to be stupid enough. That's the most important thing when attending a school of higher education: to act like the most uneducated person possible. If you want stories to be told about you for the rest of people's lives (or to write a terrible book) you have to always be willing to do something so heinously stupid it's impossible to forget.

A completely forgettable day dragged by. Hours passed slowly. Chores were getting accomplished and The Girl I was Dating tagged along, adding her charming constant sense of anxiety. It was a lackadaisical day without paying attention to classes because doing laundry was more important than going to statistics ever. I was tossing someone's wet laundry that had been sitting in a dryer whose timer had run out into the hall (college dryers usually need more than one cycle). The first load was mid-air when Chris walked across the path. "What da fuq." He jumped back, crinkling plastic bags rustling on either side of him. "Oh, hi." Stepping over the damn sloppy mess he giggled. "My mom cooked." Chris skipped over a shirt in front of him and let out, "You're a faaaggggooooott." Laundry took second place to a home-cooked meal. Assorted dried clothes were tossed in bags and the wet stuff thrown in on the longest timer at the lowest heat, allowing the most time to go by without my stuff ending up in a pile in the hallway.

The Girl I was Dating and I sprinted back through the hallway, pinching and slapping each other along the way. Giggling like children and stealing kisses, when we entered 1A neither one of us acted like we we're doing anything romantic. "My mom made a bunch of Portuguese steak, and a bunch of other garbage." Chris showed us what she had made.

"I'm going to make mouth love to your mom's meat." I tried to stick my hands into one of the bags.

"You're gonna make mouth love to my meat first."

The plastic crinkled as he pulled tray after tray of food from left-over grocery bags. "I love your mom, is she single?" I leaned on the counter and The Girl I was Dating pinched my butt.

"She makes food really spicy, she gave me this pepper." He threw a strange pepper into my hands. It was like goose down from an expensive comforter, so light I shook it to see if it was real. The noise of tiny little seeds bouncing back and forth inside dried and jerky-like skin, I noticed the darkened reds blended with fiery speckles. There was an inherent feeling of danger surrounding the light little pepper. I slung it back at Chris as hard as I could.

"She puts a tiny bit of this in food and it's super spicy."

"Tell me more things I have no interest in." I sighed and was bored.

The Girl I was Dating pinched my butt again. "Don't tell him to eat it because he will. He drinks hot sauce because he swears it makes his ulcer better."

"So how often does he shit a pool of blood?" Chris laughed.

"He has irritable bowels so I assume it he shits a scab."

"Lets keep talking about me like I'm not in the room. That's everyone's favorite game," I interrupted.

"Is it every day he shits blood?" Chris asked.

"I'm not sure, but he sits in there for hours," The Girl I was Dating informed him.

"Is it only after he drinks hot sauce, or is he just hiding from you?"

After Chris's last line, her eyes met mine with a questioning stare that made me uncomfortable. I wanted to jam bullets down his throat and throw him in a fire. I wanted to suffocate him with fiberglass. She held eye contact questioningly. Instead of answering the question, I pushed one of the containers of food off the counter.

"Aww, man," Beer Clause chimed in from the corner where he was sitting. We hadn't even noticed him.

"Are you even doing anything or just sitting there?" There wasn't a book or TV on anywhere around him. This was a time before smartphones.

"You should learn to mind your own business," Chris retorted. "You're all being faggots. Bread, eat this pepper. I dare you to eat this pepper." The speckled and seedy veggie was mid-air before he finished the sentence. It smacked me upside the head and came to a rest on the counter.

The Girl I was Dating just stared. I stared back into her eyes, picked up the pepper, and chomped down on the entire thing. I chewed it, not feeling anything besides a slightly noticeable tingle in my cheeks. "Your mom ain't shit and your food ain't shit." Proudly I showed I had swallowed the entire thing.

"Hmm. I think they're called ghost peppers 'cause you don't feel the burn right away. Then you go to the hospital. I thin—" I interrupted him.

"*Milk.*" The fire started in my mouth and sunk to the pit of my stomach. Blood rushed to my skin and sweat started dripping down my brow. "You dicth. Get me bread and milk!" My tongue was swelling.

"My mom isn't shit, huh?" Chris began dancing around in utter joy. Staggering around the counter and diving into the fridge, I snatched a gallon jug and began dousing my tongue.

"Why is your face all bloated. Is it cause you're a bitch?"

The world got fuzzy and I laid on the cold kitchen floor. I dragged my tongue across a pile of bread I pulled off the counter. "Nofink is making this bettur." I started crying and let out a scream.

"Can you keep it down? I'm pretty busy," Beer Clause sat in the corner doing absolutely nothing.

The Girl I was Dating started laughing and couldn't stop. "What burns worse babe, the pepper or humiliation?" Chris and Beer Clause nodded in approval of her shit talking.

It was only minutes into the ordeal and my body was shuttering in searing awful pain. It was like someone was flaying the skin off my face. I rubbed the bread all over my face while drinking as much milk as possible. "Why did I do hiss? Jesuth isn't real." The skin on my face and hands dried out as pains shot through my nervous system. "No hothpital!" I belted out between chugs of milk.

"No one is taking your idiot ass to the hospital anyway," The Girl I was Dating reprimanded me. She stepped over my corpse to get sangria from the fridge.

The pipes that carried air in and out of my body began to swell. Wheezing set in and I tilted my head back to try and get more air. "Dude, seriously I can't think. Can you go in another room? I'm not going to get anything done," Beer Clause sat still doing nothing.

As soon as my throat started swelling, I chugged milk. Being in college means priding yourself on how much fluid you can consume in as short a time as possible. I hadn't tried to shotgun milk before, so I gave it the old college try. Gallon of milk in one hand and a handful of molested bread in the other, I got my feet under me and leaned over the sink.

My lanky Captain Armstrong body leaned over the kitchen sink. I was completely red, the veins in my face bulged so far out of my skin a heroin addict would have been jealous. More than half the gallon of milk had been demolished and all the bread in the apartment was gone.

"I read on the Internet that booze and vinegar helps," Chris snidely remarked.

"Vinegar ith in the laundry room."

He finished putting all the food away. "I wish I could get it but I *ain't shit*." He wobbled his thighs and butt in a fake humping dance.

Instead of drinking vinegar, I grabbed a bottle of vodka sitting within arm's reach and started chugging that too. "Why aren't any of us stopping this?" The Girl I was Dating asked Beer Clause. Everyone shrugged then started a cacophony of laughing at me.

Finally a sweltering mass of peppers, milk, bread, and vodka had formed into viscous and burning plasma inside my stomach. I wanted to expel it, but I was deathly afraid of it coming out of my nose. Swirling and kneading itself in the depths of my stomach, it was only comparable to a brick fresh out of a kiln. "I've never felth thith bad. Thith was bad. Thith is bad." I darted from the kitchen to my dimly lit bathroom. I heard them all mimicking me from inside the tiled walls.

"Thith is bad," Chris laughed until he couldn't. I heaved and puked everything out in one mass into a dirty college toilet bowl. Immediately, relief washed over my mouth and out of my body. It was like giving throat birth and I vowed I'd never accept another blowjob. As I gasped for air and fell across the toilet, I had to wonder why it didn't feel as terrible anymore.

Then I remembered that the previous night The Girl I was Dating had drunk so much her liver decided to stay at its mother's for a few days to cool off. This amount of drinking led her to admit she was trying to lose weight by drinking apple cider vinegar. After her eighth vodka and girly shit, she dared me to drink the bottle. The flaming goo in my stomach was so hot it could have been Instagram famous. #Fitspo #GymLife #Squats #AnyoneWhoActuallyDoesThisShouldDie.

But, thanks to drinking an entire bottle of apple cider vinegar, the vomiting actually removed some of the heat. One dare had saved me from another dare, because stupid people never die.

As the pain subsided I flushed the pepper puke down the toilet. Exhaling and regretting my decisions, the man in the bathroom mirror looked a mess. My cheeks had swollen to a B-Cup (more than a handful is a waste). Everything I was wearing was drenched in sweat to the point where a starfish could have lived in the tide pool that formed in my extruding hipbones. A splotchy strange mix of crimson and pale Irish covered my face, arms, and hands. It was like the devil himself sat on my face and five starred my entire body.

"I'm an idiot."

"Yeah, we are." The mirror looked back disapprovingly. That age old disappointed face that parents make at their kids was now on my face in the mirror.

"At least we learned something."

"Don't eat random peppers?"

"Don't eat random peppers without a camera around."

"You are an idiot."

I pivoted away from the mirror, then stared down at my bulge. "Oh god am I lucky I didn't piss myself." I held my junk and released the vodka, water, milk mixture that was still held in my bladder. I used my piss to clean the vomit off the sides of the bowl, like any disgusting college student would. Sighing in relief that everything that could be out of my body was at this point, after an hour or so of utter hell, I could breathe and move again.

"Bread's been in the bathroom a while, think he's dead?" The Girl I was Dating slapped Chris on the shoulder.

"I'm going to drink his whiskey anyway," Chris replied. The three loafed in chairs, so lazy their limbs hung at inhuman angles. It was difficult to tell if the chairs were engulfing them or the other way around. Those bums cracked jokes and passed the bottle around. Everyone's hearts stopped suddenly when a sound more piercing than tires squealing before the inevitable noise of crumbling metal and breaking glass—I was crying and screaming in the bathroom. Their spines snapped to attention and they looked at each other questioningly.

"*It's on my dick!*"

Chris showed a little too much smile as joy overcame him. "Peppers have oils you idiot!" Everyone was laughing again.

The bathroom flew open. My hand was stuffed into the zipper of my jeans as I darted around the room screaming. "This is like herpes. This is worse than pink eye. Cut it off and I'll become a lady. I'm a fire crotch. *I'm giving birth and I won't get a tax break!*" I threw myself on the floor in front of everyone while holding my junk.

"You have pepper oil on your hands. Don't hold it." Forever in my mind I still think Beer Clause was just curious to see it. Through an unstoppable laugh, Chris let loose, "I read that running your hands through your hair helps stop the skin burning, so just rub your dick on your hair." It was the only time in my life I regretted not having pubes. I had hours of pain in front of me, but we all have years' worth of memories.

Dares are important; if I hadn't taken the dare from The Girl I was Dating, my throat could have closed. Dares are like Pringles, once you do one you never want to stop . . . Never mind, that's meth. Dares are like Pringles, people judge you if you do too many in front of them. I'm sure that's never stopped guys with "Only God Can Judge Me" tattoos, and those guys are the coolest.

Dares are nothing like Pringles, meth, or idiots—they're an easy way of making a story happen. No one has ever dared someone to do something smart, so saying, "I dare you," is a way of saying, "We're gonna talk about this for a long time." For hours, several different parts of my body were in a massive amount of pain, for the rest of my life when my friends and I get together someone will tell the story of the ghost pepper. Being a little stupid brings to life a story that changes with the years and helps keep friends together. Without someone doing something incredibly stupid, half the great stories of the world might not exist. Don't take dares to show you're brave, take them to ensure you're going to be remembered.

Baby it's Cold Inside

Mama Bauer's (?) dining hall was a special place. The hours were shorter and it was on a mostly empty part of campus where they hid the students with strange majors. Walking there felt like a horror movie; at a certain point along the way the campus grew silent and if there were any students out on that lawn they glared at you as if you were the sun and they were trolls. Once inside, it was a safe haven though. The extra-long journey had a safe end where the food was better, the choices substantial, and the hall much less crowded. It was a sacred place for those who knew about it and the security guards always let you sneak extra food back to your room. Mama Bauer's food and that dining hall were special.

A wad of fettuccine splattered across the wall behind me. One noodle stuck to the wall while the rest crawled down to the floor, leaving a viscous trail of slime on the wall. Frankie's hands flew faster than his mouth in an Italian rage. "Stop ducking, this is fucking Mama Bauer's don't waste it." The irony eluded him. A hamburger skirted through the air, spinning violently like a boomerang after a target. I swung my pool cue, a dark emerald stick with flecks of shiny forrest green that shot up from an ivory-colored base. I had separated the cue so only the stalwart base was being used, the thin well-slicked head of the pole remained in its case. The stick connected with the burger, sending a splatter of hamburger blood across Four Fingas's face and a piece of lettuce stuck to his shoulder. "I said not to get it cooked rare, fuck nuts." A meatball skimmed my cheek as he flung it in anger. Four Fingas left the blood on his face as he threw another handful of fettuccine, this time it hit the stick and splashed all over my clothing. Neither one of us could breathe for a few moments. We were bent over laughing at the stupidity.

We were in the hallway in front of The Governor's room. Frankie stood with a pile of containers at his feet throwing food at me piece by piece, trying to splatter as much as he could on the walls surrounding us. "I almost feel guilty, people in the third world would hate us," I yelled down to the pitcher.

"You're not normal," he responded by throwing as many meatballs as he could while I giggled with glee and covered myself up. Ball after ball exploded off of my body, splashed against the walls, and on the rugs below us. I picked up broken bits and tried to hit him back, knowing I didn't have the talent to get him. Other students avoided us or covered up and ran between us trying to get to the stairwells or back in their rooms.

Stevie Steve wandered out of 1A and out into the hall. He watched us for a few minutes then yelled, "What are you guys doing?" He was met with silence. Four Fingas picked up what was left on the ground and started walking back toward our apartment. I shoved his shoulder as he walked past, making him drop a container.

"What are we doing?" Both of us hung our heads lower than normal, walking in silence with Stevie Steve riding our coattails. Once back in the apartment, we put the food back in the fridge and cracked open beers. Everyone sat around the counter as if it was our war table. Max actually took time out of his busy schedule of being white and pretentious to join us as we drank. "Let's do something." All our eyes glazed over as we stared at the same empty spot on the counter.

"That guy who beat us in Beer Pong last week isn't home tonight." We stopped staring at the war table, our full attention on Stevie Steve. "His roommates left their door open. I stopped in earlier and no one was inside." All of us perked up, the chance to be mischievous lingered in the air with a palpable scent. We were drunk from excitement, beer, and mischief. The guy he was referring to was a chunky goateed weirdo who hated me. He was the type of guy who hated human beings having more fun than him. A fat repressed asshole, who constantly called me out for being the loudest in the room or the one trying to have the most fun. Worst of all, he was really good at Beer Pong.

Stevie took a few steps from the group, and stared into the courtyard. A heavy, compact snow blanketed the ground. It was too wet to glisten but, in the night reflections, haunting shades of blues and greys were adrift as the lights flickered. "Let's just fill his room with snow." No one moved. "The hallway outside his room. It's short and there is a ton of snow. We'll leave him a shovel."

I shook my head. "None of us has a shovel." Four Fingas booted the garbage can, sending the trash flying. He tore the bag from the inside and threw it on the floor.

"We got shovels, son."

"We also have a mess 'cause you kicked over the garbage like a jackass." No one paid any attention to Max. While Frankie wielded our trashcan, the rest of us found our shovels in common areas.

"We're really going to do this?" I was seething in excitement and reluctance.

"I dare you."

That's all that needed to be said. We marched outside and down two flights of snowy stairs. There were piles of snow littered outside the apartment complex that we were about to avalanche all over. We entered Count Basie hall, a clone of our apartment building, the only differing thing about the two buildings was "Staci Basie."

She was the type of girl who signed her name with a heart over the I to make up for the fact her heart was cold and lonely. She was the girl who got completely lost in college. She drank and would snort cocaine off of anything. She was an unfortunate looking girl who compensated for it using anything and everything this modern world had so she never looked like herself. Stacie applied her make up with a cannon and car sponge. Like a true patriot, she believed in quantity over quality. Her hair was dyed so often it looked ready to fall out of her head. The only thing scarier than her caked eyelashes and tri-colored lips was her medicated thin body. It was like someone took a wire frame and wrapped some skin around it, not just because her skin always appeared too tight, but both of them were hollow inside. She covered her body in designer everything. I just imagined her mother as the type to force her to wear makeup if she was running out to buy a pack of smokes. "Honey, are you gonna leave the house like that? I'm not saying its bad . . . just I'd never do something like that."

The scariest part about Staci was how aggressively sexual she was, but not in a good way. There are girls in college who learn they love sex, and those girls should be applauded and admired. If you meet one of them, high five her and don't wash your hand. Everyone wants to get laid, and those who do it with the best intentions and don't hurt others are admirable. Staci was aggressively sexual due to a complete lack of self-confidence and a need for empty validation. Her version of sexy was trying to make, "Fuck me," eyes to cover up her sad, desperately scared normal eyes. I could tell she was the type to do something because that's what she thought others wanted, instead of doing it because she loved it. It was easy to hate Staci Basie, as most people did, it was even easier to feel a sinking despair for whatever made her like this.

The doors to Basie hall opened up as our recycling bins flew through the air to land in snow banks so we could scope the scene in Stevie's friend's room without shovels. The group tried to hurry past what we thought was an empty common area, when the drab, fake voice of Stacie Basie came out of it. She stumbled in her heels and slurred her speech. My phone read 3:35 p.m.

"Hey, Bread. Jenny said you have a nice dick. Do you want to go to my room?" Stacy slurred.

"Oh Jenny? I actually used Max's dick on her." I pointed to Max to get the attention away from me.

"Max, do you have a 401K already?" Stacy moved towards Max.

We all stifled a laugh. It's difficult to give someone the validation of laughter when you dislike them as a person, Four Fingas was the only person laughing. Max stared at her with contempt until she stopped holding eye contact with him. "Stacie, we're a little busy, baby cakes." Often when he spoke to women, Stevie Steve had the diction of Vince Vaughn in *Swingers*. "Why don't you go up to your room and lay down for a bit? Frankie and Bread will come up and both fuck you. They'll bring a little cocaine." He put his arm around her shoulders and began walking her over to the elevator. "How's that sound? A little cocaine and a few familiar dicks?"

"Steve, you're like. Cute. So cute."

"I know, but you get in this elevator and you take a little lay down and we'll be right up."

He walked back through us to take the lead. "Steve, are you the whore whisperer?" Recently he transferred from getting a degree in Physical Education to trying to get an English degree, so the pun wasn't lost on everyone of the group.

He brought us to his friend's room, a dingy, smaller, less well put together version of 1A. Obnoxiously placed in the middle of their common area was a Beer Pong table that disrupted the view between the couch and TV. Sitting and watching it was impossible, and the entire room showed a lack of basic upkeep. Littered about were empty beer bottles that had led to an infestation of fruit flies throughout the room. A small swarm lingered about your head as you walked into the common area, drawing your attention away from the corners of the place where food, crumbs, and various bits of filth had collected from four men living together and not cleaning a single time. The place was filthy, the stench of spilled beer rose from the carpets twisting your mouth and nose into a crude face. The kitchen was covered in the forgotten grease of late night burgers. Nothing about the place invited people in. No one would want to steal a thing from this place, out of fear it would be too sticky. How dare this asshole say my personality sucked and I was obnoxious when he didn't have the common decency to keep his place clean enough that others would feel comfortable?

Seeing and smelling the rancid pit he called a room was infuriating while I was sober. Clearly when inebriated I had bad taste in company and setting because this place had appeared good enough. Directly to the left of the entrance was the disregarded beer bottle graveyard filled with flies . . . to the right was a short hallway with a few rooms jutting off and a single bathroom.

"That's what we're filling." The hallway had a low ceiling that my head almost touched, it couldn't have been much longer than ten feet either.

"His room is the last one on the left so we don't need to bury the entire hallway."

"We don't need to bury any of the hallway, we don't need to be here . . . But, killah, we're here so we're gonna bury this hallway. Brenjamin Watson and I will just keep doing it after you leave."

"You know me too well, Fingas."

Have you ever had an idea that you go into thinking it will turn out miserable that turned out twice as miserable as you imagined? This was worse. This was worse than an idea that lands a friend in the hospital. Everyone started off with the fervor of soon-to-be legends but midway through they realized it took hard work to be legendary. The snow started melting in the hallways before we even got it into his friend's apartment. We had to repack the slush into our snow wall. This meant two people had to run outside with the recycling bins and bring them all the way back to the room, while two people stood inside packing snow and getting completely drenched. Four Fingas and I made a contest out of bringing back the heaviest buckets, so we were exhausted after the first doorway was sealed. In a moment of compromise we decided not to fault ourselves for only filling it four or five feet high.

Four Fingas was rubbing his back and cracking his neck while I tried to find a beer in their fridge. Stevie Steve and Max took over bringing the snow in, while I unloaded and packed it because Four Fingas was obsessed with figuring out how to lower the heat. When he finally turned it off, the melted snow became an icy mess. Everyone stopped for a moment, faces glimmering with joy at the extra mess being created. After three hours of hauling snow we had barely covered five feet of the hallway. Backs ached and spines cracked, torsos moved in opposing directions to hips, lungs were filled as everyone realized how badly this was going to suck. The Egyptians had so many legends because they had manpower. Just a moment's reprieve and we all got back to our duties. Frankie and I reassumed the gathering job while Stevie Steve and Max started packing again. It was a war of wills, another half hour and we were spent. Frankie and I walked back out of the sliding glass doors, sopping wet and holding recycling cans. There was a body waiting in the middle of the sidewalk.

"Umm, Frankie, Bread." Frankie giggled at GayRA. (This was pre him being my RA but he was still *an* RA.) "Frankie and Bread. What are you doing?" Frankie kept walking forward, directly in his way. We didn't exchange words. We didn't stop to get questioned. I threw my recycling can in a freshly disturbed snow pile that was missing a chunk from our endeavor. GayRA stood in our path and we just walked straight past him making no eye contact.

It felt like I was going to walk through him, but he stepped left and stood his ground shouting questions at us. It was impossible to contain how badass I felt doing this. Frankie and I trounced back up the stairs, not acknowledging any of the smokers saying hello, and walked directly into our room.

"Let's see what happens to Stevie Steve and Max." Frankie and I soon forgot what we were waiting around for and went out drinking. Later that night we all ran into one another. The other half of 1A was complaining and whining like little children.

"Y'all just gave up and left us." Steve bitched.

"Yeah, we thought you just left." Max kept the bitching going.

"Shut up, Max." I tried to stop the complaining.

"Na, killah, we almost got caught," Frankie let them know.

"Frankie, baby, we sat around waiting for you inside." Stevie said.

"You shut up, Bread."Max whined.

"Max, I'll punch your muffin." I threatened.

"Bread, don't say muffin." Frankie said.

"Bread, don't say muffin." Steve said.

"Bread, don't say muffin." Max said.

"All right." I gave in.

"GayRA was out there and knew we were doing something." Frankie let everyone know.

"What if he came in and found us?" Stevie said.

"Bread, when was the last time you showered?" Max asked.

"I'll spit in your mouth if you speak to me that way." I hocked a loogie so he knew I was serious.

"How would he know it was that room?" Frankie asked Steve.

"So you didn't leave us?" Stevie asked Frankie back.

"You know what, what's wrong with you?" Max disregarded Frankie and Steve to continue being obnoxious towards me.

"I'll finger your cousin, I don't give a fuck." I found it my personal responsibility to piss Max off more.

"Naaa, Stevie, we didn't leave you." Frankie disregarded Max and I to keep talking to Stevie.

"We're good." Stevie said to everyone.

"No, you're good. He just said he'd finger my cousin, we're not good." Max continued being a bitch.

"We're good."

"We're good."

Come Sunday Stevie had still not received a text from his friend about a hallway of snow. There was no Facebook post. Four Fingas was itching to find out about the freak out, so he confronted Stevie Steve as he left his room holding a basketball. Four Fingas snatched the basketball and guarded it. "What happened to our snow wall?" Frankie passed to me, and I lobbed it as hard as I could at Max who was sitting on the couch behind everyone. It bounced off the wall beside him and, as Max froze in shock, Frankie rebounded off the wall.

"Oh, no one came back the past few days to clean it up. His entire room was wet but that's not a big deal for him. He had nothing on the floor. His roommate's computer got fried but he had insurance." The disappointment was staggering, essentially all we did was clean someone's floor.

Sometimes, there isn't a great end to a dare. Sometimes it's just a boring arduous task that teaches you commitment. It teaches you to have the will to win. Not all dares have an insane ending with ridiculous consequences that become a story. Sometimes you just kind of feel like a loser and take your stubbornness as a little win for yourself.

Other times a guy named Mike eats Scott Glazaar's shit out of a toilet bowl on a dare, then he gives the money back because he's so drunk. Sometimes, because of a dare, a night takes a turn for the weird and amazing and everyone remembers the story except you, because you spent two years in community college and missed the real fun. The biggest regret of my life was not being there for the night Scotty dared Mike to eat his shit. I can't devote more time to this story because I wasn't there. We know what you did Mike, and now it's in print. I digress.

Occasionally dares aren't life-changing stories. Sometimes they teach you that making a commitment to do something is binding, and that's something that will carry you post grad. Taking dares makes you legendary because of the consequences, but also because you were the only one with the devotion to your word.

Chapter 12

ACADEMICS

I'm going to be completely honest with my readers here. My publisher said I had to include a chapter about academics. I absolutely did not want to add a chapter about school in my book about school. So this chapter is meant to appease what I can only imagine are those big, balding corporate gurus smoking cigars. They're the reason why I have almost completely left the business world to be a humorist.

Self-Education, not Masturbation

There are too many flaws in the education system itself. College was a game I thought I had to play to get ahead in the world. I've been out of school for a while and now I've learned a simple rule: you can lie about where you went and if you graduated. No one really cares where you went to school, they care about the job you do . . . eh, they don't even really care about the job you do either. College is a massive waste of time and energy and it's going to be a while until society accepts that the entire foundation of our society is fucked up. Right now, we're sitting in Plato's cave waiting for someone to unchain us so we can venture outside and realize there are other ways to educate ourselves.

Self-education is more important than anything else in the world. We live in the Internet Age, a world where information is ready and waiting to be absorbed, but we are constantly bombarded by distractions. Have some discipline. Spend three hours on PornHub instead of six. Make sure amidst all the drinking, debauchery, and confusion you spend some time learning about something you really like. For some reason the idea of personal responsibility is lost on us as a society, but it is something we should all focus on. It's no one else's job to educate you, no matter what their job title says.

Get a hobby. There is a lot of down time in school—well, there is when you don't go to class and never get better than a C. Having a hobby is important because the chances of finding a fulfilling job that makes you want to get up in the morning are slim to none. Too many people appear to be playing a real life version of The Sims and it's scary and sad. Instead, find something you can't imagine your life without and get really, really good at it. Do it every moment that you can, spend every free dollar you have on it. This is going to be the creative thing that keeps you going every day. Read articles and forums on the Internet and books and get so good at something you'll be undeniable at it. I don't think any child grows up thinking he wants to be a CMO of a company. Never let those childhood dreams die (he writes as he stares at a pile of books he wrote in fifth grade).

Treat your major like a minor. Personally, comedy and nature have always been the two things I love the most. Unfortunately they don't teach those in college, those are things that I had to learn by doing and reading. I knew the chances of finding a college major that taught me how to do what I loved the way I needed to be taught was slim. So I became a publicist to help me get the connections I would someday need to sell a book or get on stage. Every free second I had, I would sneak into my room and listen to stand up recordings. I would go to friends' houses to watch HBO specials. Think of college as a means to finding your major in life. If you want to be an astronaut, become a math major because your parents never paid for you to go to Space Camp and you could never get on Nickelodeon in the nineties.

Educating yourself on what you love to do will make your life a million percent happier. When you get out of school, you'll hopefully come to realize a lot of what you did in college was shallow and meaningless while you try and find your way and identity. You'll look back on it and laugh at a lot and smile at more, but you should teach yourself the stuff you love, that will take you into adulthood. Find what you love and make sure you do it, teach yourself about everything you're interested in. Most of all never forget how you feel when you show up to work, and realize that a lot of teachers feel the same way about their job.

Avoiding Class: More Than Just Leaving the Seat Down

There are a million ways to avoid class: wearing a Hooters T-shirt, eating with your hands . . . there are many ways to be absent, as in minded. However, in terms of this book, I am supposed to explain how to never go to class and still get good grades. I spent several hours trying to figure out how to make this essay less boring so throughout I am just going to say sentences that I find hilarious.

The first and most effective way of being marked there while being absent is by just showing up late. In massive lecture halls it's easy to show up late to class without getting noticed. Show up fifteen to twenty minutes before the class has ended and take a seat. (My father's CPAP machine sounds like Randy Savage.) After class is over, walk down to the professor and explain you have terrible hearing and never heard your name get called. This sets up the foundation for you not being in class and them marking you as there just so you don't come down and talk to them more. It's an effective way to minimize time in class so you can do more important things like not be in a humanities class.

Taking classes with friends is an extremely effective way to never show up. (Please rewind the VHS of *3 Ninjas*.) When you're in a smaller class that has a sign in sheet, the best way to avoid showing up is to have a collective group. This way two or three people don't have to show up. It's like outsourcing your education. One person shows up and signs in the rest of you, takes the notes, and hands them off when they see you next. It's about time management . . . managing to have as much free time as possible.

Remember, being absent can also be a mindset. Just because you're showing up doesn't mean you actually have to *show up*. Be there in body but try astral projecting yourself somewhere more interesting, like a free Tetris game on the Internet. Literally anything is better than sitting in a class of thirty-plus students, trying to retain then spit back the stupid information you're supposed to. Being stung by bees is better, having your toenails pulled off at gun point is better, having to relive getting denied by your high school crush . . . all of these things are better than the way our education system tries to get us to learn.

Leave after attendance. Seriously, this is the one I did more than anything else. Instead of going to class, I read books about how to walk and sneak around like a ninja. This lead me to be able to sneak out of class whenever, but also made me believe in a shogunate. It's a simple formula really. It doesn't matter what your class size is. Call yourself a minimalist and show up to class without any material. No laptop, no backpack, no notebook. Then you can leave whenever you want. Just get up and if someone asks you where you're going say the bathroom or something ridiculous. If they bring up next class that you never came back, make them feel terrible by explaining you have irritable bowels or gastritis . . . maybe even explain you have horrible bleeding stress ulcers. They'll never ask you about how long you need in the bathroom again. Sure, no one in the class is ever going to talk to you, but who cares because you're not showing up anyway.

Square Pegs in Round Holes: My Un-Researched Opinion

The fundamental flaw in our education system is also the problem with any bureaucracy. They have systems in place that can handle thousands of people at once but nothing that can effectively identify and help those who don't fall into their pre-established guidelines. Since they have power as a social structure, everyone is forced into a faulty system whether they like it and it works for them or not. I will say personally, I believe, we put too much emphasis on college. We have too large a population to accommodate actual learning within a society that positively reinforces stupidity. College isn't a standard for actual learning, it is a badge you need to obtain to get to actual learning, which happens in either master's classes or the job market itself. College is no longer about education, it's about meeting a societal expectation.

We live in a service-oriented society here in America, and we can no longer handle the number of job applicants versus the number of jobs we actually have. Added to the problem is our materialism; the driving force behind people's desires to exceed. If everyone wanted less, we'd have more positions in non-service-oriented fields and see the restoration of the middle class. Instead we've convinced everyone to buy more plastic garbage that they don't need, only to be bored of it within weeks. The education system would be a million times better if more people decided academia wasn't for them, and we actually had jobs for them that could provide a healthy middle class living. Instead, we tell kids who don't want to be in college and can't afford it to try it out because it's a necessity, and accept that 20 to 30 percent will drop out and the average time it takes for a student to graduate in America is now five to six years. Accepting a huge drop out rate is insane. Those kids could have saved that money for *anything* else. Instead they have debt and nothing to show for it. So, instead of being able to get a loan for a business or for any idea they have that could result in them making money, their first concern is paying off a high debt with an insane interest rate with no feasible way of doing this. It's a vicious cycle.

The large bureaucracy of college is like fitting a square peg into a round hole. There are plenty of people who would be more adept at learning if education styles weren't so robotic and actually had individualized attention to help people master what they want to do. Realistically, none of what I just said actually matters though, because to change things we'd need an entire generation of students to say, "We've had enough of this shit, give us something for our money."

I tried. I really tried to have one semi-meaningful article in this book. I gave it my best try but I just can't take any of this seriously because I'm acquainted with the amount of apathy people now have for others or themselves. It's sad, all of it. It's depressing. Well, fuck you, reader, because you could probably change this.

A B-Line to an A

I think the only thing that ever really kept me from being 100 percent bro was my lack of number skills. There are varying degrees of bro, but none more stereotypical and classic as the Finance bro. This is the stereotypical imagine of a Bro, and what most frat brothers and business school men are taught to be the pinnacle of success. If you have a family of five, there better be ten collars on that family Christmas card. For better or worse, I discovered that I would never make it completely out of the middle class and into the J. Crew catalog. I gave up on ever becoming rich the day I entered college-level finance. I was a marketing and public relations student for a reason. They just make up numbers.

I can best explain finance thus: Finance is the art of confusing people with ADHD and number dyslexia. Every time a problem was proposed, it felt like my professor was throwing a knife at me, and not just because he was Japanese and hated the shogunate. My professor was widely regarded as one of the best businessmen in Taiwan. He could project, he could analyze, he could do super complex math, but languages really weren't his thing. He always came in wearing a suit, blue or black, from an expensive brand. Even a perfectly tailored suit couldn't hide the gut he had developed from living so comfortably. I wish I remembered his face, but in all honesty I can't. So, imagine his face as just a mouth that spewed noises you can't understand. His round head and straight black hair were constantly overshadowed by the fact his face was just an enormous mouth. When he laughed, the entire top of his head tilted back at a 90-degree angle and he bobbled. He was a mouth-breather, because he had no other choice. Every time he spoke, flecks of spit would cover the front row, and a stream of babble we could never understand flew out of his mouth at us not to us.

Every class started with every person there not actually being there. Whether it was simple online video games or a cell phone, hidden, no one was where they actually were. Then our teacher and his teacher's aide, who had a normal face, would stand in front of the class. He never took attendance because he assumed that if people didn't show up because of how successful he was, they'd show up to see a mouth on a head say nothing because that's what they had paid for. He would stand there momentarily then his mouth would move and a constant incessant stream of noise would come out of his mouth. He'd shuffle papers and then ask everyone to turn in the homework that no one ever did. It was impossible to do homework when you couldn't understand what the homework was, and even if you could, you wouldn't be able to understand that it was time to turn the homework in.

Bread Foster

After shuffling his papers to get everyone's attention, he was not attentive enough to see that none of us were paying attention. At the a dry erase board he would mumble to himself, and do complex analysis, and draw graphs that none of us could understand. He would unabashedly keep his back to the class until the problem was over then reveal his answers dramatically with a wave of the arm, and his lips would pucker together then vibrate and send spit into the front row. The teacher knew he was so good at business and teaching because students showed up early, and filled the back of the class. After revealing his perfection of an answer, he often went back and double-checked his perfection, changing numbers on the board to make his already correct answer some of us had copied down even more correct. He did this over and over until he thought we had learned everything we needed to learn that day, which should have meant a never-ending class since no one learned anything.

Our very first test was wonderful; everyone in the class ended up passing, once he added fifty points to our scores. He tried to explain his version of a grading curve, keeping his back to us then revealing the future of our GPAs and not going back to correct the perfection of this graph. He pointed and spit and babbled, students holding their tests in front of them for cover. More than three-fourths of my test had been scribbled over in red pen, alerting me that I was wrong, or right because it was written in a different language. All that mattered in his class was a circled grade at the top. No one was there to learn, we wanted our numbers and to stop paying attention to the mouth-faced man who controlled our futures.

After seeing his graph, I decided I would no longer go to the talking mouth finance class, because by not showing up I was still passing the class. The way his insane grading curves worked, by getting a zero I was getting a C. While everyone else wasted hours a week trying to learn finance, I spend my time trying to learn how to say, "You're a talking head that no one understands," in Taiwanese. If he wasn't going to teach me anything, I was going to have to teach myself. He was such a good teacher that by the end of the semester I knew curse words and how to say, "My name is not Yossarian," in Armenian. He didn't even have to teach it for me to learn it.

After tracking my progress through the semester and seeing how much I had learned and what good grades I was getting, it frightened me when I realized I didn't know anything. I was so proud to be getting a D in a very difficult math-based class, but very confused why I still didn't know anything. It was even better when people dropped the class because then sometimes I would get a C. He was such a good teacher than I never even had to see him for him to know what I was learning. While everyone I knew came back from that class moaning about how hard it was, I tried to explain to them that if they all got zeros we'd all get Bs, but it's very hard to unionize students.

When the finals grades came in I was personally offended to see that I had received a C. I was so proud of all the hard work I wasn't doing that a C simply would not fly. On a very drunken night I decided to write mouth-breather a scathing email explaining to him he was nothing but a mouth that couldn't communicate. At 2:00 a.m. I expressed to him everyone else's concerns besides my own: his class was very hard to follow, he made mistakes on the problems then didn't show us how to correct them, and often he refused to repeat himself and made the students feel like we were the problem. I explained to him what everyone else had explained to me about his harsh grading practices that we often couldn't understand. While everyone else studied to compensate, I wrote an email explaining his faults as a man with no hearing, smell, or vision. After hitting send on the email I returned to drinking heavily and sleeping heavily as well.

When I woke up the next day I was livid. I had still not learned any finance, but I had forgotten sending the email. I marched right to his office hours with a hangover and piss-poor attitude. I was not going to get a C for doing nothing, I wanted at least a B for all the work I never did. His offices sat on the third floor of a quiet hall with a marble floor, terrible white drop down ceilings, and the stink of Clorox. Everywhere there was salt from not slipping on the ice. In the two years of me staying on campus no one ever got hurt from ice, but I imagine plenty got sick from licking delicious sidewalks. It was the adjunct professor's office where I waited outside for him to spit at someone else and until they left the room smiling.

When it was finally my turn to enter, the previous student wished me awful luck, as if bringing my grade down would somehow bring everyone's up, that was untrue because as the worst grade in the class that student actually owed me. I stepped across the threshold and there behind a desk covered in paperwork and massive quantities of used floss sat a head with just a mouth, a body covered in a suit that has elbow covered in cow skin and as far as I could see no legs at all.

"Where did your legs go?" The mouth sat open and panting, greedily sucking in the air from the small office. "How dare you try to outbreathe me, you are the best businessman, however, I am a much better breather." I inhaled and exhaled as much as possible to show him the extent of how good I was at breathing, since he had never seen me in class to know how good of a breather I was. "You're very good at mouth breathing, sir, but I need to explain to you that I do not deserve the grade you're giving me. In fact, I deserve to get a better grade for all the finance I didn't learn. Do you know how hard it is to not know anything about finance and still get a grade at all? The fact I never showed up and I still have a seventy should show you how good of a student I am. I am a student who deserves to get his grade bumped up for all the work I never did."

The mouth closed and opened again but no words were coming forth. A slimy tentacle of spit rolled off his tongue and landed on his desk. His mouth was agape and his breath came out forcefully. "You should understand that you're impossible to understand? If I cannot understand you, clearly you cannot understand me, but whose fault is that? That's your parents' fault, so I will have my parents call your parents if you do not give me a better grade. Not only will I have our parents talk, which will be fruitless as your parents will not be able to talk either, I will explain to your boss that my parents called you parents and they don't speak and English, so neither do you. Do you understand this? Of course you don't."

He began writing on a piece of paper a complex mathematical formula that my grades showed I already knew. "Sir, I have the paperwork to show that I know that." His head tilted upward while he didn't make eye contact with me because he had no eyes and stopped writing. He began writing another complex formula on a piece of paper. In an effort to communicate, I began writing complex mathematical formulas of my own.

$$A = P\left(1 + \frac{r}{100}\right)^n \quad \text{Whereas both A and R = 0.}$$

"Do you understand me now?" he stared at the formula for a while without any eyes. My mathematical prowess impressed him enough that he wrote an A on the page and in a tiny little book. The most important part about having no interest is the ability to tell a teacher such.

When I went home I logged onto my email. There was a reply to an email I had clearly written, even though I had also clearly never written it.

"Hello Mr. Foster,

Your email was strongly worded and I understand your concerns. You also need to understand my lack of caring about your concerns. I am a very important businessperson, and a very important adjunct professor who does not have the time to read every email from a student. I have much more important things to do besides waste all my time teaching when I could be wasting my time on other projects. Please consider this: I have a proven track record of being a teacher with a proven track record of being a good business man. I am in fact the best businessperson in Taiwan. So why would I care that you're not able to learn the way I learned? It's clear by how much money I have, I know this, so all I can do is tell you and expect you to understand because clearly I know and you don't. After much deliberation that I did not have time to do, I will bump your grade to a B because I will make my already perfect grading scale even more perfect than it was. Thanks."

That was it. I had gone from a C to an A in twelve hours, thus proving how much I actually deserved an A. I was angry because I knew I deserved an A from the beginning, but instead I had to waste several hours I did not have to get a grade I didn't deserve. If they had just given me a grade I didn't deserve to being with, all of this would have been easier. All it takes to get an A is to play within their rules by breaking their rules.

Much like this story, the college system is a confusing ass-backward joke. I honestly failed my finance class because a teacher, who had all the credentials of an amazing businessperson, lacked the credentials of an educator. Colleges want the prestige of having amazing-sounding teachers who are completely unable to teach. I never showed up to that class because a zero on a test meant getting a seventy and that was much easier than ever trying to learn from someone so inept. I honestly did write an email and forget then visit the teacher the next day only to be bumped up again to an A, which shows how much of a joke college actually is.

My generation was told that if we went to college and got good grades, we'd come out with a job and a house and an amazing life. We graduated to no jobs, huge economic problems, and a housing bubble bursting around us. The institutions that they put us in were a joke. College isn't about learning the way it used to be, now it's about remembering information, putting it on paper, and spewing it back to the person who gave it to us to being with. It's a vicious cycle of regurgitating into each other until we forget how it started and why we even did it in the first place.

Grades are an illusion; if you're willing to cause a stink, you can get a degree without a problem. Classes, grades, institutions as a whole are so screwed up and confusing it's like going to war. Treat every class as such, go in knowing that it's you against that teacher for the imaginary prize of an A that actually means nothing when you get into the real world. I've been lucky enough to revisit colleges doing stand up, and from what I can tell . . . nothing has changed. The people who do the least work and refuse to get bullied will always get an easier A than the hardworking kids. The real lesson you should take out of college is that it's never the person who works the hardest who turns out the best, it's the person most willing to work their way around the system with people who will do anything to avoid having more paper work.

The Game: You Just Lost

Honestly, my publisher asked me to write an entire chapter on academics and I'm the person least fit to do that. I graduated with a high in-major GPA and I never got below a B, but I can confidently tell you, do not listen to my chapter on academics. I slept in class, I found ways around assignments. By my calculations, I had four childhood dogs and five uncles die in two years. That would have been news to my mother since she only had two brothers. The crowning achievements for me academically were the time I got an A in statistics after drawing a bear as an answer on my final, and the time I beat a game designed by Harvard to test their business students.

It was mandatory to take some global business class that was supposed to help every student understand the wacky world of globalization. Globalization is easy. The world is smaller and more accessible and everyone is different, so try not to be a dick and you'll be fine. Instead of teaching common sense, a bunch of Harvard students got coked out of their brains and made some simulation that they were selling to colleges across the country. "We're from Harvard," they'd tell the business school, "trust us, this game is going to teach your students how to run a multinational footwear company with several different brands under its umbrella and a complex system of finances." that was completely impossible to make funny even in the slightest. Grand Theft Auto teaches you more about business than this glorified MS-Dos Prompt. Essentially the game consisted of plugging numbers into slots and never really understanding the outcome. The entire class was divided into groups of CEOs and given a company. I remembered playing pretend in school used to be a lot more fun. I got teamed up with a bunch of jaggoffs, who typed numbers into the prompts without understanding the simulation, and I secretly wished I was teamed up with smarter people, like the monkeys we send into space. Hell, after watching my peers I was so happy I slapped them on the back and said, "You run a company like this, you're gonna be captains of industry some day," then mumbled under my breath, "industrial waste."

The problem with telling this story is that I never wanted to interact with my peers in this class. I know we met on occasion and they remained friendly, but they managed to get us third-to-last place in the end of the game. Without the reaction of my peers I am going to come off as a megalomaniac braggart so . . . let's take a minute and talk about something else shall we? College kids, don't pee in the shampoo bottles. Everyone knows the trick and checks for it. Anyone who eats their roommate's food or holds a party in their room should understand they are at the risk of shampoo tampering and smell it before use. If you *really* hate someone and need to get back at them try cuming in their conditioner bottle. It's much harder to detect, and conditioner-like jizz will leave hair shiny and silky smooth. Yeah, the person you do it to might get better skin and softer hair, but know they only look wonderful because you have immaculate aim. Ladies, since you can't jizz into the conditioner it's a much harder situation for you. I suggest the good old butt on the toothbrush. If you're going to be a jerk off, don't be one that gets caught.

While my teammates explained to me that you can buy celebrity endorsements and run both a mass AND name-brand line, I told them that made me so excited I could almost imagine not being lower middle class. While they jabbered on, I did what any child of the eighties would do: I tried to find cheat codes. It was incomprehensible that someone could create a game like this and not put in some backdoor cheat codes for unlimited money or GodMode, hell, I'd even take a mini-game to break up the monotony. CEOs have a god complex, their game should have a God cheat code. Instead I found that everyone online had written complex strategies on how to beat the game depending on the actions of your other classmates. I was playing glorified chess on a screen that looked like a Zenith 4000. The future sure was here.

I left class for a cigarette and came back in, where I was met with more explanations, *yay*. I was so overjoyed that I imagined cumming in my classmates' conditioner bottles. I understand trying to get an understanding of something like this for a grade, but celebrating what some asshats from Harvard were putting us through seemed asinine. Finally, they explained how insane and intense the lending system was. Overjoyed, I bit my lip until it bled then doodled me being hung in my book with the blood. As the teacher said, "So the game runs for twelve weeks and at the end of twelve weeks the winner gets an A," my colleague said, "So in the bank you can take out three-year, five-year, and ten-year loans." I thought about what other acts of self-mutilation might amuse me.

As the class ended, everyone tried to exchange numbers and I explained I didn't have a phone because someone had tricked me into giving them mine for an omelet and a copy of *Animal Farm*. While they were looking at each other confused, my phone rang in my pocket. I answered, pivoted military style on my heels and continued down the concourse marching and raising my right hand in a salute to everyone I walked passed.

The next class the amorphous blobs of teammates chuckled and made business jokes that made me gag, while I wished I was back in my apartment making jokes that had nothing to do with splitting dividend or having to hear the explanations that people with no sense of humor gave about why the joke was funny. "So this week begins the actual game. After the last class, we have in the lead teams blah, blah, blah, blah, blah." The professor droned on about the mechanics of the game I had already studied at night. In school, it's important to study smart, not hard. If you can put in a few hours of extra work, that will save you from going to class or having to waste an entire night cramming . . . just do it.

Once he let the entire class go to strategize, I grabbed my monkeys and explained the strategy. "The game is for twelve years. There is a ten-year loan. So we wait for it to be nine years, take out a massive loan then take out another ten loan to pay the fees on the ten-year loan. Essentially our company will fail at thirteen years but who cares?" Everyone was shocked. "Guys, it's pretty easy. This isn't a real company. You understand that right? This is 80 percent of our grade. We do this, we can get a B while getting a zero on the final." My teammates mingled among themselves while I excused myself for a cigarette and from hearing the peons be shocked I'd be willing to destroy their twelve-week baby.

"Excuse me do you have a spare cig?" A stranger asked.

"Only if you kiss me on the cheek."

The guy in the MSU football jersey looked shocked. He was enormous and seemed offended by the suggestion of a kiss. At least that face would get me through a few hours.

Back upstairs, my team had appointed me leader and decided they all agreed with my plan. With eight weeks left, we were in the number one spot. Everyone in the class wondered where we got the capital to buy out all the celebrity endorsements, perfect our mass label, and purchase superior materials to make our sneakers. Everyone reading this is wondering why the fuck they're bothering; college has nothing to do with classes. I was riding high on the fact I had outsmarted everyone when, with six weeks left, another team took first. Livid, I asked their team how they figured out the loan trick, each pointed to the asshole on my team who ruined it. The only thing I ever learned about business and life in that class was the only way to keep a secret is to never share it.

Back with my group, I asked the kid who told them how much of a simulation he wanted. When he answered, I smacked him as hard as I could on the back of the head and screamed, "You're fucking fired, you fucking numbskull!" Now everyone in the class would know the trick and I'd end up with a D. Still managing to keep our heads above water as the playing field leveled, by the last week we were in the number one spot and I had plugged in all the numbers we needed to stay top five. The night before the final class, everyone met up in the library, judging me for having a flask.

"Look, just leave the game alone, we're not going to win but we won't fail. Besides, I'm fucking pissed I have to take a final now."

The next day I showed up and took the final, knowing that if I got a C or better my entire grade would be a B. This was all I ever strived for in college. Before the final we received our standings and we were second to last place. I stared at my team with the same face I had after the ghost pepper got on my genitals. "Who fucked with my numbers?" The same asshole who had told the other team how to cheat the game had botched my numbers, worse than this story is botching my book. I dead-eyed the weasel, who thought he knew better, until we saw the final was an essay question, "What are the practical applications of the game, and what were variables that they missed?" I wrote the second half saying they didn't take into account being able to fire idiots and hire from within, because it increases productivity.

Now, let me first apologize to the reader. This story comes off like I'm some drunken Stanford man, drinking scotch alone and talking to the bust of Benjamin Franklin in his study. Also he's wearing a polo and his name is something obnoxious like Steven Napier, Johnathan Healy, or Bobby Sullivan, Esquire. Those types of guys know what equity is and have bank accounts that are called something besides "savings." They're private equity firms, I've always been more of a Ponzi scheme.

Now that I've apologized, there is something to be learned here besides that whole shampoo bottle thing. If you're stupid like I am, you'll have to learn to bend and break rules. There are plenty of people who will never retain information and regurgitate it like the entire system seems to be geared toward. If you're someone who can't sit still or concentrate in a classroom, it's up to you to teach yourself and work really hard to get good at what you love. Unless you take control of your own education, they'll have you on ADHD medicine, doing accounting until you finally die by hanging yourself in an autoerotic asphyxiation accident.

There is a serious lack of self-reliance in this world. It's glaring in the educational system. Remember if you don't fit into a system, find a way to make it work for you. If you learn differently don't try to learn the way you're being taught. Don't be an asshole and say no one has anything to teach you and that people are stupid, that's how you end up at The Gathering Of The Juggalos. Take the system and exploit every single flaw you can that's in your favor. There is an entire network of teachers and supervisors just waiting to be exploited by any student smart enough to try. Don't forget, they accepted you into their institution, but you're still paying their salaries. Demand more than just what's handed to you.

In college, getting good grades is the easy part. Once a girl told me she was going to stab my entire bloodline and my response was, "Those are called veins, not bloodlines you idiot." If someone like me can get above a 3.2 GPA, anyone who's willing to do a little manipulation is going be on honor roll. Your real education comes from the interactions you have with those who wield power over you and your peers. Focus on what makes people tick and how social interactions work, that will get you farther in life then regurgitating anything from your humanities classes.

Chapter 12

GRADUATION:

It's Finally Over

WHAT COLLEGE ACTUALLY TEACHES YOU

Post-graduation feels like being a freshman all over again in the real world. You've paid thousands of dollars to ensure the next year and a half of your life is spent getting coffee and answering phones. Within months you'll realize your degree prepared you for the working world about as well as a sharpened stick prepares you to fight a bear. You used to think you'd hang that degree proudly on a wall, now you're burning it for thirty seconds of warmth. The real world has a way of showing you that everything you learned in school is already dated, or that the company you work for uses techniques that are even older than what you learned. There is hope though. There are a few things you learn in school that actually translate into real life.

Ambivalence. College is where you learn to give zero fucks. It's here where you start to understand the only things in life that are for sure are pregnancy scares and death. People flake and teachers change the rules. After a while you'll learn to accept the fact that plans will get broken, and PornHub is the only thing that will never let you down. In fact PornHub tailors itself to your tastes, which is more than you can say for anyone else. Instead of getting sad about it, get drunk alone.

How to Lie. Your grandma has been in the hospital four times this semester, which is weird because she died in 2001. Who knew a horrible family tragedy could help you procrastinate on a paper? College is where you learn to make excuses because you didn't have the initiative to leave your bed. It starts with professors, but soon you'll find yourself lying to everyone. Telling your girlfriend you think you got strep throat is a lot better than saying you couldn't meet her parents because you don't care.

Staying Awake. It's much easier to treat your body like shit now, so it's ready for when you do it later. When you're in your late twenties it's a lot easier to stay up working all night and still function the next day after you remember that three-day spring break bender. Sure, deadlines help you to stay awake to get everything done but so does Irish coffee and 20 mg of Adderall. In college, you have the time to figure out the perfect combination of stimulants and hardheadedness that can help you through your adult life.

How to Cheat. Cheating is an essential part of adult life. In college you learn how to write on your body, make a cheat sheet, or text a friend while being watched. As an adult these lessons carry, taking credit for what other people have learned is the best way to get ahead. Nothing feels better than a business presentation where everyone congratulates you, unless of course it was just a rehashed version of previous ideas that only took you twenty minutes. Remember to distract everyone with as many visuals as possible. Even adults love shiny things.

Cooking. You're going to learn to make one impressive meal, but probably nothing more than that. One meal is all you need to make when you have friends over for dinner. One meal is enough to impress the opposite sex when they come over. Most people hate cooking, but putting Chipotle in new wrapping isn't clever enough for people not to notice.

In college you're also going to learn about your alcohol tolerance and how to do drugs, but the five skills above get used the most post-graduation. It's disheartening to know that you paid thousands upon thousands of dollars to learn five things. Just know the best part about those five things is that, when used together properly, they can get you farther ahead in life than anything a textbook ever taught you.

I'm HOOOOOOME: Now What?

With the crappy economy and awful job market, more and more people are being forced to move back in with their parents post-graduation. It's a terrible and oppressive decision to make after having four to six years of freedom, but it's the only way to save enough money to be able to afford a couch when you move out. Moving back in with your parents is a terrible and awful thing, they're going to ask questions and want to keep an eye on you while you pretty much just want to be left alone. There are going to have to be major adjustments for it to work out, and a few have pretty common fixes.

Answering Questions. Your parents are old by now. Once you graduate college you have to realize you and your parents have become much more distant than you were in high school and before. They're going to be obnoxious about asking questions and worrying about you. The first question you'll probably get a lot is, "Why are you drinking so much?" You may be cutting down from the amount you drank in college, but you're still drinking a lot in their mind. They're next going to questions about your day, depending on your relationship, they could be prying or sadly actually interested in you life. It's annoying to have to answer to someone again, just remember that you're probably living pretty well.

Paying Rent. A study a guy at a bar told me about says more parents are having to charge their kids rent when they move back home. It's not just them being assholes (they are being assholes though) it's because everything sucks monetarily after college. The world is going to fuck you for money around every corner so your parents see you as a way to offset the costs of you being around. Paying rent on your own can be obnoxious, but it is a decent way to start learning more responsibility since the rent is all your own.

Bringing People Home. In college you had plenty of complete strangers in your place. That's not going to happen much anymore. Now when you bring someone home you have to worry whether they're going to be a drunken mess around your parents, or steal their stuff. Bringing a strange girl home is going to have to be awkwardly timed to avoid your parents or they'll interview her about her life. Explaining to them you met her on the Internet will not only make them question your judgment, but your dad will probably question your game.

Hours. Your schedule is going to be scrutinized. Coming home at 3:00 a.m. is no longer going to be a weekly occurrence. When they see how you've been living for the past few years, they're going to be concerned and drop little hints about you life choices. When you come home at sunrise and see your mom or dad getting up and ready for work, the guilt and shame will be unparalleled. Get used to a more tame lifestyle until you can move out on your own.

Real Life. Real life is going to start creeping in slowly while you live with your parents. They're going to ask you to find a job, be hygienic, and worry about every dollar you spend. Getting day drunk has to be done outside the house and someone has to be a designated driver. Slowly but surely, they'll have you start to become more of an adult and try to impress life lessons on you so that you'll move out quicker and be out of their hair. It's all about getting you out of the house so they can retire.

Moving back in with your parents can be cumbersome and obnoxious, and neither one of you really wants to be in that situation. It's like being in high school again when you feel like an adult (guess what, you're not yet). If it were easy, everyone would still live with their parents, but it's not. It's incredibly annoying to both parties to have people at different of life stages crammed in the same house. Just be as nice as you can to them, they're helping you save money.

Graduation

Graduation was the scariest day of my life. I had seen friends turn blue, had my stomach pumped, gotten in more fights than I could count, told a girl "I love you" for the first time, been scammed, scammed others, and opened up to groups of people I had never thought I would have. Nothing was scarier than graduation and the feeling of, "It's over." The entire day I felt like I wanted to puke, Four Fingas (whose last name was always directly after mine, so we walked together) made fun of me for not ironing my robe and looking like a mess. I cranked back a joint before The Girl I was Dating showed up with us. None of my family was there, being the youngest meant they'd done this twice already. The only reason I walked at graduation was because she forced me to (things were not going well by now).

We waited in line and watched everyone assemble in the outdoor auditorium on a warm day. Everyone was sweating under their robes, and Four Fingas had snuck a beer in to drink while the boring commencement happened. It was all "Pomp and Circumstance" and some people did better than others. When the communications majors walked, there were murmurs of, "There go the most educated future plumbers of America." The only highlight to the graduation was that my favorite teacher, Dr. Knoll, was visibly high and kept taking his cap off. Whenever he exposed his bald head and white hair, the dean would turn and demand him to put it back on, only moments after his back was turned would it come off again. Dr. Knoll looked to be enjoying himself. As he was one of the smartest people I had ever met, I actually thought about how much I was going to miss him. More speeches and more pomp and my mind was dwelling on everything I was going to miss. It all felt like the end of my entire life's goals. Everyone tells you for years, "You have to graduate college," then when you do there's a subtle emptiness mixed with the excitement of finally saying, "It's fucking over." I was sad and scared as I walked to get my diploma and handshake

I looked over everyone's faces. They were filled with excitement and overwhelmed with joy. I thought about all the people who I'd never be able to keep up with, hundreds of people I saw on a daily basis would now slowly fall into the grey area of forgotten memories. We'd never create new stories. From here on out, we would only be reminiscing over the times we did this or that, when everyone lived together in a harmoniously immature and like-minded fashion. I ached at the memories of seeing these people drunk outside at the stone tables or high on the common lawns reading Salinger and Kerouac because they still spoke to us. I knew how much I'd miss the spirit of college as the occasional familiar student met my eyes and nodded in acknowledgment.

I shook a hand, I got a piece of paper, I nodded at Dr. Hill whose cap was off again. Soon everyone tossed their caps into the air, cheering. I felt empty and sad. I walked around the grounds meeting my friends' families. Everyone's mothers and sisters and cousins were with them, and most of my friends knew I'd be alone and were curt and respectful about it. I think that day was when a lot of my friends figured out I was always going to be a bit of a loner. Everyone was jubilant. I wasn't living with Four Fingas at this point, so he and I stuck together like glue for a few hours afterward.

Everyone else was excited.

That night I introduced Four Fingas to Chris, Beer Clause, and the roommate I wanted to talk about more but didn't have the pages to, Leonardo. The mixing of worlds didn't go over well, Fingas was too crazy for my new roommates who didn't cause near the mayhem he and I did. The awkwardness of the situation was fitting to how I was feeling as a whole. We all drank a few beers and talked about what was next for us. Four Fingas had a job waiting for him with his extended family and my prospects were slim to none. I had been working in public relations since I was eighteen, so I figured I'd keep going down that road. It was sobering and quiet with my friends and me. I knew soon I'd have to leave campus entirely. The world was changing, it was scary and we all wondered where we would go and where we would live.

The insecurity that happens after college is intense. You realize the decisions you make matter and affect your life and future. Everything feels heavy for a while until you get to the real world and everything feels new, tingly, and exciting again. The fear is overwhelming but a slight spirit of possibility lingers, that's what gets you through the first years after graduation . . . there is still potential.

I graduated mid-semester so there was no senior week for me, there was no crazy last party. I took most of my stuff and threw it in my car, looked at the campus I had just spent a year and a half graduating from and muttered, "See you next weekend when I'm back to see The Girl I Was Dating." An hour and a half drive home, I had my laundry, a fish tank full of turtles, and some furniture. I walked in through the garage door. "Mom! Dad! I'm home. I graduated college. Now what?"

Anime: Don't Tell Anyone

Just a quick note as this book draws to a close. You're going to experiment and do drugs and do art you'd never normally do. You'll hang out with a ton of different types of people and watch worlds collide. There will be humiliating social disasters and apologies given to people for inebriated actions that were terrible. Once my friend Doug called me because his girlfriend was mad at him. There was a three way the night before and he forgot to involve his girlfriend. I explained he had to apologize for cheating on her twice. Doug asked me if I'd ever have a three way, and I said if I wanted to disappoint two women at once I'd get married and have a daughter. All of that is less embarrassing than the one thing you'll experiment with in college that you can never tell anyone about: Anime.

Right now tons of people who are reading this are looking at your Sailor Moon outfits, your *Gundam Planet* toys, even your *Neon Genesis Evangelion* toys and getting pissed. Guess what, fuck off. Anime is embarrassing to watch. Anime's sense of humor is terrible and douchey. What's even worse is people to explain to others how, "Only they get it." I'm not sorry, anime can be okay to watch during college, but most of it is garbage with up skirts and creepy perverted sisters and brothers being romantic. Of all the embarrassing shit you've done during school, anime might be the worst.

Do not tell anyone ever that you watched anime. If you find someone else who's really into it avoid them like the plague. Anime is a gateway drug to pillows with characters on them and being a lonely person who jerks off to tentacle porn.

I'm bored, wanna watch some anime?

Fine, as long as there are no upskirts, creepy old men, sex between siblings, 13 year olds with gay undertones, women with comically large breasts, creepy rape stuff or a young man not knowing how to interact with women.

So, no?

EPILOGUE

Guess what, reader? We did it. You did it. You sat through some meandering paragraphs and some imperfect descriptions. We had some moments when you laughed and other moments when you felt terrible about the things you were reading. Primarily, I want to thank you for reading my first book. Getting this thing published was a beast of burden and I spent a full year of my life sitting around and wondering how I could connect to you. I hope I did.

It's over now though. You've gotten to know me and I don't know a single thing about you. It's unfair really how books work. The only things I know about you are that you had twenty dollars lying around and you are now fully equipped with more information than I ever had before college. I hope this book has helped you a little bit, I hope it's entertained you at the very least. So let's take a look at everything you've learned: Don't be the Ultimate Frisbee guy. Crap, Sam Haft told you that not me. I think he wrote the only thing worth reading in the entire book.

I hope that college is as awesome for you as it was for me. I don't think I'll ever have as much fun in life as I did during those years. I wrote this book hoping you would take on the responsibility of being an instigator. This entire book was written so that you'd be willing to shotgun a beer and instigate some insanity. Take the responsibility to make sure every night you have in college is the best night you could possibly have had.

For those of you who've read this after school . . . what the hell are you thinking? Now you're going to be convinced you need one more night of college like craziness. You might call up a friend you haven't talked to in years and get too drunk; you might order a drug you haven't done in a while. Don't be that guy. During the writing of this book, I had to revisit people and places I hadn't in years. I puked on myself, I got drugged at a frat party, I saw people I hoped I'd never have the embarrassment of seeing again . . . it's not worth it. College is a golden time in our lives when we had as much fun as our bodies could take. It sucks, but we as graduates don't have that kind of energy anymore. Go be productive, write your own book, face rejection after rejection, and do something creative instead.

College was college, let sleeping dragons lie.